THE LUCCHESE FAMILY

A History of New York's Lucchese Mafia Family

ANDY PETEPIECE

The Lucchese Family
Copyright © 2022 by Andy Petepiece

All rights reserved. No part of this publication may be reproduced, distributed, or transmitted in any form or by any means, including photocopying, recording, or other electronic or mechanical methods, without the prior written permission of the author, except in the case of brief quotations embodied in critical reviews and certain other non-commercial uses permitted by copyright law.

tellwell

Tellwell Talent
www.tellwell.ca

ISBN
978-0-2288-7437-9 (Paperback)
978-0-2288-7438-6 (eBook)

Acknowledgements

To Patti
The Love of My Life

To David, Doug, and Bill
Three terrific brothers

To Dr. Howard "Magic" Stidwill
A great friend for 74 years

To the MacPhee Group
"The Mutts"
Jim MacPhee
Chef Ricky Kalil
Tomaso Good
Peter LeClair
Lenny Currier
Bear Lalonde
Larry Gabri
Tilton Donihee
Andre Poirier
Claude McIntosh

Note:
Not one of the above mutts bought any of my books.

To Dr. Ron Tremblay
A super friend/doctor

To Rod Grant
A class act

To Dan Poirier
The most loyal friend ever

To Brian "The Cat" Rouleau
Thanks for your service in Vietnam.

In sympathy to Colin and his New York Giants

To Jerry Capeci, Peter Edwards, and Gaetan Pouliot
Thanks for the support

To all my buddies from the Green Berets, the FBI, the CIA, and the RCMP. (See below)

To my psychiatrist, Dr. I M Aquack, who has been working with me for forty years, hoping I will stop making up stories about my life. I take pills for delusions of grandeur, but sometimes I forget to do so.

CAUTION

I am not a great writer, and my editing skills are less than perfect. So if these things bother you, please do not buy this book. But, on the other hand, if you are looking for thousands of details on the Lucchese Family, you are in the right place.

BOOK SUGGESTIONS

Mob Boss by my boss Jerry Capeci and Tom Robbins
The Brotherhood by Guy Lawson and William Oldham
The Good Rat by Jimmy Breslin

OTHER BOOKS BY ANDY PETEPIECE

The Commission
The Colombo Family
The Bonanno Family

I did a tremendous amount of research for "The Complete Idiots Guide to the Mafia" by Jerry Capeci.

For many years I have contributed research for Jerry Capeci's terrific website, "Gangland News."

Over the decades, I have periodically contributed an "Ask Andy" piece for Capeci's website. Jerry tells me that his readers consistently email him complaining about my boring writing, lack of knowledge, and poor humor. But, of course, those slings do not bother me; at $800 a week, I can buy a lot of junk food.

Introduction

This book attempts to summarize the more than 100-year history of the Lucchese Family. It is impossible to include every event during this period. Hopefully, I have captured the major points and characters.

The writings of David Critchley, Nicole Gentile, and Joe Bonanno provided much of the information from the early years. Other insights came from government agencies, court documents, a few informers, and newspaper accounts.

More detail began to emerge after the famous 1957 debacle when New York State Troopers and Agents from the Bureau of Alcohol and Tobacco came upon a National Meeting of La Cosa Nostra in Apalachin, New York. The endless hearings and inquiries produced much information on the Lucchese Family and others. As the decades passed, the floodgates opened on the once-secret society. Informers, the Freedom of Information Act, electronic surveillance, and new laws were the main reasons for this change.

Unfortunately, there are many pitfalls with material on La Cosa Nostra. FBI files sometimes contain errors due to lies or exaggerations by informers. Also, there have been instances when agents deliberately entered falsehoods to deceive various people. Even electronic surveillance transcripts may contain untruths. Not surprisingly, the bad guys often lie to each other.

Constant material comparison is imperative if you hope to get near the truth. Unfortunately, I have made many errors over my career. For example, I believed Anthony "Fat Tony" was the Genovese Boss when he wasn't. The newspapers said he was the Boss, as did the FBI, and many hoods. Rudy Giuliano's boys listed him as the Genovese Boss in their famous Commission Case from the mid-1980s. We were all wrong.

So, this book is the result of more than fifty years of researching La Cosa Nostra. I have tried to avoid errors, but some will jump out and bite me.

It might be a simple typo, a lack of knowledge, or a misinterpretation of fact. My apologies in advance for these, but hopefully, you will enjoy the endless list of details anyway.

Notes

NOTE ONE:

The proper name of the American Mafia is Cosa Nostra. I use La Cosa Nostra since that is the practice of the FBI.

NOTE TWO:

I will use the names of the five New York Mafia Families that came into public use in the 1960s to indicate their histories. This decision is not technically correct, but hopefully, it will make following the accounts easier.

Table of Contents

Acknowledgements iii
Introduction. vii
Notes. ix

Chapter One: Boss Tommy Reina. 1
Chapter Two: Boss Joe Pinzolo. 6
Chapter Three: Boss Tommy Gagliano 9
Chapter Four: Boss Tommy Lucchese 20
Chapter Five: Boss Carmine "Mr. Gribbs" Tramunti 49
Chapter Six: Boss Anthony "Tony Ducks" Corallo. 62
Chapter Seven: Boss Vic Amuso. 78
Chapter Eight: Boss Vic Amuso Continued. 106
Chapter Nine: Capo Paul Vario. 123
Chapter Ten: Capo John Dioguardi 129
Chapter Eleven: Consigliere Vincent Rao 146
Chapter Twelve: Unions. 154
Chapter Thirteen: The New Jersey Crew 167
Chapter Fourteen: Frankie Carbo Boxing Czar. 186
Chapter Fifteen: Two Lucchese Drug Dealers. 194
Chapter Sixteen: Capo Eddie Coco 207
Chapter Seventeen: Underboss Salvatore Santoro 214
Chapter Eighteen: Capo James Plumeri 218

Appendix A: The History of the Lucchese Family Administration 231
Appendix B: Comedian Billy Crystal and Mafioso John Ormento 239
Appendix C: The FBI's List of Lucchese Soldiers in 1963 245
Appendix D: The NYPD's List of the Lucchese Administration
    Circa 1988. 253
Appendix E: The FBI's List of Lucchese Soldiers Circa 1988 259
Appendix F: NJ Commission of Investigation 1989 Report. 267

CHAPTER ONE

Boss Tommy Reina

Gaetano "Tommy" Reina was the first known Boss of what we now call the Lucchese Family. The best information suggests his organization evolved from the Morello (Genovese) Family, which dominated the Mafia scene in New York in the early 1900s. When it's Boss, Giuseppe Morello, went off to prison for counterfeiting in 1910, opportunities for ambitious underlings arose. It wasn't long before Reina headed up his own Family and had accumulated considerable wealth and power. Below is a chronological outline of the known parts of his short life.

DOB
September 27, 1889
Sicily

DOD
February 26, 1930
NYC

Residences

107 St, Manhattan
Circa 1910

227 E 107th St, Manhattan
Circa 1913

1906
Reina immigrated to the US aboard the SS Sicilian Prince.

1910 US Census
Reina lived at 107th St in Manhattan
and listed his occupation as laborer.

1913
Hoods placed a bomb outside the home of poultry dealer Barnet Baff on Long Island. Later testimony by Antonio Cardinale revealed that he had an employee Joseph Sorro, Frank Burke, and Tony Nino plant the explosive. Eventually, the first two men admitted their participation in this event.

November 24, 1914
Two hoods gunned down poultry dealer Barnet Baff. He had become a power in the West Washington Poultry Market by various means. Several other dealers hated Baff, and some did something about it.

Eventually, several versions of the plot emerged, with one involving Tommy Reina. Turncoat Giuseppe Arichiello told the police that saloon-keeper Ippolitto Greco forced him to participate in the action. He said that he and Tommy Reina shot Baff, with Reina receiving $700. Arichiello named some other participants, their roles, and payments. To the turncoat, the two leading players were Greco and Antonio Cardinale.

It appeared that Reina was in trouble, but things changed when Arichiello testified at his own trial. Not only did he deny any involvement in the killing, but he also testified that he did not recognize Reina when police brought him into the courtroom. The jury convicted Arichiello of first-degree murder. However, in September 1917, an appeal court granted Arichiello a new trial. He made a deal, and the judge handed out a suspended sentence for manslaughter.

Frank Ferrara was another hood arrested in the Baff case. He gave three statements to authorities, but the one to the DA is the most important to this work. Ferrara said he drove a group of men to the sight of the Baff slaying and that Reina shot the victim. However, at his trial, Ferrara recanted and said the police beat him and gave him Reina's name. In the end, the jury convicted Ferrara, and the judge sentenced him to death.

In July 1917, Ferrara became a state witness hoping to save himself. He confirmed his earlier story that the police gave him the names of Reina and another man. Now the killers were Charles Dragna and Ben "Tita" Rizzotta.

After the recantations of two witnesses, the authorities had nothing against Reina. Therefore, it is impossible to know whether he did play a role in the Baff hit.

Note:
Thanks to the author and superb Mafia historian Dave Critchley, we know Charles Dragna was Jack Dragna, the future Boss of the LA Family. Police arrested Dragna on the Baff case in 1917, but authorities dismissed the charge two years later.

Note 2:
Around 1914, Jack Dragna and Tommy Reina both worked at the Columbus Wet Wash Laundry at 339 E 107th St in Manhattan.

July 5, 1917
Reina registered for the draft.

1924
A judge sentenced future Lucchese Soldier and boxing czar Frank Carbo to 20 months in prison for killing taxi driver Al Weber in a Bronx poolroom.

ORIGINS OF THE LUCCHESE FAMILY

It is unfortunate, but I have been unable to find any primary evidence as to the beginning of the Reina Family that the FBI labeled the Lucchese Family in the 1960s. However, some historians have speculated that Reina used his connections to the Morello Family (Genovese Family) to form a crew that grew into his organization. Some relationships that support this theory include:

Joseph Morello was a stockholder in the United Lathing Company, with future Lucchese Family Boss Tommy Gagliano.
Long-time Lucchese Underboss Stefano LaSalle lived in the same apartment building as Joe Morello. He also worked at a laundry with Tommy Reina, and both operated in the Morello milieu.

October 10, 1928

A protracted rivalry between Sal D'Aquila, Boss of the Gambino Family, and Joe Masseria, Boss of the Genovese Family, came to a head on this date. At the corner of 13th St and Avenue A, three gunmen blasted D'Aquila with nine shots ending the long-time Boss of Boss' reign. Masseria was on top but wanted more.

The spheres of influence of Masseria and Reina were close. This fact was a potential problem. Long after the D'Aquila murder, Joe Bonanno wrote, "Reina had to be careful not to offend him (Masseria) and generally toed the Masseria line."

Ice Wars

A 1925 study indicated that New York used 4,000,000 tons of ice each year. Ice-making plants produced 98% of the product that 7,000 dealers sold. The competition was fierce, leading to violence of varying levels.

Smaller dealers complained to authorities that the big companies formed cartels to control the price and competition. In 1927 Referee Edgar F Hazelton held hearings about allegations that the Metropolitan Retail Ice and Coal Dealers Union Inc. dominated the market by illegal means.

Tomaso Reina, the Boss of the Lucchese Family, prospered in the ice trade in the Bronx. Newspaper accounts after his death related stories that he had amassed $1,000,000 over the last few years and had eight trucks. In addition, Reina had enough money for a 16 room house, three automobiles, a wife's and nine kids' expenses, not to mention a mistress.

Success like this would provoke jealousy and envy.

February 26, 1930

A shooter blasted Reina with shotgun slugs just as he was to enter his car parked in front of 3181 Rochambeau Ave in the Bronx. The killer and his accomplice escaped quickly. A passing taxi took Reina and his girlfriend Mary Ellis to Morrisania Hospital, where he died. In his clothes, officials found a .32 pistol and $804 in cash. A police search of his vehicle discovered a hidden compartment behind the front seats that contained a loaded .22 rifle and 100 bullets.

The police speculated that the killing was due to a cut-rate war among wholesale ice dealers. Ice likely had something to do with the murder, but Genovese Family Boss Joe Masseria wanted to place someone more cooperative on the Lucchese throne. Reina loyalists believed this theory.

Reporter Stanford Jarrel of the Daily News provided a colorful account of the Reina hit and its immediate aftermath. He described the $100 a month apartment occupied by Reina's girlfriend as a "Love nest," located at 1521 Sheridon Ave in the Bronx. Maria Ennis was a "gorgeously attractive blonde" who looked on in terror as the shooting took place. She accompanied her mortally wounded lover to the hospital.

Maria Ellis and Mrs. Angelina Reina found themselves in the Bathgate Ave Police Station an hour later. When Mrs. Reina saw her rival, she "charged like a tigress with venom in her heart. 'You were not satisfied with one man. You had to take mine away from me and my children.'"

Perhaps unnecessarily because it was apparent, Jarrel added that Reina was a man "who seems to toy with women's affections in a careless manner."

Comment:
It must have been lousy enough for Reina's nine children to lose him but to see his dirty laundry splashed across the papers couldn't have helped.

1930

With the support of Boss Joe Masseria (Genovese Family), Joe Pinzolo took the Lucchese Family throne. Unfortunately, we have no primary evidence of whether there was a vote or Masseria openly ordered Pinzolo's ascension.

CHAPTER TWO

Boss Joe Pinzolo

Joe Pinzolo was the second Boss of what we now call the Lucchese Family. From what little primary evidence exists, it appears that he was imposed on the Lucchese group by powerful Genovese Boss Joe Masseria. Unfortunately, we are stuck with that theory because what we know about his reign comes from the victor's side of a conflict. We learned from Joe Valachi that only a handful of Lucchese members secretly rebelled against Pinzolo. In any case, what follows below is a chronological list of what little we know of this character.

DOB
January 9, 1887
Palermo, Sicily

DOD
September 9, 1930
NYC

Descriptions

Joe Valachi's description

Ugly grease ball
Fat belly

Flowing handlebar mustache
A distinct odor of garlic

August 1906
Pinzola arrived in the USA.

July 1908
Police were investigating a series of blackmail attempts against apartment owner Francisco Spinelli. They caught a young Girolamo Pinzolo attempting to light a stick of dynamite to destroy the building at 314 E 11th St in Manhattan. In his pocket, the officers found a blackmail note. Pinzolo was toast.

The young hood quickly gave up his superior, Giuseppe Constabile but refused to testify against him. A judge sent Pinzolo up the river for two years and eight months to five years.

October 1922
Police arrested Pinzolo for violating the Sullivan law. (The carrying of a gun).

1930
Dominick, "The Gap" Petrilli, brought gangster Joe Valachi to Pinzolo at the Boss' request. Immediately Valachi was put off by Pinzolo's appearance and manner. Furthermore, he was insulted when Pinzolo asked him to bring some girls from the Rainbow Room. Valachi complained to Petrilli, who quietly told him that Pinzolo didn't have long to live.

Note:
When shooters killed Boss Tom Reina, a handful of his supporters vowed revenge. Tom Lucchese, Petrilli, Steve Runnelli, and a few others were in that group. They had to keep their plotting secret for their safety but needed new men for support. So the Reina loyalists brought Valachi and a few other independent gangsters into the fold.

June 1930 approximately
Tommy Lucchese rented offices in suite 1007 at the Brokaw Building at 1487 Broadway. Pinzolo ran his California Dry Fruit Importers from this 10th-floor location.

September 9, 1930
Girolamo "Bobby Doyle" Santucci gunned down Pinzolo in his office around 4 PM. Santucci told Valachi, "I caught him alone in the office." A shocked

cleaning lady discovered the body at 10 PM. Pinzolo had been shot two times in the back, another two in the chest, and the fifth slug in his side. A .32 semi-automatic pistol lay on the floor beside the late Boss with six slugs gone. Cops found $1,600 in his pocket but not much else.

The police visited Mrs. Carmela Pinzolo at 8516 2nd Ave in Brooklyn. She explained that her husband had left in the morning for parts unknown. However, the widow did add that Pinzolo ran a dry fruit importing business. She thought the dead man's description fit her husband and agreed to come in and try to identify him.

Police brought Lucchese in for questioning, but nothing came of that investigation.

The members of the Pinzolo Family (Lucchese Family) held a meeting to attempt to discover who killed their second Boss within a year. Gagliano, Lucchese, and the other plotters attended the meeting to avoid suspicion.

They acted innocent just like John Gotti and his fellow plotters did when the Gambino Family held a gathering after the murder of Boss Paul Castellano in December of 1985.

The membership must have elected Tommy Gagliano as Boss, and he selected Tommy Lucchese as his Underboss. It wasn't long after these events that the Lucchese crew realized others were plotting against Joe Masseria. As a result, an alliance was formed with Salvatore Maranzano, unofficially leading the Bonanno Family.

CHAPTER THREE

Boss Tommy Gagliano

DOB
May 29, 1883
Corleone, Sicily

DOD
February 16, 1951
NYC

Description
Joe Valachi's description of Gagliano
Big tall guy
A little bald
Looked like a businessman

Residences
638 E 227th St
213 E 102 St, NY
Circa 1921
138 E 227th St
Circa 1925

Businesses
Lathing and Hoisting in the Bronx
With brother-in-law Nunzio Pomilia.

Monopoly on the ice business in the Bronx

May 18, 1905
Gagliano entered the USA from Palermo.

June 23, 1915
Gagliano filed a naturalization petition in New York State Superior Court.

January 17, 1920
The USA granted Gagliano a passport. The details stated that he was in the hay, straw, and grain business. Also included was an upcoming trip on June 28, 1920.

May 3, 1920
Gagliano arrived in NYC aboard the SS President Wilson. It appears he took a European trip before the one stated on his passport papers.

October 23, 1921
Gagliano married Giuseppina Pomilia.

December 5, 1921
Gagliano filed a naturalization petition in New York State's Superior Court.

March 17, 1925
New York State issued incorporation papers for Montforte and Gagliano, a metal lath and plastering concern capitalized with $5,000 from Antonio Montforte, Gagliano, and Frank Cassella.

October 10, 1925
Washington renewed Gagliano's passport.

August 1, 1926
Gagliano and his wife arrived in NYC aboard the SS Giuseppe Verde. They must have been on a trip.

August 1926
Gagliano and Antonio Monforte formed the United Lathing Company. Other directors included Anthony Cecala, Genovese Family Underboss Joseph Morello, and Ignazio Milone.

April 1927
Thomas Gagliano and Antonio Monforte formed the Plaster's Information Bureau. This enterprise would furnish pricing information to its members, who would pay a percentage of a gross contract price in return. Other stockholders included Frank Casella and Antonio Merziano. Over the next three years, the firm took in $1,500,000, resulting in a net profit of $1,000,000. The stockholders received a $3,800 dividend on each $1,000 share.

July 15, 1929
DA John F. McGeehan ordered raids on the offices of the Plasterers Information Bureau, Union Lathing, and Williamsburg Investment Corp, all located at 3550 White Plains Ave in the Bronx. The agents seized company books from each enterprise. The DA was investigating a series of mysterious fires in the construction business in the Bronx.

July 22, 1929
Special auditors hired by DA McGeehan went through the books of the Plasterers Information Bureau, Union Lathing, and Williamsburg Investment Corp. All three were located at the same address but in different offices. DA McGeehan disclosed that the auditors found a close association between the three entities.

August 21, 1929
Fire destroyed an 11 story apartment building under construction in the Bronx.

August 26, 1929
Fire Marshall Thomas Brophy investigated a fire that destroyed an 11 story apartment under construction. He questioned Montforte, president of the Plasterers Information Bureau and Union Lathing Corp. The Daily News described Monforte as chief of the latherers and plasterers in the Bronx.

October 21, 1929
A grand jury indicted Joseph Sindona, an organizer for the Plasterers Information Bureau, for perjury in their investigation of apartment fires in the Bronx.

November 2, 1929
Fire destroyed an apartment building under construction at 501 W 183rd St in the Bronx; a worker died in the incident. Police arrested Charles Chinquinano for starting the blaze. He worked as a latherer at the site. He was an ex-con and admitted that a contractor employed him at the site of another apartment fire at Jerome Ave and 165th St in the Bronx.

Note:
There were ten police officers in the courtroom during the extortion trial described below, and the sequestered jury also had guards in their hotel.

February 20, 1930
In the extortion trial of Gagliano allies Anthony Monforte and Michael McClosky, David Dorward, a plasterer contractor, testified that he paid Anthony Monforte $540 to start work on a job site at Plymouth Ave and Middleton Drive in the Bronx. Monforte headed the Plasterer's Information Bureau. Dorward said he regularly took his jobs to Montforte for approval. On one occasion, Monforte told Dorward to raise his bid on a job from $8,600 to $10,800. This action strongly suggests that the Plasterer's Information Bureau was an instrument to control plastering in the Bronx and the prices and kickbacks involved.

February 26, 1930
A hitman gunned down Lucchese Boss Tommy Reina in front of 3113 Rochambeau Ave in the Bronx. Boss Joe Masseria of the Genovese Family attempted to assert control of the Lucchese group. Capo Joe Pinzolo became the new Lucchese leader.

February 27, 1930
Before Judge James Barrett, the defense lawyers for Monforte and McCloskey filed a motion for a new trial. They claimed that DA Charles S McLaughlin violated their rights by discussing the case before a Rotary Club meeting. The judge rejected their motion.

March 3, 1930
In the extortion trial of Gagliano Associates Anthony Monforte and Michael McClosky, a contractor gave details to the jury. McClosky, a Wood Lather's Union Local 60 delegate, threatened to call a strike on a building construction site at Rosedale and Lafayette Ave. The contractor paid McClosky $800 to call off the union action. In a similar fashion contractor, Victor Scally testified that

he paid McClosky $200 then $2,000 to avoid strikes by the Wood Latherer's Union.

March 4, 1930
After the prosecution concluded its case, the defense lawyer asked for an adjournment, but Judge Barrett denied their motion.

March 6, 1930
Defendant McClosky testified that the Wood Lather's Union purchased him four new cars over seven years. In addition, documents showed that the union members approved $5,100 to McClosky's lawyer for his defense in the extortion trial. In its report on these matters, the Daily News sarcastically said, "Wood Lathers' Union officials apparently scorn riding in slightly soiled motor cars."

March 10, 1930
A jury convicted Monforte and McClosky of extorting $800 from contractor Bernard Lyons to call off a strike.

March 18, 1930
County Judge James M Barrett sentenced Anthony Monforte to 71/2 to 15 years in Sing Sing for his extortion conviction. He described Montforte as the "Mastermind of a sinister combination that brought havoc and destruction to the building industry in Bronx County. In addition, the judge gave Wood Lather's Union Local 60 delegate Michael McClusky a 5 to 10-year term.

CASTELLAMARESSE WAR

1930
Joe Valachi and Nicky Padovano beat up a union man giving Gagliano problems. They did not accept payment, hoping to gain favor with Gagliano.

At the invitation of Gagliano, a friend brought Joe Valachi to see him. Gagliano explained there was trouble in the air, including with Ciro Terranova, whom Valachi hated. He asked Valachi if he would shoot someone if asked to which Valachi replied in the positive. This interchange indicated that Valachi was now an Associate of the Lucchese Family.

April 15, 1930
Shooters killed Genovese Family Underboss Peter Morello and two others in his Manhattan office. Morello was second in command to Boss of Bosses Joe Masseria, making him a target of Masseria's rivals.

May 31, 1930
Rivals of Detroit Boss Gaspar Milazzo killed him and an ally. Boss of Bosses Joe Masseria of New York supported the Detroit rebels. He wanted a Detroit Boss who would back him.

This murder set off a chain of events. The primary battle took place in New York, where the Bonanno Family united around Salvatore Maranzano.

Key players in the Lucchese Family who resented Masseria's killing of their Boss Tommy Reina joined the Maranzano forces.

Gagliano is the new Boss

September 5, 1930
Tommy Gagliano and Tommy Lucchese led a successful coup that killed Boss Joe Pinzolo. Joe Valachi said that Girolamo "Bobby Doyle" Santucci was the shooter. Gagliano became the new Lucchese Boss.

November 5, 1930
Valachi rented an apartment on Pelham Parkway S on instructions from his superiors. Steve Ferrigno, the Underboss of the rival Gambino Family, had a unit there. One day Valachi spotted Boss of Boss Joe Masseria (Genovese Family) entering the apartment complex and alerted his companion killers.

On November 5, the hitmen, Valachi, Bastiano "Buster from Chicago" Domingo, Bobby Doyle Santucci, and Nick Capuzzo rented a ground-floor apartment C1 at 760 Pelham Parkway South. The later three fired shotgun blasts at Ferrigno and Boss Al Mineo as they walked by their window. The two mob leaders died instantly.

1931
At a gathering of about 40 Mafia men, Salvatore Maranzano inducted Valachi, Salvatore "Sally Shields" Shillitani, and Nick Padovano into La Cosa Nostra.

Maranzano explained that they were at war with Joe Masseria, attempting to subjugate all Castellammarese Mafia members. In addition, he had ordered the murder of Lucchese Boss Tommy Reina. The leaders would place groups of men in apartments around the city where they would be on call for action. Maranzano mentioned that the war could never end unless they killed Masseria.

February 3, 1931
Joe Valachi accompanied Nick Capuzzo and Salvatore Shillitani when Bastiano "Buster from Chicago" Domingo gunned down rival Joseph "Joe the Baker" Catania. Six shots hit Catania, who died later in Fordham Hospital.

August 1931
Valachi and many others attended a banquet hosted by Maranzano. Maranzano gave the recruits a choice of whether to stay in his Family or join the Lucchese group. Because Gagliano had made no effort to convince Valachi to remain with him, Valachi joined Maranzano. This decision greatly angered Tommy Lucchese, but he couldn't persuade Valachi to change his mind.

September 10, 1931
Gagliano and Tommy Lucchese were in Boss Salvatore Maranzano's outer office when a group with badges entered. First, they lined the two hoods and others up against the wall, then two went into Maranzano's inner office and killed him. Valachi would have been present in the office, but a Bonanno member told him not to come in. Additionally, Dominick "The Gap' Petrelli, a Lucchese Soldier, took Valachi away from the city. After the hit, Valachi later stated, "Now I realize they were all in on this." Tommy Gagliano was front and center in the plot.

September 12-14, 1931 approximate
Fearing for his life due to his closeness to Maranzano, Valachi persuaded the son of the late Tommy Reina to hide him in his attic while the dust settled. Then Valachi phoned Tommy Lucchese, who arranged a meeting with Boss Tom Gagliano.

At the sit-down, Lucchese peppered Valachi with a series of questions. Did he know Maranzano was hijacking Luciano's trucks? Did he see Maranzano with piles of money? Did he know that Maranzano had hired freelance gangster Vince Coll to kill Genovese and Luciano? To all these questions, Valachi vehemently asserted his ignorance. Finally, Lucchese said, "Now Tom Gagliano wants you to come back with us, providing you are telling the truth." Now off the hook, Valachi retreated and began soliciting advice. Unfortunately for him, Valachi decided to go with Underboss Vito Genovese of the Luciano Family. (Genovese Family)

October 1931
At the First National Meeting of La Cosa in Chicago, the nation's Mafia Bosses decided to form a Commission of seven. This body would replace the previous system of having a Boss of Bosses to arbitrate inter-family disputes, approve Bosses' election, set broad La Cosa Nostra policy, etc.

The five reigning New York Bosses, Bonanno, Luciano, Gagliano, Profaci, and Mangano, joined Bosses Steve Magaddino of Buffalo and Al Capone of Chicago to form this new body. They were to serve a five-year term, at which time the mob Bosses would hold a second National Meeting to ratify the Commission's membership.

October 5, 1931
LA Boss Joe Ardizzone disappeared. It is a reasonable guess that the new Commission gave their stamp of approval to this action. They then recognized Jack Dragna as the new leader. Gagliano would have voted on this matter.

1932
Gagliano attended Joe Valachi's wedding reception out of respect for bride Mildred Reina, daughter of the late Tommy Reina.

February 28, 1932
A federal grand jury indicted Gagliano and four other Bronx building racketeers for conspiracy and perjury to evade taxes. They accused Gagliano of not reporting a net income of $270,000. All five accused held stock in the Plasterer's Information Bureau and United Lathing. Officials said that neither entity had any legitimate function but extorted contractors in the Bronx.

May 21, 1932
A judge sentenced four Bronx construction figures for their perjury and tax fraud guilty pleas. He gave Gagliano two one-year and three-month terms to be served concurrently in the Atlanta Penitentiary.

May 25, 1932
A jury found Soldier Salvatore "Sally Shields" Shillitani guilty of killing Benedetto Bellini that January. The judge sentenced him to a twenty-year term, of which he did 14.

August 7, 1932
Pittsburgh Boss John Bazzano wiped out some major rivals without the Commission's approval. So they ordered him to New York and killed him.

Gagliano was in prison, so a reasonable guess would be that Underboss Tommy Lucchese cast his vote. They approved Vince Capizzi as the new Pittsburgh Boss.

February 1933
A jury convicted Gagliano, a Bronx building trades racketeer, of tax fraud.

1933
BOP (Bureau of Prisons) officials released Gagliano after 15 months.

June 29, 1933
Beer baron Waxey Gordon's crew member, Murray Marks, died on a Bronx street after being shot three times. According to Joe Valachi, a tip from Gagliano that Marks used one of his garages contributed to the hitman knowing where to find the victim. Gordon was battling with the Myer Lansky and Bugsy Siegel gang over territory. Lansky was close to Lucky Luciano, a Commission member like Gagliano. A Lansky crew whacked out Salvatore Maranzano back in 1931 for Luciano et al.

August 19, 1933
Gunmen entered the fifth-floor offices of the Five Boroughs Truckmen's Association and shot Genovese Capo Dominick "Terry Burns" Didato and Lucchese Associate James Plumeri. Didato took slugs to the back and shoulder while Plumeri received bullets to the stomach and chest. Ambulances rushed the two men to St Vincent's Hospital in critical condition.

August 21, 1933
Didato died of his wounds at 10 AM while Plumeri struggled but eventually recovered.

Nicolo Gentile, the old-time Mafioso who wrote his memoirs in the early sixties, spoke about this hit. A summary of his take follows below.

Vito Genovese feared that Didato might move for Lucky Luciano's throne now that Lucky was in prison. So Genovese allied with Gambino Boss Vince Mangano and had Didato murdered to forestall that possibility. Interestingly Gentile claimed to have set Didato up, even holding his arm while a gunman shot the gangster. Nowhere does he mention the attempt on Plumeri's life.

Note:
Didato, Plumeri, and Vincent Rao were all involved with the Five Boroughs Truckmen's Association. So that means both the Genovese and Lucchese Families had an interest in that extortion vehicle.

1935
Gagliano petitioned for bankruptcy with assets of $79,800 and liabilities of $352 676.

August 17, 1936
Rivals gunned down Philadelphia Boss John Avena. The Commission probably approved this hit and the elevation of Joe Bruno to Boss.

1936
The Second National Meeting of La Cosa Nostra took place in some unknown location. The membership approved Gagliano for a second term on the Commission.

1937
Pittsburgh Boss Vince Capizzi resigned. Gagliano and the Commission approved Frank Amato as the new Boss.

April 20, 1939
Gagliano and his wife arrived in NYC aboard the SS Rex. They must have been on a trip to Europe.

1942
Gagliano began another five-year term on the Commission.

October 22, 1946
Gagliano and the Commission approved Joe Ida as the new Philadelphia Boss after the natural death of Joe Bruno.

1946
Parole officials released Soldier Salvatore "Sally Shields" Shillitani after completing 14 years of his 20-year sentence for killing Benedetto Bellini in January of 1932.

1946
Gagliano began another five-year term on the Commission.

February 16, 1951

Gagliano died of natural causes. On his tombstone, the inscription reads, "In Loving Memory of My Dear Husband Tommaso Gagliano."

Gagliano had a solid reign and never appeared to be challenged by rivals within his Family or outside. He was an original member of the Commission and served four five-year terms on that body. His biggest problems were personal criminal matters connected to his businesses.

The papers rarely mentioned his name despite his powerful position. His long-time loyal Underboss Tommy Lucchese took the throne.

CHAPTER FOUR

Boss Tommy Lucchese

After Al Capone and before John Gotti, Tommy Lucchese was one of two best-known Mafia Bosses. He unwillingly burst on the scene in the early 1950s when a mayoralty candidate claimed he was a political power. A decade later, famous informer Joe Valachi named him as Boss of one of the five New York La Cosa Nostra Families. But his story goes back long before those headlines. A summary of his Mafia life follows below.

DOB
December 1, 1899
Palermo, Sicily

DOD
July 13, 1967
Lido Beach

The Spelling of his Name

I chose to use Lucchese to spell this Mafia Boss' name after seeing it on the Family charts from the 1963 Valachi Hearings. To be consistent, I have used it ever since. Unfortunately, although courts and the FBI have used this version, it is incorrect. The proper spelling is Luckese, and it is this label that appears on his tombstone.

In a private session before the New York State Investigation Committee on August 1, 1952, Lucchese partially explained the many versions of his name. He said that during a 1920's prison sentence, fellow convicts were pronouncing his name, Luckese, as "la cheese" and soon gave him the nickname "cheese" that he hated. Consequently, he changed the spelling to Luchese.

Lucchese acknowledged that he and others used the following versions over the decades; Three Finger, Three Finger Brown, Tommy Brown, Gaetano Lucchese, Thomas Lucase, Thomas Lacase, and Thomas Arra. He explained that he used "Arra" once after being arrested. He did not want his parole board to be aware of his arrest for fear they would send him back to prison.

During his 1921 arrest for auto theft, a local cop sarcastically compared Lucchese to a famous pitcher Mordecai Brown who had only three fingers on his right hand but did have a thumb. Lucchese had lost his right thumb and index finger in an industrial accident in 1917. Police and the media often used "Three Finger Brown" to identify Lucchese. The gangster said he hated that label, and no one used it to his face.

Bureau of Narcotics description circa 1960
5'5"
150 lbs
Brown eyes
Grey hair, balding
Glasses
Medium built
Dark complexion

Three fingers on his right hand lost his thumb and index finger in an industrial accident in 1917.

Joe Bonanno's description of Lucchese circa 1957
"Short, fair-haired man."
"Clean-cut face."
"Dressed with care."
"Appearance was a little too slick."
"It looked like he'd been varnished."

Joe Bonanno's description of Lucchese circa 1962
"His face was beginning to sag."
"His hair had thinned."

"Age had dropped his varnished features."
Keep in mind that Bonanno hated Lucchese.

Malcolm Johnson, an Immigration Agent, described Lucchese as "squat and swarthy."

New York Times description on November 22, 1952

"Short, trimly built man of 52 who could pass for 40."

Parents
Baldassari
Francesca

Siblings
Anthony
Joseph
Pietra
Rosalie
Concetta

Wife
Concetta "Katherine" Vassallo
DOB 1908
DOD 2007

Children
Robert Thomas
DOB 1928
DOD 2006
Graduate of West Point, member of US Air Force

Frances
Married Thomas Gambino, son of Carlo Gambino

Lucchese's Businesses

Braunel Ltd
225 W 37th in NY
Circa 1952
Coats and suits

Lucchese testified he paid $10,000 for 1/3 interest.
His partners were Louis Kaufman and Joseph Lagana.
Lucchese testified that he declared $250,000 in income between 1942 and 1951. He said most came from Braunel limited.

Wine Brick
1457 Broadway NY
Workers compacted raisins in the shape of a brick. It was then soaked in water to ferment, creating rough alcohol. In 1930, Lucchese shared an office with Lucchese Family Boss Joe Pinzolo, where assassins killed Pinzolo on September 5.

Harvic Sport
1007 Capouse Ave, Scranton and Sweet Valley, LI
Stopped business in 1958, and buildings sold.
Lucchese was an officer in the company.

Bal-Fran Company
140 W 36th, NY
Circa 1947
Out of business in 1950

Empire Lathing Company
2373 Washington Ave, Bronx, NY
Circa 1952
Its president Nunzio Pomillo testified that Lucchese had a piece of this concern.

Fordham Hoisting Equipment Company
Circa 1948
President was Nunzio Pomillo, while Lucchese was secretary/treasurer.

Bab-France Blouse Company
140 36th Street, NY
Circa 1947
Lucchese was president, with Andimo Pappadio, the secretary/treasurer.

Kaska Manufacturing Company
Kaska, Pennsylvania
Circa December 1955 to May 30, 1956
Lucchese was part owner with Nicholas Fiorillo

Pleasant Coat Company
Pleasant, NJ
Circa the 1960s

Lou Kaufman and Company, Inc.
He said he owned it on February 1, 1946, and he filed legal papers on March 1, 1946. The following year Lucchese changed the company name to Brown then dissolved the entity on May 18, 1956.

Malba Partners Development Company

Wawarsing Sand and Gravel

Pilgrim Dress Company

Ku Kris Kringle Company

V&L Hat Company

Lucchese Residences

213 E 106th Street, NY
Circa 1930

1093 Briarway, Palisades, NJ
1936 to 1942 approximately.

106 Parsons Blvd, Malba, Queens
Ten room house in his wife's name
Since 1942.

71 Royat Street, Lido Beach, LI
Built 1951
Millie Rao, the wife of Lucchese Family Consigliere, Vincent Rao, held the mortgage.

Early Life in the USA

November 21, 1911
Lucchese arrived in New York aboard the Duca D'Agosta, which departed from Palermo.

1917
Lucchese lost his right thumb and forefinger in an industrial accident.

October 2, 1921
Police arrested Lucchese and John Spina for stealing a Packard worth $3,000. They had stolen the vehicle minutes before the police caught them in front of a Bay Shore theatre.

October 21, 1921
Court authorities re-arraigned Lucchese and Spina before Judge Furman, who set bail at $5,000.

January 19, 1922
A Riverhead, Long Island jury convicted Lucchese and Spina for auto theft.

March 27, 1922
In Riverhead, Judge Furman sentenced Lucchese to three years and nine months to ten years. He would serve 13 months before being paroled. Lucchese labeled himself as a grocer.

April 21, 1927
The New York State Parole Board released Lucchese from all restrictions.

June 25, 1927
Lucchese married Concetta Vassalo.

June 25, 1928
A shooter killed Louis Cerasulo.

July 18, 1928
Police arrested Lucchese, Joe Rosato, and John Gudio for the murder after Cerasulo's wife and daughter identified them. The documents listed Lucchese as Thomas Lucase.

July 24, 1928
Court authorities dismissed charges against Lucchese, Rosato, and Guido after Cerasulo's wife and daughter withdrew their identifications.

There is no evidence to prove when Lucchese first began associating with Mafia members. Nor are there any details as to the date of his induction. However, it is reasonable to conclude that the Family leaders brought him into the organization sometime in the 1920s.

July 5, 1929
Gaetano "Tommy" Lucchese was born. He would later graduate from the US Military academy.

Joe Pinzolo become Boss

February 26, 1930
A gunman brandishing a double-barrelled shotgun blasted Boss Tommy Reina with ten slugs. Boss of Bosses Joe Masseria supported Joe Pinzolo's taking of the throne. However, Lucchese and a few others were very unhappy. Bonanno called Lucchese "The second leading figure of the Reina (Lucchese) Family, which meant he was the Underboss.

The Castellammarese War

In the late 1930s, Boss of Bosses Joe Masseria of the Genovese Family began interfering in various other Families' leaderships, including the Luccheses, the Detroit Family, and the chaotic situation in Chicago. Most of his rivals were of Castellammarese del Golfo origins in Sicily. The Bonanno Family in New York was predominantly of that background, especially in its administrative positions.

Salvatore Maranzano, formally just a Soldier in the Bonanno Family, desired to return to a position of power as he enjoyed in Sicily. Maranzano described Masseria's actions as an attack on all Castellammarese people and thus on the Bonanno Family. This theory gained significant traction, and soon Maranzano had become the de facto leader of the Bonanno Family and all others opposed to Masseria for one reason or another.

Castellammarese groups in Chicago, Detroit, Buffalo, Philadelphia, and elsewhere funneled into New York to aid the Maranzano alliance in their war with Masseria.

Gagliano become Boss

September 5, 1930
Bobby Doyle Santucci killed Boss Joe Pinzolo in Suite 1007 of the Brokaw Building, 1487 Broadway, according to Valachi. He ran California Dried Fruit Importers and rented the office from Lucchese. Pinzolo died of five gunshots.

According to Joe Bonanno, Lucchese was among a tight group of Reina loyalists who plotted against new Boss Joe Pinzolo. When the cops looked for Lucchese, his friends said he had left town, and they didn't know where he went.

September 8, 1930
The Daily News ran a small story saying that Lucchese had turned himself in for questioning on the Joe Pinzolo murder on September 5. It said police would hold him without bail and that his residence was 213 E 106th Street.

November 5, 1930
Bonanno wrote that Lucchese had recruited new Associates, including Joe Valachi. The latter noticed Boss Joe Masseria entering his apartment complex and alerted Lucchese. Bonanno Boss Salvatore Maranzano then sent orders for Masseria to be killed. However, the shooters failed in getting Masseria but did murder the two top men in the Gambino Family, Al Mineo and Steve Ferrigno.

December 1930
Lucchese joined other supporters of Boss Salvatore Maranzano for a party held at a farm near Hyde Park.

February 24, 1931
A grand jury did not indict Lucchese for the Pinzolo killing.

April 1931
Allies of Boss of Bosses Joe Masseria gunned him down after realizing their side was losing the war to the Maranzano forces. This hit brought Lucky Luciano to the top of what we now call the Genovese Family.

June 6, 1931
Francis Lucchese was born. She would later marry Tommy Gambino, a son of Mafia Boss Carlo Gambino.

July 4, 1931
Police arrested Lucchese, Charles "Lucky" Luciano, and Joe Biondo at a boxing match in Cleveland but released them after questioning.

September 10, 1931,
According to Lucchese's testimony decades later, he accompanied Tommy Gagliano to the offices of Salvatore Maranzano. Lucchese was uncertain why they went there but guessed it might have been to buy lottery tickets or for Gagliano to obtain renovation work from Maranzano. Instead, four men with badges entered. Two held the people in the office at gunpoint while the other two stabbed and shot Maranzano to death and fled. The police questioned Lucchese but laid no charges. In 1952, Lucchese told a New York Crime Commission that he saw nothing.

The Commission Era Begins

October 1931
After the death of Maranzano, the leading Bosses of La Cosa Nostra agreed to form a Commission of seven Bosses to set policy, confirm leadership changes and arbitrate disputes among Families. Previously the strongest Boss had those powers, but this method had led to constant bloodshed. So everyone was ready for a change in 1931. Lucchese Boss Tom Gagliano became one of the seven original members of the Commission.

November 11, 1935
Police arrested Lucchese (they listed him as Lacase) for vagrancy, but Judge Klapp dismissed the charges.

Naturalization Problems
After much media attention to Lucchese's connection to political and criminal figures, the Immigration authorities attempted to remove Lucchese's naturalization beginning in 1952. The government tried to use this legal means to remove alleged criminals from the United States. They had some success, but many well-financed mobsters could fend off this method of government attack. Lucchese was one of these men.

A simplified explanation of this battle between Lucchese and the feds follows. I will get into more detail on the role of publicity in another section.

October 9, 1936
Lucchese filed his first papers for naturalization in Newark.

November. 1936
Luchese was living at 1093 Briarway, Palisades, NJ.

July 13, 1940
Lucchese filed his final papers for naturalization. He stated that he had only one arrest for car theft in 1921 and no others.

December 16, 1940
Lucchese filed his alien registration and stated he had only one arrest in 1921 and no others.

November 21, 1941
A naturalization examiner questioned Lucchese on his background. Lucchese repeated that he had only one arrest (in 1921) and always spelled his name the same.

1942
Lucchese was living at 106 Parsons Blvd, Malba, NY.

January 25, 1943
Lucchese obtained his naturalization in Newark. The witnesses were Thomas Valente and Anthony Vadala. Years later, the feds would argue that he received his citizenship fraudulently.

1944
Lucchese voted in Queen's as Gaetano Lucchese.

1949
Armand Chankalian was the administrative assistant to US Attorney Myles Lane. He was also a good friend of Lucchese. Chankalian met with New York Governor Thomas Dewey in the hopes of receiving a pardon for Lucchese's auto theft conviction from January 1922. Instead, Dewey referred Chankalian to his secretary, who was to put him in touch with the New York Parole Board. This meeting would make headlines in 1952 when Chankalian appeared before the New York State Crime Commission.

Fall 1950

In 1949 popular Democratic Mayor William O'Dwyer won re-election as New York's leader. However, a series of police corruption scandals plagued his regime such that both federal and state authorities were on his tail. Democratic President Herbert Hoover suddenly appointed O'Dwyer as the United States Ambassador to Mexico in the hopes of ending the controversies.

When O'Dwyer resigned as Mayor at the end of August 1949, Vincent Impellitteri, the City Council President, stepped in to complete the rest of O'Dwyer's second term. However, when Impellitteri decided to run for election in 1950, the Democratic Party surprisingly changed horses and selected Judge Ferdinand Pecora. Although the Democrats offered Impellitteri a consolation prize of a judgeship, he decided to run independently under the Experience Party label. The Republicans picked Edward Corsi as their flag bearer.

Candidate Corsi brought Lucchese's name into public view in October 1950. First, he charged that Lucchese had aided Impellitteri in winning the Democratic nomination for City Council President in 1945. Then Corsi described Lucchese as a man with a police record operating legitimate coat and suit businesses as a front for his underworld activities. Finally, he also alleged that other gangsters were backing candidate Judge Pecora. These accusations led to a huge uproar and heavy press coverage.

The result was that everyone wanted to talk to Lucchese. The press, the Kefauver Committee, and a local grand jury pursued him relentlessly. For our purposes, I will focus on the activities of the New York State Crime Commission.

Lucchese reluctantly agreed to be interviewed in private but legally fought any attempts to have his testimony in public. Commission officials questioned Lucchese seven times over a period stretching from September 29, 1952, until November 10, 1952. All his testimony resulted in more than 500 pages on the record.

Frustrated by Lucchese's legal attempts to prevent his public examination, the Commission decided to read a summary of his private inquiry. This public event happened on November 14, 1952. It caused a sensation and was national news. (Please see the section on Lucchese and the press).

November 22, 1950
District Attorney Frank Hogan impaneled a grand jury to look into charges during the mayoralty campaign.

February 1951
Rudolph Halley, the counsel of the Kefauver Senate Committee, announced he would call witnesses to inquire into the New York mayoralty race and all the allegations of gangster/politician tie-ups.

Lucchese is the new Boss

February 16, 1951
Boss Tom Gagliano died of natural causes. So Underboss Tommy Lucchese became the new Boss and took his seat on the Commission.

February 19, 1951
The Kefauver Committee subpoenaed Lucchese. They wanted to talk to him about the mayoralty campaign in NY City. US Marshalls served Lucchese at his lawyer's office, Arthur Swartz of 19E, 70th Street.

April 19, 1951
Mangano had been the Boss of what we now call the Gambino Family since 1931. Towards the end of his reign, Joe Bonanno told us that the growing ambitions of Underboss Albert Anastasia began to worry Mangano. According to Bonanno, Mangano felt him out in the hopes Bonanno would help eliminate Anastasia. Bonanno refused.

In brief, Mangano disappeared on April 19, 1951, and some plotters killed his brother. Anastasia, the natural suspect, did not admit to the hits but claimed the Mangano's had been plotting against him. Boss Frank Costello supported Anastasia's right to self-defence. The Commission, including Lucchese, then approved Anastasia as Boss of the Gambino Family, and he took a seat on the ruling body. Frank Costello was content, for he now had a strong ally against Vito Genovese.

October 4, 1951
Shooters killed Genovese Family Underboss Willie Moretti in Joe's Elbow Room restaurant in Cliffside, NJ. Boss and friend Frank Costello had become disenchanted with Moretti, who felt slighted by Costello's growing closeness to Albert Anastasia.

Costello felt the need to form an alliance with Anastasia, the Boss of the Gambino Family, to counter the ambitions of Vito Genovese. The latter had been Underboss in the Genovese Family before fleeing to Italy in the late 1930s. After World War Two, the authorities brought Genovese back to America to face a murder charge, but a Judge freed Genovese. He then continued angling to find a way to unseat Costello.

Moretti's outgoing personality, his frustration with his loss of prestige, plus his total obliviousness that he might be in danger because of his opposition to Boss Frank Costello's moves all created unease in Mafia circles in New York. Soon rumors began flying that syphilis caused Moretti's loquaciousness. The worry then became that Moretti might spill Mafia secrets; thus, he was a danger to all.

Joe Bonanno wrote, "Willie's mind was rapidly disintegrating. He was an embarrassment... Costello and Anastasia said that Moretti was a sick man. We could not disagree. Poor Willie."

The irony was that Moretti did not have syphilis, and at autopsy, Bergen County Medical Examiner Dr. Ralph Gilady found no evidence of brain damage. Unfortunately, most profiles of Moretti do not include this critical fact.

The murder of Moretti removed a potential troublemaker from the leadership of La Cosa Nostra. In hindsight, his loss eliminated another potential obstacle to the ambitions of Vito Genovese. It is safe to assume that Lucchese supported the hit on Moretti.

October 29, 1951
Former mayoralty candidate Corsi went on WNBC and repeated his charge that Lucchese had supported Impellitteri in his successful run for the 1945 chairmanship of New York City Council. (He also said that other well-known gangsters were helping Pecora.) Not surprisingly, everyone concerned denied these charges.

September 29, 1951, to November 10, 1952
Lucchese made seven private appearances before the New York State Crime Commission.

September 20, 1952
Shooters killed Lucchese Soldier Eugene Giannini on this date. Joe Valachi, in 1963, publicly revealed the details of this hit. A summary follows below.

Joe Valachi and his Capo Anthony "Tony Bender" Strollo met in Rocco's tavern. Bender relays that the exiled Lucky Luciano told Vito Genovese that Giannini was an informer. Valachi mentioned that Giannini owed him a few thousand dollars.

A month later, Valachi met with Bender in the Gold Key Club. Bender indicated that the Lucchese guys were having difficulty finding Bender. Valachi offered to hit Giannini to avoid any suspicion he didn't reveal Giannini's location due to the money he owed Valachi. Bender said he'd have to get the OK from Genovese.

Bender passed on the word Genovese approved of Valachi doing the hit the next day. He then rounded up Associates Pat Pagano, Joe Pagano, and his nephew Fiore Siano to commit the murder. Valachi schooled the trio on the proper method of whacking someone.

Valachi discovered the Giannini was working at a crap game run by Paul "Paulie Ham" of the Lucchese Family. He then sought permission from Bender to carry out the hit at another Family's gambling spot. Bender checked with Genovese and relayed his approval.

One of the three-person hit teams killed Giannini with two shots, and the group fled successfully. Valachi later proposed the trio for membership which Boss Frank Costello approved. Unfortunately for Siano, when Valachi rolled in the early sixties, someone made him disappear permanently.

November 14, 1952
Armand Chankalian testified before the New York State Crime Commission. He described how he met with Governor Dewey in 1949 in the hopes of gaining a pardon for Lucchese for his 1922 auto theft conviction. Instead, according to Chankalian, Dewey referred him to the New York State Parole Board.

November 17, 1952
Attorney General James McGranery directed US Attorney Frank J Parker in Brooklyn to file a petition in US District Court to cancel Lucchese's naturalization on grounds he concealed his criminal record and fudged his name. Unfortunately for the government, they did not file the required affidavit of good cause with the complaint.

November 18, 1952
US Marshalls failed to find Lucchese at either of his homes to serve him with a subpoena. The New York papers covered the attempt.

November 21, 1952
Attorney General James McGranery told the press that his office had been investigating Lucchese for possible deportation for three months. As asked when Marshalls would find Lucchese, McGranery replied, "We'll have him, we'll get him."

November 28, 1952
FBI Agents served Lucchese with a deportation writ at lawyer Louis F Frohlich's office at 19E 70the Street. Frohlich arranged this meeting. Lucchese quietly accepted the summons to which he had 60 days to reply in Federal Court.

Lucchese left a message for the press. What follows are the main points.

The pursuit of Lucchese was a political stunt by Rudolph Haley, President of the City Council.

Lucchese wrote that Haley claimed to have provided important information to the Crime Commission, but that body denied it.

The mobster stated that the office of US Marshall Eugene Smith had refused to serve the summons at the lawyer's office on November 18, despite Lucchese waiting more than three hours for the Marshalls.

Instead, the Marshalls went to two of Lucchese's homes, accompanied by the press knowing full well that Lucchese wasn't there.

The FBI's November 19 announcement of a nationwide search was a fraud. The Agents could only serve Lucchese with this summons in New York State.

Lucchese wrote that he had no reason to avoid being served, for the authorities had not indicted him, and he had not committed any crimes.

Lucchese promised to tell the whole story of his persecution later.

Denaturalization Premise

When filing his naturalization papers, Lucchese stated he had been convicted of auto theft and had served time. However, the feds alleged that Lucchese deliberately did not reveal that he had been arrested twice for murder along with some other minor offenses. Lucchese countered that the officials only asked if he was in trouble after filing for naturalization.

1955
Lucchese's Plot against Anastasia
According to Joe Bonanno, Tommy Lucchese and Vito Genovese were very close. Lucchese envied Costello's political clout in New York while Genovese coveted the leadership of the Family. Bonanno wrote about their alliance, "The expression I like to use is 'They were making love.'"

In an attempt to pre-empt any attack by Lucchese and Genovese, Costello went before the Commission and accused Lucchese of plotting against Anastasia. He presented two Lucchese Soldiers who confirmed the charge. To further the seriousness of the matter, Costello said that Anastasia was aware of the plot and didn't intend to stand idle. In other words, war might break out.

Joe Bonanno gave a lengthy explanation of the Commission meeting that was to decide Lucchese's fate. As usual, he gave himself a starring role using his brilliance and understanding of people to get the result he desired. According to Bonanno, Lucchese confessed his Anastasia plot but explained that he had discovered Anastasia planned to kill him, so Lucchese was only defending himself. Anastasia forgave Lucchese, and everyone was friends. Bonanno had saved the peace. (Yeah, right!)

June 4, 1955
Lucchese attended the marriage of Boss Joe Profaci's daughter, Carmela, to Anthony Tocco, a future Boss of the Detroit Family.

October 27, 1955
Lucchese moved to dismiss the US petition to permit his deportation. He claimed that the order was not valid, for the government failed to file an affidavit of good cause with the paperwork.

November 23, 1955
The US filed the affidavit to support the Lucchese petition of deportation in an overdue move. It was dated November 17, 1955, the same date as the

original deportation order. But, unfortunately, someone had forgotten to file it back then. Nevertheless, Judge Inch denied the Lucchese motion to dismiss the order of deportation.

March 26, 1956
Once again, Lucchese filed a motion to have his denaturalization order dismissed. His focus was on the affidavit that the government had filed late. Judge Inch denied the Lucchese motion.

May 1956
Basing his decision on a recent relevant court ruling, Judge Inch ruled that the government had fatally errored when it did not file the affidavit of good cause at the same time as the petition for denaturalization. He then dismissed the order of denaturalization.

October 1956
1956 National Meeting of La Cosa Nostra
The Bosses of the many La Cosa Nostra Families around the United States gathered at the estate of Joe Barbara near Apalachin, New York. Back when the Commission was formed, in 1931, the Bosses agreed to hold a National Meeting every five years to put their blessing on the Commission members in their new term. The Mafia leaders also discussed other matters of national interest, including whether to ban or allow drug dealing.

This National Meeting concluded undetected, and we can assume that Lucchese was present, although there is no evidence to prove he was. Bonanno Underboss Carmine Galante was stopped for speeding when he was departing the area, but this event had little significance at the time.

November 15, 1956
John and Ben Nicolosi told the FBI that Lucchese was a former partner with Tommy Gagliano in the Central Lathing Company. John Nicolosi was the son-in-law of Thomas Valenti, the man who witnessed Lucchese's citizenship papers back in 1943.

May 2, 1957
Boss Frank Costello was entering the lobby of his apartment building when Soldier Vince Gigante wounded him in the head. Gigante fled before finishing the job, but it didn't matter. Costello got the message and promptly "retired," leaving the Boss position to Vito Genovese.

Background:
When federal prosecutors convicted Boss Lucky Luciano in 1936, his Underboss Vito Genovese briefly became Acting Boss. But a murder accusation caused Genovese to flee to Italy, where he remained till 1946. This action opened the door for Capo Frank Costello to become Acting Boss.

In the early 1950s, Costello became a celebrity when his contacts with high-powered politicians became known. Unfortunately, this publicity made him a huge target, and the resulting crush greatly handicapped him and opened the way for the ambitions of Vito Genovese.

In brief, Costello's legal problems included a prison sentence for contempt before the Kefauver Committee, tax sentences, and an attempt by the feds to remove his denaturalization. These actions meant Costello was constantly in and out of court and prison as cases unfolded and he undertook appeals. As a result, there was little time for La Cosa Nostra's business, and Genovese pointed this out to everyone.

June 17, 1957
The Second Circuit Court of Appeals reversed Judge Inch's ruling that dismissed the denaturalization petition against Lucchese.

October 25, 1957
The Death of Albert Anastasia
Anastasia was a long-time Mafioso who spent many decades as the Underboss to Vincent Mangano, the Gambino Family leader. As discussed above, Anastasia shot his way to the top of the Family in 1951. However, by 1957, his Consigliere, Carlo Gambino, had formed secret alliances, including with Boss Tommy Lucchese. Sensing the intrigue, Anastasia had his Underboss, Frank Scalise, whacked out on May 2, 1957. There is no evidence that I am aware that Scalise was plotting against Anastasia. Nevertheless, he ended up dead.

Theoretically, the Commission would have voted on whether the plotters could kill Anastasia. It is reasonable to assume the Boss Tommy Lucchese supported his long-time friend Carlo Gambino. Joe Bonanno wrote that he was opposed to any action against Anastasia. There is no direct evidence of the vote of Commission members Vito Genovese, Joe Profaci, Stefano Magaddino, and Sam Giancanna, the Chicago Outfit Boss. However, the future indicated they gave their blessing.

On October 25, 1957, two gunmen allied with Carlo Gambino killed Anastasia in a barbershop. Later, the Commission approved Gambino as Boss. Still, many New York leaders felt it necessary to hold a National Meeting to inform other Bosses around the nation that everything was tranquil in the Big Apple. But, unfortunately, that decision would prove to be a disaster.

November 14, 1957
1957 National Meeting of La Cosa Nostra at Apalachin
When the Mafia Bosses and their aids gathered at Joseph Barbara's Apalachin estate, they were minutes from disaster. Sgt Edgar Croswell of the New York State Police and an assistant were nearby. They had become suspicious of a few out-of-town autos in nearby Binghamton and at Barbara's home. So the following day, they and two officers from ATF drove to Barbara's estate and found many vehicles parked there.

The officers started taking down plate numbers from their unmarked vehicle when some of Barbara's guests discovered them. Trooper Vasisko backed the car out of the driveway, and the officers set up a roadblock at the bottom of the hill leading to Barbara's.

Eventually, 58 men were stopped and identified, either at the roadblock, in the surrounding fields and forests, or at the Vestal Trooper station. Lucchese was not among these men, although Capo John Ormento was. It is safe to assume that at least Boss Lucchese was invited. Whether he was able to flee successfully or arrived late remains a mystery. Various courts sentenced some Mafiosi to prison for refusing to testify before a Grand Jury or Committee. The bottom line is that Lucchese's absence protected him from the wild publicity and endless legal battles.

April 7, 1958
The US Supreme Court dismissed the denaturalization proceedings against Lucchese because the US government failed to file the required affidavit of good cause with their petition back in 1952.

June 4, 1958
The Federal Bureau of Narcotics arrested Andimo Papadio for a vast drug conspiracy. However, the judge released him on $5,000 bail.

July 3, 1958
Background: The McClellan Hearings

The US Senate Select Committee on Improper Activities in Labor and Management began operation on January 30, 1957, and ran until March 31, 1960. The Committee was to investigate criminal activity in unions and management and then recommend changes in US laws to right the problems. They conducted hundreds of investigations, interviewed more than a thousand witnesses, and created a media storm. The most remembered events were the televised clashes between Committee counsel Robert Kennedy and Teamster leader Jimmy Hoffa. The Committee and its work is a book in itself. However, I will concentrate on the appearance of Lucchese.

Before the McClellan Committee, Lucchese testified that he was not a member of the Mafia and not connected to illegal activities:
He testified that he lost his right index finger in an industrial accident in 1917.

When the cops arrested him in 1921, Lucchese stated they named him Three-Finger Brown after famous pitcher Mordecai Brown.

Lucchese testified he was a dress contractor from Long Island.
He refused to say whether he was a partner in "Budget Dress Corp" of NYC.
On any questions about his Associates, Lucchese took the 5th.

A photographer took a picture of Lucchese as the Committee swore him in. It clearly showed that his right thumb and forefinger were missing.
Lucchese escaped relatively unharmed from the McClellan Committee and its powers compared to many other witnesses.

1960
FBI's list of Lucchese Capos
Joseph LaRatro
Joseph Lucchese
John Ormento
James Plumeri
Joseph Rosato
Salvatore Santora
Carmine Tramunti
Paul Correale

February 20, 1961
The US Supreme Court ruled that the US government could re-file a petition of denaturalization against Lucchese.

1964
An informant told the FBI that Lucchese had taken over illegal gambling in Queen's. His brother Joe Lucchese was in charge with Joe LaRato doing the grunt work.

February 1964
A special federal grand jury began investigating the affairs of the Lucchese Family. But unfortunately, most of the gangsters who appeared refused to testify. Among those were: Underboss Stefano LaSalle, Capo Joe Plumeri, Consigliere Vince Rao, Capo Joe Rosato, Capo Andimo Pappadio, Capo Carmine Tramunti, Soldier Tommy Dioguardia, Anthony Castaldi, and NJ Capo Salvatore LoProto.

1964-1968
Carlo Gambino and Tommy Lucchese accused Boss Joe Magliocco of the Colombo Family and Joe Bonanno, Boss of his Family, of plotting to kill them. As a result, Magliocco appeared before the Commission, which refused to recognize him as Boss. Instead, they ordered him to pay a fine of $40,000 and call a new election for Boss.

After many excuses, Bonanno never turned himself into the Commission. Instead, they voted to dethrone Bonanno and recognize one of his long-time Capos as the new Boss. Finally, after four years of sporadic violence, Bonanno threw in the towel and retired to Arizona. Lucchese and Gambino were triumphant.

July 1964
A judge sentenced Soldier Salvatore "Sally Shields" Shillitani to two years for refusing to testify before the Lucchese grand jury. The judge ruled no bail.

August 1964
A judge sentenced Soldier Anthony Castaldi to two years for refusing to testify before the Lucchese grand jury. However, he released Castaldi on $20,000 bail.

September 29, 1964
The FBI learned that a group of Mafia powers met at Runyon Sales Company at 45th St and 29th Ave. Present were Genovese Acting Boss Jerry Catena, Genovese Underboss Tommy Eboli, Lucchese Capo Carmine Tramunti, and Gambino Boss Carlo Gambino.

According to the informant, Catena told Eboli that Lucchese was working on finding out where they might find renegade Boss Joe Bonanno. Catena indicated that Lucchese might need help from the Genovese Family.

October 30, 1964
After receiving immunity, Andimo Pappadio still refused to testify before a federal grand jury. The panel wanted to ask him five questions about his meeting with Boss Tommy Lucchese. A jury found him guilty with the result. Judge William B Herlands sentenced Andimo Pappadio to two years and ruled no bail.

US Attorney Robert Morgenthau told the press that Pappadio was the principal stockholder in Tempo Fashions located at 230W 38th St and drew a salary of $30,000 to $40,000.

Pappadio was also on $5,000 bail from drug charges.

Carmine Tramunti became the Boss

July 13, 1967
After a long battle with cancer, Boss Tommy Lucchese passed away. Capo Carmine Tramunti became Boss.

Samples of Media Coverage of Lucchese in the 1950s

Like many other mob Bosses of the era, Lucchese attempted to present a legitimate life and sought the acquaintance of influential figures. But, as Jimmy Breslin used to write, he succeeded until he didn't.

October 29, 1950
Edward Corsi, the Republican candidate for Mayor, went on WNBC TV and charged that one of his opponents, Vito Impellitteri, had been supported by Lucchese for the New York Council Presidency in 1945.

October 30, 1950
The local newspapers covered Corsi's charges, but the Lucchese allegation was just one of many aspects of the fierce campaign covered in the article.

November 25, 1950

District Attorney Frank Hogan released a statement to the press announcing a special grand jury to look into the claims of collusion between gangsters and politicians. The papers included Lucchese's name in the Hogan story. (Page 10 in the Daily News).

February 20, 1951
The Daily News reported that Marshalls had served Lucchese with a subpoena for the Kefauver Hearings. (Page 36)

February 24, 1951
The media covered the announcement that it had scheduled testimony from Mayor Impellitteri and former candidate Ferdinand Pecora. The Daily News reported that Edward Corsi had already testified and repeated his Lucchese and Impellitteri allegations.

March 16, 1951
Fortunately for Lucchese, the media focused on the startling walkout of Boss Frank Costello before the Kefauver Hearings in New York. However, the Daily News reported that Bureau of Narcotics Agent Sam Levine had testified that drug dealing connected Lucchese and Lucky Luciano. (Page 48)

March 22, 1951
The media reported that Mayor Impellitteri had written to the Kefauver Committee denying the Corsi claims about him and Lucchese. (Page C12)

September 4, 1952
When Lucchese, accompanied by Superior Court Justice Ferdinand Pecora, attended Foley Square for a New York State Crime Committee appointment, the New York Daily News Photographer waited. Lucchese was furious that the photographer had snapped his picture in an elevator. He yelled, "Let me alone! Let me alone!" The Mob Boss was probably even angrier when the image appeared on the front page of the Daily News on September 4.

November 10, 1952
The New York Daily News wrote an extensive story on Lucchese. (Page C3)

November 11, 1952
The Daily News wrote another lengthy piece on Lucchese.

November 12, 1952
The Daily News continued their series on Lucchese.

November 13, 1952
The Daily News carried another long article on Lucchese.

November 14, 1952
The Daily News published stories about why the FBI initiated an investigation into Lucchese's friend, Armand Chankalian.

The Miami News p 17 headline
LUCHESE CALLED NEW MOB CZAR

The Chicago Tribune Lucchese headline on page 11
KEY TAMMANY AIDS BAR CLOSE GANGSTER TIES

November 15, 1952
The previous day, a New York State Crime Commission member read a summary of Lucchese's seven appearances before that body. The Daily News gave it extensive coverage. A summary follows:

"The frightening story of how Thomas "Three Finger Brown Lucchese, murder suspect, dope peddler, and thug stamped his influence on the political life of New York and into high place to extract favors."

"Luchese could move politicians of both parties to obtain favors and could reach into City Hall and the Executive Mansion in Albany for special privileges through his many friends."

"He manipulated federal officeholders through his political contact and used his influence in Washington to put through his naturalization although he was already notorious and neglected to mention two homicide arrests."

The Montreal Gazette story headline on page 2
"Three-Finger" Takes New Job As Mob Czar

The Philadelphia Inquirer Lucchese headline on page 6
Several High Officials Linked to Costello Heir

The Los Angeles Times Lucchese headline
Costello Pal Described as Crime Boss

The Chicago Tribune headline about Lucchese on page 3
NY Crime Quiz Ties High Officials to Racket Leader

The New York Times headline about Lucchese on page 10
Excerpt from the Testimony of Luchese and Chankalian at the State Crime Hearing

November 16, 1952
The Daily News front-page headline.
LANE IS GATHERING ALL LUCHESE DATA FOR RACKETS JURY

November 18, 1952
A Daily News sub-headline stated, "Act to Deport Lucchese, Other Crime Biggies."

The New York Times headline on page one
McGranery Acts to Deport Luchese to His Native Italy

November 19, 1952
The Daily News carried an article describing the US Marshall's failed attempt to serve Lucchese with a subpoena from the Kefauver Committee.

The Miami News page 12 headline
US Acts To Strip Mob King Luchese of His Citizenship

The New York Times on page 24
CRIME BODY DROPS THREAT TO LUCHESE

November 21, 1952
The New York Times Luchese headline on page 20
FBI SEEKS LUCHESE WHO EVADES MARSHALLS

November 22, 1952
The Daily News headline on page 84
FAVOR TO LUCHESE DENIED BY WICK

The New York Times on page one
Lawyer Seeks to Force the State Crime Unit to Void Racketeer's Immunity

November 28, 1952
The Philadelphia Inquirer Lucchese headline on page 18
LUCHESE GIVES UP TO AGENTS OF THE FBI

November 29, 1952
The Chicago Tribune Lucchese headline on page 9
TOP US RACKET BOSS GIVES UP, ENDS FBI HUNT

The New York Times headline on page one
DEPORTATION WRIT SERVED ON LUCHESE

Lucchese's Influential Friends

Note:
Knowing Lucchese did not necessarily mean there was anything criminal going on.

July 31 and August 1, 1950
Washington's Mayflower Hotel had Lucchese and Armand Chankalian registered as guests. Chankalian was the chief assistant to US Attorney Myles Lane.

August 21 and 22, 1950
Washington's Mayflower Hotel had Lucchese and Chankalian registered as guests.

September 14, 1950
Washington's Mayflower Hotel had Lucchese and US Attorney Myles Lane registered as guests.

November 14, 1952
Officials of the New York Crime Commission raked Chankalian over the coals about his close association with Lucchese. Below is a list of some of the revelations.

In 1949 Chankalian asked Governor Dewey to issue a pardon to Lucchese for his 1921 car theft conviction. Instead, Dewey's office directed him to the New York State Parole Board, which gave Lucchese a Certificate of Good Conduct.

Chankalian approached Federal Judge Thomas F Meaney of Newark to meet with Lucchese. The latter wanted to intercede for a man awaiting sentencing. However, Meany refused to meet with Lucchese on two occasions.

Chankalian attended many formal dinners in New York with Lucchese. At these events, he would introduce Lucchese to many prominent citizens.

Chankalian retained a room at the Hotel Astor from 1945 to 1952. To many, it seemed he was living beyond his means. Lucchese stayed in the same hotel between March 18 to 20, 1948, but his bill went to Chankalian.

Between January 16 to February 6, 1949, the Miami Beach Hotel had Chankalian and Lucchese as guests. Chankalian, in 1952, testified this was just a coincidence.

After the controversial 1950 New York mayoralty race, a candidate exposed Lucchese as a hood. Chankalian claimed it was when he cut off all contact with Lucchese. However, police surveillance spotted his vehicle near the mobster's home several times in February, March, and April 1951.

February 3, 1953
Attorney General Herbert Brownell ordered the resignation of Armand Chankalian.

Carmine DeSapio
Long-time New York Democratic power

Thomas Murphy
New York Police Commissioner and later a judge
Testified that he had visited Lucchese's home twice, Lucchese went to his home twice and that he had met with Lucchese about 12 times.
Murphy invited Lucchese to sit at his table at the 1949 Friendly Sons of St Patrick dinner at the Hotel Astor.

Irving Saypol
US Attorney for the Southern District and later a Justice on the New York Supreme Court

Charles E Ramsgate
A New York Magistrate

Louis J Capozzoli
Democratic Representative in Congress ((1941-1945), a lawyer, then various positions as a Judge including sitting on the New York Supreme Court

James Bruno
Republican District Leader in East Harlem and
Confidential Secretary to the Supreme Court

Myles J Lane
US Attorney
Lane admitted accompanying Lucchese to see a West Point Football Game and other meetings.

Charles Neal
Chairman of Tammany Hall Election Committee

Hugo Rogers
Tammany Hall power

Frank Sampson
Tammany Hall Power

Harry Brickman
Politician

Vito Marcantonio
Representative
"Long-time friend"

Francis X Mancuso
Judge

Arthur W Wicks
State Senator
He met with Luchese and then arranged an investigation of his character. He passed on the report to parole officials responsible for issuing good conduct certificates. Wicks said he did not include any recommendations in the document.

Ferdinand Pecora
Supreme Court Justice
Lawyer

John J Merli
New York City Councillor
Lucchese drove back from Florida with Merli and another man.

Despite all the negative publicity and the many violent enemies, Lucchese survived in the world of La Cosa Nostra for many decades. It is a testament to good luck, smarts, and an ability to impose his will on some tough characters. More than fifty years after his death, the Lucchese (or Luchese) name still designates the Mafia Family he once controlled.

Next on the throne was Capo Carmine Tramunti, whom you will learn about in the next chapter.

CHAPTER FIVE

Boss Carmine "Mr. Gribbs" Tramunti

Tramunti is one of the lesser-known Lucchese Family Bosses. The membership voted him as their new Boss when Tommy Lucchese passed away in 1967. It may have seemed like a beautiful experience, but things went bad quickly.

Tramunti spent much of the 1960 and early 1970s before grand juries investigating various crimes. So, naturally, he would refuse to testify, resulting in a seemingly endless round of court cases. His costs must have been terrific.

By the mid-1970s, Tramunti's future looked grim. A grand jury indicted him for a drug conspiracy, and a jury convicted the Boss at the subsequent trial. His many appeals failed, leaving him to rot in prison until he died in 1978. What follows is an outline of his career in La Cosa Nostra.

DOB
October 1, 1910
Casala, Italy

DOD
October 15, 1978
In prison

Descriptions
5'10"
200 lbs
Brown eyes
Dark brown hair
Heavy build

Daily News
May 1973
Portly hood

Daily News
October 1973
Jauntily attired in a maroon
Shirt, grey checkered coat, and black slacks.
Rotund

Daily News
October 1973
Fat but not jolly, man

Wife
Lillian Anelli

Sons
Robert
Louis-deceased

Father
Luigi

Mother
Rosa DeRosa

Sister
Ermiland Fioranventi

Residences

215 E 112th Street, NYC
1429 Leland Ave, Bronx
Circa 1930

145-79 6th Ave, Whitestone, LI

Businesses
Imperial Truck Co
37th St, NYC
Closed around 1964

Rosalie Florist
645 Lexington Ave, NYC
Circa 1964

Eiffel Classic Dress Co
263 W 38th, Manhattan
Part owner

September 1, 1913
Arrived in the USA aboard the Duca D'Abuzzi

April 18, 1929
In the US Court for the Southern District of NY, Carmine Tramunti applied for his Declaration of Intention, a step to Naturalization. He listed his occupation as a truck helper.

November 22, 1930
Two hoods robbed a rent collector in a hallway at 1638 Madison Ave. He claimed they took $917 in cash and $2,000 in jewelry.

December 9, 1930
Police arrested Carmine Tramunti and Paul Correale on suspicion of robbery from the November 22, 1930 incident.

December 25, 1930
Magistrate McKiniry discharged Tramunti and Correale. Police suspected them of committing a robbery on November 22, 1930.

May 23, 1931
Tramunti discharged a revolver at a detective during a robbery.

June 2, 1931
Someone carried out a $1,000 holdup in City Fuel and Ice Company offices located at 219th St and 9th Ave. One of the victims identified Tramunti as the gunman at a later date.

July 24, 1931
A magistrate released Tramunti, whom the police held on suspicion of burglary.

July 25, 1931
Magistrate Francis Irwin held Tramunti for wounding a police detective during a holdup on May 23, 1931. While in court, the June 2, 1931 holdup victim identified Tramunti as the culprit. The magistrate set bail at $3,000.

December 8, 1932
Judge Allan sentenced Tramunti to prison for his second-degree assault conviction for firing on a detective during a robbery on May 23, 1931.

December 13, 1932
Prison officials took Tramunti into their care at Sing Sing prison. His admitting form said his crime was a second-degree assault and that he had been in jail for 112 days. I assume he did that after a judge revoked his bail before trial. They listed his sentences as 1-0-0/5-0-0 and 5-0-0/10-0-0.

Tramunti told prison officials that he worked eight months at NY and Queens Electric Power Company in 1929. Before that, Tramunti said he spent eight weeks at JG Ellis Clothing Manufacturing in 1928.

December 12, 1933
BOP officials released Tramunti from prison.

Note:
I cannot figure out how Tramunti got out on parole so soon. Perhaps the prison officials messed up their calculations on his admittance papers.

December 1, 1937
Tramunti married Angela Anelli.

1940
The US Census takers found Tramunti residing at Ossington Prison (Sing Sing). I assume the parole people busted him in a violation; thus, he ended up back at Sing Sing.

September 9, 1942
Tramunti registered for the draft. He listed his employer as United Sportswear at 72 Spring Ave in NYC. His address was 1429 Leland Ave in the Bronx.

October 12, 1944
Police arrested Tramunti for shooting two men at 74th and York Ave.

January 22, 1945
Authorities held Tramunti in jail, without bail, for the alleged shooting of two men.

February 20, 1945
A judge dismissed all charges against Tramunti for the shooting of two men.

November 14, 1957
During the investigation of the National Meeting of La Cosa Nostra at the Apalachin estate of Joe Barbara, New York State Troopers found a business card with Tramunti's name on it. A guess would be that some hood dropped it, for there is no evidence that Tramunti was there or in the vicinity.

January 15, 1962
Tramunti told two FBI Agents that he had several dice games in East Harlem but added they weren't doing too well the last two weeks. He bragged that he would cover any wager a person wanted to make. (He would loan the person the money if he lost the bet.)

February 13, 1964
Tramunti refused to answer questions before a Southern District grand jury investigating narcotics law violations.

April 23, 1964
Tramunti again refused to answer questions before the Southern District grand jury. They wanted to ask Tramunti about narcotics and the Lucchese Family, as well as Tramunti's possible role in drug trafficking.

May 7, 1964
Once again, Tramunti refused to answer the grand jury's questions.

August 4, 1964
The US Attorney for the Southern District applied for an order to compel Tramunti to testify before the grand jury. Judge Lloyd F MacMahon granted

Tramunti immunity and ordered him to testify. He gave Tramunti a couple of days to consult his lawyer.

November 10, 1964
Although the Judge had given Tramunti permission to consult his lawyer outside the grand jury room, the gangster again refused to answer.

November 12, 1964
Officials brought Tramunti before Judge Wyatt, who held hearings on Tramunti's refusal to testify.

November 19, 1964
Judge Wyatt held a hearing on Tramunti's refusal to testify.

November 27, 1964
Judge Wyatt held a further hearing on Tramunti's refusal to testify.

December 2, 1964
Judge Wyatt held Tramunti in contempt and sentenced him to one year in jail. The Judge rejected the three objections Tramunti had about being given immunity. However, Tramunti could negate the sentence by changing his mind and testifying. The jail time would also end when the grand jury's term finished in perhaps 18 months.

April 5, 1965
The Second Circuit Court of Appeals affirmed Tramunti's contempt conviction from December 2, 1964.

June 20, 1966
The US Supreme Court set aside Tramunti's one-year jail sentence because the contempt charges should have been civil and not criminal.

November 6, 1966
Federal Judge Harold Tyler cited Tramunti for civil contempt. Tramunti had refused to testify about drugs and the Lucchese Family before a grand jury. As a result, the gangster might remain behind bars for the rest of the grand jury's term unless he talked.

Tramunti Becomes the Boss

October 20, 1967
An FBI report concluded that Tramunti or Anthony Corallo would be the next Lucchese Family Boss. But, in the end, it turned out to be Tramunti.

March 23, 1968
An informer told the FBI that Tramunti, Joseph Vecchio, and Attorney Schectel held a meeting in the New Yorker Hotel. Tramunti told the informer that the Lucchese Family were partners in $180,00 that two New York bookies invested in a Los Angeles area Pan Club. The informer was to relay this message to the relevant people in Los Angeles.

November 1968
Police conducted a raid on the Eastchester-Biltmore Gardens.

1969
Lucchese Capos list by the FBI
Joseph Lagano
Joseph LaRatro
Joseph Lucchese
John Ormento
Joe Rosato
Chris Furnari
Paul Vario

January 20, 1969
An informer told the FBI that he had known Tramunti since 1934. He added that Tramunti trusted hood Sam Cavalieri.

April 9, 1969
Judge Myles J Lane charged Tramunti and others for criminal contempt before a Bronx grand jury.

September 11, 1969
Justice Myles J Lane found Tramunti guilty of 37 counts of civil contempt in the Bronx. Lane set bail and released Tramunti until sentencing on November 10, 1969.

November 10, 1969
A judge sentenced Tramunti to one year for contempt before a grand jury.

November 11, 1969
The judge set Tramunti's bail at $5,000 while appealing his contempt sentence.

November 19, 1970
In a large stock fraud case, a federal grand jury indicted Tramunti, Vinnie Aloi, and others. The group had gained control of a worthless Miami concern called Imperial Investment Corp. By hard sell tactics, they managed to pump up the value of the stock then dumped it, leaving innocent investors with significant losses.

December 15, 1970
An appeals court denied Tramunti a stay in his one-year contempt sentence.

December 16, 1970
Tramunti surrendered to begin his contempt sentence.

January 13, 1971
US Attorney Whitney North Seymour announced an indictment of an aide to Hiram L Fong, a Senator from Hawaii. The indictment accused the aide of offering a $100,000 bribe to US Deputy Attorney General Richard Kleindienst to fix the Tramunti case. There was no suggestion Kleindienst accepted the bribe.

July 7, 1971
The Second Circuit Court of Appeal dismissed civil contempt charges against Tramunti from September 11, 1969.

October 18, 1971
A grand jury indicted Tramunti and others for stock fraud.

December 23, 1971
In the stock fraud case, a jury acquitted Tramunti, Vinnie Alo, and three others of conspiracy and 16 counts of mail violation.

February 3, 1972
Agents for the Joint Task Force confiscated a suitcase while arresting a hood. They believed it contained heroin, but it was money. The prosecution would use the money as evidence of drug dealing in a later Tramunti trial.

May 25, 1972
Tramunti called Bargain Auto Parts in the Bronx and left a message for Capo Paul Vario.

June 2, 1972
Tramunti again called Bargain Auto Parts and left a message.

October 16, 1972
A raid on the Canarsie junkyard of Paul Vario began a long period of headaches for the Lucchese leaders. Bargain Auto Parts was at 5702 Ave D.

November 18, 1972
Detectives from the District Attorney's office arrested Tramunti at his home. Justice John R Starky took Tramunti's innocent plea then released the hood on $2,500 bail.

November 29, 1972
Bronx DA Eugene Gold announced that a special rackets grand jury charged Tramunti with three counts of criminal contempt. The charges stem from Tramunti's responses to questions about phone calls to the bugged trailer of Paul Vario at Bargain Auto Parts in Brooklyn. Justice John R Starkey took Tramunti's innocent plea then released the hood on $2,500 bail.

According to Gold, Tramunti had left an urgent phone message at Vario's business that the Capo should meet him at the corner of 114th St and Broadway. However, when the grand jury questioned him on this, Tramunti claimed he didn't know what the call was about nor why it was so urgent. Tramunti also testified that he had no business dealings with Vario. These answers were the basis of the criminal contempt.

April 3, 1973
A grand jury produced the first indictment of Tramunti and many others for drug dealing.

May 1, 1973
US Attorney Whitney North Seymour announced an indictment of Tramunti and Vincent Gugliari for perjury. The allegation said the two lied in testimony during the stock fraud trial in December of 1971. Judge John M Cannella released Tramunti on $25,000 bail and a lesser amount for Gugliari.

May 22, 1973
Agents of the Joint Task Force arrested minor league hood Frank Stassi. They promised him money, a new ID, and a plane ticket if he worked against a drug ring. Stassi would become the most critical witness against Tramunti in a later trial.

May 30, 1973
A jury found Tramunti guilty of three counts of criminal contempt before a grand jury.

May 31, 1973
US Attorney Whitney North Seymour announced an indictment of Tramunti and Vincent Gugliari. The grand jury charged that the two had committed seven acts of perjury during their December 1971 stock fraud trial. Seymour complained that the men "Had deliberately lied under oath about their meetings with certain co-defendants and certain co-conspirators." Judge John M Cannella set Tramunti's bail at $15,000 and Gugliari's at $500.

August 6, 1973
DA Eugene Gold requested the court sentence Tramunti to four years on each of his three contempt convictions. Gold described Tramunti as "One of the five most important criminal figures in NYC." However, Justice Raymart Alter sentenced Tramunti to three years on each count, with the sentences to run concurrently.

October 3, 1973
US Attorney Paul J Curran announced a 17 count drug indictment against Tramunti and others. He described Tramunti as" The top man and prime mover of the conspiracy." The Grand Jury charged Tramunti et al. with conspiracy and the distribution of heroin and cocaine going back to 1969. US Magistrate Martin D Jacobs set Tramunti's bail at $25,000.

October 25, 1973
Tramunti is found guilty of committing six counts of perjury in the December 1971 stock fraud case.

December 3, 1973
Authorities updated the drug indictment from October 3, 1973.

January 17, 1974
Judge Kevin Duffy heard arguments to suppress evidence in the upcoming Tramunti drug trial. At issue was a suitcase filled with nearly $1 million in cash. The judge rejected the motion but had some harsh words for a police detective involved in the seizure of the evidence. Judge Duffy said, "John Spurdis is a liar. I reject entirely the testimony of witness John Spurdis."

January 26, 1974
Opening arguments begin in Tramunti's drug trial. Assistant US Attorney Walter M Phillips Jr described Tramunti as "Mr. Big, the chairman of the board, he never sold, delivered or handled drugs but he was the bankroll behind the ring."

January 31, 1974
In a crucial part of the trial, witness Frank Stassi stated he was walking past Tramunti and fellow defendant Iggi Inglese and heard Inglese say, "I expect some goods. I'm going to need some money." To this, Tramunti nodded his head. Stassi also claimed that Tramunti sent him to a local jail to see Inglese, who was in on a driving rap. Tramunti wanted to know if "Yes or No," Inglese needed money for drugs. Inglese replied "No" and explained that nothing was happening in the drug acquisition efforts at the time.

Note
In the movie "Goodfellas," there is a scene where Capo Paul Cicero warned Henry Hill about being involved in drugs.

"Listen, I ain't gonna get fucked like Gribbs, understand? Gribbs is 76 years old, and the fucking guy is gonna die in prison. I don't need that... Gribbs got 20 years just for saying 'Hello' to some fuck who was sneaking behind his back selling junk."

The movie character Paul Cicero was Capo Paul Vario of the Lucchese Family. For some reason producer, Martin Scorsese changed the name.

February 27, 1974
Judge Arnold Bauman sentenced Tramunti to five years for each of the six counts of perjury from October 25, 1973. However, he ruled that the sentences would run concurrently.

March 13, 1974
The jury convicted Tramunti and 14 other men of running a vast drug ring operating in Washington and New York City. US Attorney Paul Curran said that Tramunti is in "The top echelons of organized crime." Judge Kevin T Duffy set sentencing for April 22, 1974.

May 7, 1974
US Attorney Walter Phillips asked for a stiff prison term for Tramunti since he had spent most of his life in criminal activities. Then, federal Judge Kevin Duff told Tramunti, "You are a dangerous man," and handed out a 15-year sentence.

June 12, 1974
The Second Circuit Court of Appeals upheld Tramunti's conviction and sentence from the perjury trial of October 25, 1973.

March 17, 1975
The Second Circuit Court of Appeals affirmed Tramunti's drug conviction.

September 24, 1976
A gunman killed veteran soldier Andimo Pappadio with 11 shots outside Pappadio's home in Lido Beach, Long Island. Years later, turncoat Al D'Arco explained that Pappadio's superiors whacked him out for not correctly sharing the illegal income from the garment center.

October 15, 1978
Tramunti died in prison.

Trivia
Tramunti kept his 1968, 28-foot speedboat, the Coho, at Ray's Marina at 503 City Island Ave in the Bronx.

In 1968 Tramunti was driving a two-door bronze Buick.

Tramunti visited a social club at 114th and Pleasant Ave in Manhattan each morning in the 60s.

Tramunti Headlines

December 3, 1964
Cosa Nostra Can Say Good-by, Mr. Gribbs

December 16, 1970
Tramunti Due to Start Term

May 31, 1973
TRAMUNTI IS GUILTY AT CONTEMPT TRIAL

October 5, 1973
Tramunti Is Charged

October 26, 1973
TRAMUNTI GUILTY OF PERJURY HERE

CHAPTER SIX

Boss Anthony "Tony Ducks" Corallo

Anthony "Tony Ducks" Corallo led a long, successful career in La Cosa Nostra until the government got serious. Then, he had the misfortune of riding around in a beautiful Jaguar, talking away, totally unaware the good guys were listening. Even when he visited his buddy, Anthony "Fat Tony" Salerno, Underboss of the Genovese Family, the feds recorded poor Corallo. It only got worse when two FBI agents photographed him leaving a Commission meeting. However, Tony knew none of this until it all became public, and the feds jacked him up in the famous 1986 Commission trial. It was all over but the crying then. A summary of Corallo's Mafia life follows.

DOB
February 12, 1913
NYC

DOD
August 23, 2000
In prison

Description
Bureau of Narcotics 1964
5'6"
170 lbs

Daily News 1961
A short, hulking figure
Wearing heavy, horned-rimmed spectacles

Wife
Ann Ryan

Stepdaughter Madeline
Son Jerry

1935
Police jail Corallo for consorting with criminals.

1941
The Authorities gave Corallo six months in Rikers Island (a prison) for a narcotics violation.

March 12, 1948
Two hoods held up the office of Mike Kraisilovsky's warehouse at 228 Mulbury Street in Manhattan. They stole $2,000 in payroll money just brought in by Anthony Corallo, a rigger foreman with the firm. In hindsight, it is reasonable to guess that this might have been a set-up job between Corallo and a few buddies.

February 2, 1955
A wiretap overheard Corallo and a gambler discussing a police raid on one of their floating crap games. For our purposes, this event shows Corallo's involvement in illegal gambling.

Background of Corallo's Union Battles
In the 1950s, the Teamsters did not elect their president by a direct vote of its membership. Instead, it had a convoluted system designed to keep its top people in power. Delegates for each local had a vote, but so too did the joint councils. They were a regional organization composed of representatives from all the locals in its territory.

The Corallo/union story focuses on his control of many union locals and his efforts to help Jimmy Hoffa win the Teamster presidency. He expected the future rewards to be great. Instead, he received reams of negative publicity.

1955
In 1955, Teamster VP Jimmy Hoffa made a move for the union's presidency. Hoffa wanted control of Joint Council 16 from the New York area as part of his election strategy. He hoped to oust Martin Lacey, the Joint Council president, and replace him with James O'Rourke, a strong Hoffa supporter.

August 1955
DA Frank Hogan taped many phone calls involving Corallo, Dioguardi, and others in New York unions. The McClellan Rackets Committee would reveal these tapes to the public in 1957.

November 8, 1955
A vital part of this move was the creation of seven "paper locals" by Teamster president Dave Beck. None of these entities had any members when they came into existence. Hoffa, Corallo, et al. hoped the votes of these new locals would help win control of Joint Council 16.

January 9, 1956
Superiors in the Teamster Union overruled Lacey's objections to seating the seven new locals on his joint council. However, Lacey refused to back down.

January 26, 1956
The executive board of Joint Council 16 overruled president Lacey and approved the seating of the seven new locals.

February 1, 1956
Teamster president Dave Beck ordered Lacey to seat the seven locals.

February 14, 1956
Much to the chagrin of Corallo, Dioguardi, and Hoffa, president Lacey retained control of Joint Council 16.

March 9, 1956
DA Frank Hogan announced that Dioguardi, Corallo, and Irving Slutsky were attempting to gain control of Joint Council 16. He said three grand juries would be investigating the matter the following week.

January 1957
An ill and worn down Martin Lacey, president of Joint Council 16, decided not to seek re-election. Hoffa's man, James O'Rourke, won the position.

April 30, 1957
DA Frank Hogan said Corallo was "fast emerging as one of the most powerful underworld figures in the field of labor."

1957
Corallo was VP of Local 995 of the UAW-AFL. VP of Local 229 of the Teamsters and allegedly in control of Teamster Locals, 275, 522, and 875. His influence covered Local 405 of the Retail Clerks Union and Local 229 of the United Textile Workers.

August 15, 1957
While Corallo appeared in front of the McClellan Rackets Committee, they played a tape of a conversation Corallo had back on February 7, 1955. Corallo and a crony were discussing a business matter involving doing a favor for Martin Lacey, then president of Joint Council 16, in return for a massive reduction in the fees their local owed.

A cousin of Lacey headed up Teamster Local 719. John DeLury wanted the workers from Rutgers Metals Company moved from Local 875 to his local. This change would bring in dues and many opportunities for extortion etc. Not surprisingly, Corallo took the 5th on questions about this matter.

October 1957
The Teamsters Union elected Jimmy Hoffa as its president.

November 14, 1957
New York State Troopers stumbled upon an emergency National Meeting of La Cosa Nostra. But unfortunately, troopers did not identify any prominent Lucchese Family members there.

January 3, 1961
Authorities served Corallo with a subpoena to appear before the McLellan Rackets Committee. They found him at 71 Prospect Road in Centerpoint, LI. Corallo's buddy Felice Falco had rented the place for his Boss; however, the cops found Corallo by following Falco from New York.

January 25, 1961
Officials of the Senate McLellan Rackets Committee played a legally taped phone conversation between Corallo and Jimmy Hoffa. In summary, Hoffa told Corallo it was alright to steal as long as he didn't get caught. Not surprisingly, Corallo took the 5th rather than answer questions about that call.

December 7, 1961
A federal grand jury indicted Corallo, minor hood Sanford J Moore, New York Judge J Vincent Keogh, a former assistant DA Elliot Kahaner, and Dr. Robert Erdman of conspiracy to bribe a judge.

Background:

On March 9, 1961, a grand jury accused Moore and two other men of carrying out a bankruptcy fraud involving jukeboxes. Afraid of substantial legal fees, Moore took advice from Kahaner, who introduced him to Dr. Moore. For $35,000, Dr. Moore said he could get Kahaner and Superior Court Judge J Vincent Keogh to speak to Moore's presiding judge. The plan was to get Judge Leo F Rayfiel to order a suspended sentence.

Moore pled guilty to the indictment, but Judge Rayfiel hit him with a three-year sentence. The judge had heard rumors of a bribe attempt and lowered the boom on Moore.

April 9, 1962
Judge Rayfiel ordered the opening of court records sealed in the fall of 1961. An affidavit of Sanford Moore accused then Assistant US Attorney Kahaner of coercing him into pleading guilty to the March 1961 fraud indictment. Moore stated that Kahaner used the possibility of a lengthy prison term and hefty lawyer fees to extort $35,000 from him.

May 14, 1962
The bribery trial of Corallo et al. began before Judge Edward M Weinfeld.

June 16, 1962
A federal grand jury brought down guilty verdicts for Corallo, Judge Weinfeld set Corallo's bail at $50,000 but released the other two defendants into the custody of their attorneys.

During the proceedings, damaging testimony came from Dr. Erdman, whom the government severed from the trial as long as he testified. He said he got the $35,000 bribe from Corallo and gave $12,500 to Kahaner and $22,500 to Keogh. The jury must have believed him.

August 2, 1962
Federal Judge Edward Weinfeld sentenced Corallo, Keough, and Kahaner to two years for their bribery conviction. The judge commented, "There are

no mitigating circumstances. The crime was calculated. It was deliberate." Weinfeld continued Corallo on $25,000 bail while the other two remained free on their own recognizance.

November 1963
Corallo began his two-year sentence in Lewisburg prison.

1965
BOP officials released Corallo from prison.

September 22, 1966
Around 2:30 PM, police from the 112th precinct arrested 13 men having lunch in the basement dining room of La Stella restaurant in Forrest Hills, Queens. Among those arrested were: Santo Trafficante, Boss of Tampa, Carlos Marcello, Boss of New Orleans, Boss Carlo Gambino, Boss Joe Colombo, and Acting Boss Tommy Eboli of the Genovese Family.

There is no definite prime evidence to prove the purpose of the gathering, but one theory suggested the severe illness of Boss Tommy Lucchese had to be on the agenda.

January 1967
Corallo, Tom Mancuso, and Herbert Itkin traveled to Britain to see their legal casinos. However, the British border people would not permit Corallo's entry due to his criminal record. The FBI most likely tipped the British off about the visit.

December 17, 1967
Former New York Water Commissioner James Marcus, Corallo, and four other men appeared before a Grand Jury investigating corruption in New York City's administration.

December 18, 1967
US Attorney Robert Morgenthau announced an indictment involving former New York's Water Commissioner James Marcus, Corallo, Herbert Itkin, Danny Motto, construction magnate Henry Fried, and another man. Police arrested all of the accused.

The feds alleged that Marcus got into debt gambling on stocks and turned to shady characters for money. Itkin led him to Motto, a local union president, who brought in Corallo. The plan was to award a contract to clean the Jerome

Park Reservoir without rival bidding. The contractor, Henry Fried, would kickback $40,000 of the $835,000 contract to the conspirators who would cut it up. Judge Constance Baker Motley released five men without bail but set $10,000 for Corallo.

March 13, 1968
Judge Wyatt of the District Court denied Corallo's motion to move the trial to another location due to excess publicity. He also rejected the motion to dismiss the charges.

May 3, 1968
Acting on appeal motions, Judge Weinburg denied Corallo's motion to sever him from the scheduled proceedings, declined to move the trial, and rejected the idea of a delay.

June 9/10, 1968
Herbert Itkin testified against his former co-defendants. Along with the testimony of James Marcus, both insiders in the bribery plot, the remaining accused were in big trouble.

June 19, 1968
A jury found Corallo, Danny Motto, Henry Fried, and his company ST Grand guilty of interstate conspiracy to bribe. Judge Edward Weinfeld set Corallo's bail at $25,000, Fried's at $50,000, and Motto's at $10,000.

December 20, 1968
A grand jury indicted Corallo, Carmine DeSapio, a former Tammany Hall power, Corallo, and businessman Henry Fried for conspiring to bribe James Marcus, then New York's Water Commissioner. They wanted Marcus to award contracts for work on Consolidated Edison facilities to Fried's firm. A judge later severed Fried from the case due to ill health.
Judge Tyler set Corallo's bail at $25,000 and let DeSapio free on his own recognizance.

July 8, 1969
The Second Court of Appeals rejected all the claims of Corallo's appeal of his June 19, 1968 conviction involving bribing Marcus.

November 12, 1969
Judge Harold R Tyler seated the jury in the Marcus/Con Edison bribery case involving Corallo and DeSapio.

December 13, 1969
In the Marcus/Con Edison case, the jury found Corallo guilty of one count of conspiracy to use interstate transportation to commit a crime. (He used a phone to call across state lines). Judge Harold R Tyler doubled Corallo's bail to $50,000. The jury ruled Carmine DeSapio guilty of three counts of conspiracy to bribe. Judge Tyler continued DeSapio on his own recognizance despite US Attorney Paul K Roney's request for $25,000 bail.

December 29, 1969
Corallo turned himself into the court to begin serving his three-year sentence for conspiracy to bribe Marcus. However, contractor Henry Fried asked for a suspended sentence due to ill health, and Judge Weinfeld agreed to hold a hearing on the matter.

February 6, 1970
Judge Harold R Tyler Jr sentenced Corallo to four and a half years for his bribery conviction of December 13, 1969.

February 27, 1970
Judge Tyler of the District Court denied Corallo's appeal for a new trial.

September 12, 1973
The Second Court of Appeals upheld Capo Paul Vario's tax conviction and sentence of three years and a $20,000 fine.

December 21, 1976
Judge Robert L Carter sentenced Matthew Madonna to 30 years and a $50,000 fine for drug trafficking.

1980
Professor Robert Blakey held a seminar on the RICO laws at Cornell University. Blakey explains that the good guys have to strike at the heart of the Mafia with wiretaps, bugs, and the RICO law.

1981
Blakey suggested it would be an excellent idea to indict the Commission.

1982
The New York office of the FBI reorganized into five groups, each taking a specific NY Mafia Family.

September 1982
The Second Court of Appeals affirmed Madonna's 1976 drug conviction.

January 11, 1982
Matthew Madonna refused to testify before a grand jury investigating drug dealing.

February 17, 1982
Judge Edelstein granted Madonna immunity before the grand jury and ordered him to testify.

March 16, 1982
Despite having immunity Madonna refused to testify before the grand jury. Judge Edelstein ruled he was guilty of civil contempt and must stay in jail until the grand jury term finished. In addition the judge ruled that Madonna's on going drug sentence was on hold until his contempt term finished.

March 18, 1983
Two agents of the New York Organized Crime Task Force planted a bug in the dashboard of Capo Salvatore Avellino's black Jaguar parked at the Huntington Town House. Avellino was attending a private party there. This success would lead to the devastation of the Mafia Commission.

March 28, 1983
The Jaguar bug listens in as Avellino and Underboss Tom Santoro talk of former Boss Joe Bonanno who was recently on 60 Minutes promoting his autobiography. When Avellino mentioned to Corallo that Bonanno talked about the Commission, Santoro responded this was gold to the good guys listening in.

April 6, 1983
The car bug hears Corallo dismiss Joe Bonanno's claims of being kidnapped. Tony Ducks stated that Bonanno cooked that plot up to avoid the government and the mob.

June 83
The Task Force's Jaguar bug hears of an upcoming Commission meeting set for June 14.

June 14, 1983
The Task Force tails the Jag to Bari Restaurant and Pizzeria Equipment Company in lower Manhattan. Unfortunately, the mob guys panicked and escaped the building before the officers could take photographs.

Later that day, from the bug in the Jag, the Task Force heard Corallo explain to Avellino that Gambino Boss Paul Castellano thought he saw FBI Agent O'Brien looking in the window, so they all bolted.

In later Senate testimony, Genovese Soldier Vincent "Fish" Cafaro talked about that meeting. He said he drove Salerno to Bari's. He said Corallo, Santoro, Castellano, Gigante, Joe Gallo, Castellano, Langella, Donny Shacks, and Baldy Dom were there.

July 19, 1983
While in the Jaguar, Corallo expressed his feeling about drug dealers. "We should kill them... we should make some examples, anyone with us, anyone near us, comes near us, you know, we'll kill them."

August 16, 1983
An FBI bug caught Lucchese power. Frank Manzo say, "We rule the airport." That quote would come back to haunt Manzo a few years later.

August 25, 1983
The term of the grand jury that Matthew Madonna refused to testify to expired. This meant that Madonna's drug sentence could resume. His civil contempt sentence pushed Madonna's parole eligibility on his drug sentence from November 18, 1986 to April 19, 1988.

1983
The FBI recorded a conversation between Peter Vario and Lucchese Underboss Salvatore Santoro. Vario explained the split of a $21,000 construction payoff that didn't impress his Underboss. According to Vario, $19,000 of the payoff had nothing to do with Boss Paul Castellano of the Gambino Family. Instead, it was money for a previous deal not involving Castellano. That meant there was only $2,000 to split between three mob Families. Dreading having to explain this to Castellano, Santoro responded, "This is pretty petty on your part." Ironically, we don't know if Castellano ever got his $666.66.

August 1983
Ronald Goldstock presented an outline of a Commission case to Giuliani.

August 1983
The FBI opens a case file on the Commission. They put Pat Marshall in charge.

September 1983
Giuliani presented the idea of a Commission Case to Attorney General William French Smith and FBI Director Webster. They backed the project and offered nearly unlimited resources.

1984
A report stated that JFK Airport's 200 Freight Forwarding companies handled about $50 billion worth of cargo each year.

January 31, 1984
At Tony Salerno's Palma Boy Social Club, a bug catches him, Underboss Tom Santoro, and Consigliere Chris Furnari discussing the Commission. The issue was whether Phil Rastelli, Boss of the Bonanno Family, could sit on the Commission. The talk of the Commission by Mafia guys was a treasure to the FBI Agents listening in.

February 15, 1984
At a social club located at 2244 1st Ave, FBI agents heard Consigliere Chris Furnari, Capo Neil Migliore, and Vincent "Fish" Cafaro of the Genovese Family discuss the construction business. Their conversation about how the Families whacked up the jobs and money would be significant evidence in the upcoming Commission trial.

May 15, 1984
Two FBI Agents conducted surveillance on a Commission meeting held at 34 Cameron Avenue Staten Island. They took pictures of the hoods leaving the home.
Below is a summary of what they saw.
4:00 PM approximately
FBI saw Gambino Capo Frank DeCicco drive slowly by in a maroon Chrysler. Then Salvatore Barbato pulled up in his gray Buick and went into the house, exited a few minutes later, and drove off.

4:39 PM
Colombo Soldier Ralph Mosca walked out of the home.

4:40 PM
Genovese Underboss Anthony Salerno left the residence, followed by Soldier Carmine Dellacava. Colombo Soldier Ralph "Funzi" Mosca picked them up in a red Oldsmobile.

4:41
Colombo Underboss Gerry Langella exited, followed by Tom Bilotti and Ralph Scopo. Frank DeCicco picked up Bilotti.

4:44
Bilotti returns in Gambino Boss Paul Castellano's blue caddy. He goes into the house.

4:47
Gambino Capo Frank DeCicco drove up and parked.

4:53
Frank DeCicco drove Lucchese Underboss Salvatore "Tom Mix" Santoro and Capo Aniello Migliore away.

4:55
Boss Paul Castellano left the house, followed by Tom Bilotti. He drove Castellano away in the Boss' Caddy.

This picture would prove invaluable in helping prove to jurors that the Commission existed.

December 12, 1984
At the Palma Boy Social Club, Underboss Anthony "Fat Tony" Salerno of the Genovese Family questioned his buddy, Boss Anthony Salerno of the Lucchese Family, if he was in trouble with the bug in Avellino's Jaguar. The news of this bug had recently become public. In hindsight, Corallo was whistling in the woods when he responded, "That case I shouldn't be Tony, I shouldn't be in trouble because you, you ask me something... and I say, 'Well, well what are you, fucking crazy? Don't you know there's an investigation goin' on there? What do you want to do, throw gasoline on the fire"

January 8, 1985
Joseph Zingara tells Salerno, "Listen, they got eight hundred hours of tape on Tony Ducks. Eight hundred hours." This comment was from the bug at Salerno's social club.

February 21, 1985
Assistant US Attorney Brock announced a 23 count federal indictment concerning criminality at JFK Airport. Among the charges was laundering illegal payments by buying municipal bonds on Wall Street. Also, the hoods made $340,000 on illegal insider trading of the stock of a company they were shaking down. Among those the feds charged were Lenny Manzo, Salvatore Santoro (Lucchese Underboss), Paul Vario (Lucchese Capo), Frank Calise (president of Teamster Local 295), and Harry Davidoff (VP of Teamster Local 851).

February 24, 1985
The Daily News breaks the story on the Commission indictment.

February 25, 1985
The FBI decided to go ahead with their arrests so that no target could flee. Below is a list of where they found the hoods.
Gambino Boss Paul Castellano- arrested at his home. $2 million bail. He paid for it the next day.
Genovese Underboss Anthony Salerno-arrested at his apartment. $2 million bail. He paid for it the next day.
Colombo Soldier Ralph Scopo-arrested in a hospital.
Gambino Underboss Aniello Dellacroce-arrested in hospital.
Lucchese Boss Anthony Corallo-arrested in hospital.
Colombo Underboss Gerry Langella-arrested in jail.
Bonanno Boss Phil Rastelli-arrested in prison.
Lucchese Underboss Santoro- arrested. $1.75 bail. Santoro couldn't meet it the next day.
Lucchese Consigliere Chris Furnari was arrested. $1.75 bail

February 26, 1985
The feds announced the original 22 count Commission indictment.
They charged each defendant with racketeering conspiracy and racketeering. These charges meant each defendant planned and committed at least two

racketeering acts (serious crimes) on behalf of the criminal enterprise (The Commission)

The indictment stated that the Commission was behind three conspiracies; the Concrete Club, which illegally controlled much of the construction industry in NYC, and the Commission approved murder of Carmine Galante of the Bonanno Family.

The feds also charged Boss Anthony Corallo and Underboss Salvatore Santoro with a separate RICO Conspiracy and RICO charge. The bugs caught the two talking about a loansharking matter, so they threw those charges into the mix.

Commenting on the historic indictment FBI Director, William Webster said, "The ruling body of the most powerful organized crime elements in the US… has now been brought to the bar of justice." US Attorney Rudy Giuliani added, "This is a great day for law enforcement but a bad day, maybe the worst, for the mafia." He was right.

June 26, 1985
The feds announced a superseding Commission indictment. It added Colombo Boss Carmine Persico and Bonanno Consigliere Steve Cannone to the list of defendants.

November 12, 1985
The feds announce another superseding Commission indictment. It added Bonanno Soldier Anthony Indelicato and charged him with participating in the murder of Carmine Galante on behalf of the Commission.

December 2, 1985
Gambino Underboss Aniello Dellacroce died, taking his name out of the Commission case.

December 16, 1985
John Gotti and his allies killed Gambino Boss Paul Castellano, taking his name out of the Commission case.

April 24, 1986
Heino Benthin, the owner of two trucking companies at JFK, decided to become a government witness. He admitted to sharing $132,000 in shakedown money from Schenker's International Forwarders with Frank Manzo.

October 1, 1986
Heino Benthin, owner of Hi's Airport Service at JFK, testified that he paid Frank Manzo $600 a week to operate. Manzo told Benthin that he would have to pay if he expected to work without union labor.

October 8, 1986
Frank Manzo, Paul Vario, and two others pled guilty to racketeering charges related to JFK Airport.

September 8, 1986 - November 19, 1986
The feds used; 85 witnesses, 85 taped conversations, including some from the famous Jaguar bug during the Commission trial.

November 1986
At a Lucchese Family meeting on Staten Island, Boss Anthony Corallo named Vic Amuso the Acting Boss, Anthony Casso as the Acting Underboss, and Neil Migliore as the Acting Consigliere. If the jury found the Lucchese administrators guilty in the Commission case, these positions would become permanent.

November 19, 1986
The Commission jury found the entire Lucchese Family administration and the other defendants guilty of all counts. Boss Anthony Corallo, Underboss Santoro and Consigliere Chris Furnari were finished as La Cosa Nostra powers. As a result, Judge Owen revoked bail for all those defendants still free.

January 13, 1987
Commission case sentencing
Note: The 100 yrs. is five consecutive 20 yr. terms.
Note: These sentences were BEFORE the end of federal parole; thus, these mutts were eligible for parole.
Note: Judge Owen RECOMMENDED no parole for any of the defendants.
Salerno: 100 yrs., $240,000
Persico: 100 yrs., $240,000
Corallo: 100 yrs., $250,000 (extra $10,000 was for loan sharking)
Langella: 100 yrs., $240,000
Furnari: 100 yrs., $240,000
Santoro: 100 yrs., $250,000 (extra $10,000 was for loan sharking)
Scopo: 100 yrs., $240,000
Indelicato: 40 yrs., $50,000 (two racketeering counts)

The long Mafia careers of Corallo, Santoro, and Furnari were over. They oversaw committing many violent crimes and murders, but the Lucchese Family membership would look back and long for the relative peace of the Corallo era. But, unfortunately, what was to come for them all was horrendous.

CHAPTER SEVEN

Boss Vic Amuso

Boss Anthony Corallo, headed off to life behind bars, anointing long-time Capo Vic Amuso as his successor. It would be interesting to know if Corallo had second thoughts before he passed. For years after taking the reins, Amuso led a dysfunctional Family, and he and his Underboss, Anthony Casso, used murder as the solution to any problem, big or small.

What follows is a long, long summary of events during his ongoing reign.

DOB
November 4, 1934

Residences
164-33 Cross Bay Blvd
Queens, NY.

1965
Anthony "Gaspipe" Casso shot and wounded a man. Capo Chris Furnari worked out a deal with the victim that fell apart. However, eventually, the victim claimed he couldn't identify Casso as the shooter. Casso walked away a free man.

Early 1970's
Thanks to the sponsorship of Capo Chris Furnari, the Lucchese Boss Carmine Tramunti inducted Casso into the Family. He teamed up with Vic Amuso and ran bookmaking, collections, and other rackets for Furnari. However, one of their most significant scores was kidnapping. Pretending to work for the family, Casso made off with the $2 million ransom.

July 19, 1972
Brooklyn US Attorney Robert A Morse announced an indictment that charged Anthony "Gaspipe" Casso and three other men with a bank robbery at a branch of the Chase Manhattan Bank in Brooklyn on April 29.
A Holmes Burglar Alarm Company employee disconnected the alarm on the safety deposit vault for a payment of $32,000. As a result, the hoods made off with an estimated $400,000 in cash and jewelry from the looted boxes.

December 21, 1972
Bronx DA Burton B Roberts announced a series of indictments involving parole schemes. The grand jury charged Vic Amuso and Anthony Casso with an attempt to win early parole for three police officers serving time on Rikers Island for shaking down drug addicts in the Bronx. Interestingly Roberts labeled Casso as a Gambino Family member.

March 27, 1973
Before Judge Edward R Neaher, a jury found Anthony Casso and other men not guilty of a bank robbery in 1972.

1977
From prison, Boss Carmine Tramunti approved the induction of Anthony Casso.

May 27, 1977
Brooklyn Strike Force Chief Thomas Puccio announced the arrest of Amuso, Caso, and Vince DiNapoli for possession of three pounds of heroin from Thailand. The magistrate set bail at $50,000 for Amuso and Casso but $75,000 for DiNapoli.

1978
James Bishop, secretary-treasurer of Painters Union District Council 9, approached Peter "Big Pete" Chiodo to help oust a trustee imposed by union headquarters.

Chiodo discussed the matter with Lucchese Consigliere Chris "Christy Trick" Furnari, who ordered Chiodo to beat the trustee. With the help of another man, Chiodo followed orders with the result the trustee left town after he got out of the hospital. This action solidified the Lucchese Family's control of District Council 9.

1980
Boss Anthony Corallo promoted Amuso to Capo and bumped Chris "Christy Trick" Furnari up to Consigliere.

1982
When a judge sends someone off to prison, they don't just go to sleep until their release date. Some do their time quietly while others engage in various crimes. In the example below, the parole authority committed an injustice, if not a crime.

On May 7, 1974, Lucchese heavyweight Joe DiNapoli began serving a 21 year and four-month sentence for several crimes involving tax fraud and drug dealing. In 1981 DiNapoli applied for parole but was denied. He then launched a series of litigations hoping for a reversal. However, on May 8, 1991, a district judge ruled that DiNapoli had to work with the parole system before asking the court for help.

The Third Circuit Court of Appeals finally weighed in ordering the District Court Judge to consider the matter. DiNapoli had exhausted all the administrative moves with the parole authority.

On January 27, 1982, the District Court rejected DiNapoli's motion again. This decision set off another series of exhausting appeals and hearings.
On March 31, 1982, US Magistrate John Havas ruled that the parole authority had appropriately treated DiNapoli.

Probably worn out this time, DiNapoli went to the Third Circuit Court of Appeals and finally made some progress. The judges ruled that the US Parole Commission mistreated DiNapoli during the lengthy process. Accordingly, they granted DiNapoli's writ of habeas corpus. Oops---The Parole guys appealed!

August 23, 1982
The Lucchese Family inducted Al D'Arco, Louis Daidone, and four other men in a ceremony. Among those present were Boss Anthony Corallo, Underboss Sal Santoro, Capo Paul Vario, Capo Vic Amuso, and others.

1984
An internal NYPD trial found Detective Lou Eppolito not guilty of giving a police file to a Gambino Capo. However, officers found the file in the gangster's possession, and it had Eppolito's fingerprints on it. The failure to convict the detective at this stage would prove to be a disaster for many.

1984
Lucchese Associate Frank Santora finished his prison term and quickly headed for a store run by his prison mate Burton Kaplan. Then, Santora told Kaplan about his crooked cop cousin Lou Eppolito. He explained that Eppolito had a high-placed partner in the NYPD, and the two were willing to sell secrets for the right price.

February 15, 1985
Rudy Giuliani announced the Commission indictment signally the beginning of the end of the reign of the Lucchese administration.

February 10, 1986
Rogue cops Lou Eppolito and Steve Caracappa stopped jeweler Israel Greenwald on a fake charge. They drove the unsuspecting man to an isolated garage, where they killed and buried him. Burton Kaplan had allegedly been involved in an illegal deal with Greenwald and feared he might testify against him.

April 13, 1986
Genovese Boss Chin Gigante and Lucchese Boss Anthony Corallo decided to kill John Gotti for his unsanctioned hit on Gambino Boss Paul Castellano. Amuso and Casso arranged for an unknown Associate named Herbert Pate to place a bomb under the car of Gambino Underboss Frank DeCicco. They believed the new Gambino Boss John Gotti would be with DeCicco. Unfortunately for the plotters, Pate mistook a Lucchese Soldier for Gotti and pushed the bomb, killing DeCicco but wounding the other man.

November 1986
At a Staten Island meeting called by Boss Anthony Corallo, the Family settled the future leadership question. Underboss Sal Santoro hoped his protégée, Buddy Luongo, might take the throne, but Corallo nixed that idea. So instead, Vic Amuso became the Acting Boss.

September 14, 1986
James Hydell, Bob Bering, and Nicky Guido local hoods shot and wounded Anthony Casso. Gambino Associate Mickey Paradisio hired Hydell. In turn, Hydell conned Vincent "Fat Vinny" DiPierro, a Casso cousin, into believing he had a bunch of stolen checks to sell. Casso took the bait and agreed to a rendezvous with DiPierro. Hydell et al. were waiting but failed in their hit attempt. Casso was livid and sought revenge.

A Casso Associate named Burton Kaplan approached the Underboss and explained that he had a connection to two rogue cops who had helped him in the past. Kaplan felt these two might aid Casso track down his attackers and those behind it. Kaplan added that he had connected with the cops through a fellow inmate, Frank Santora, a cousin of bad cop Lou Eppolito.

From his position at the 63 Precinct, Lou Eppolito obtained the file on the Casso hit attempt and passed it along to Kaplan. Then the Associate gave it to Casso. Nevertheless, Casso et al. were unable to find the would-be assassins.

Kaplan passed on an offer from Frank Santora that the cops would be willing to snatch James Hydell. Pleased, Casso agreed to pay $35,000 for this service.

October 18, 1986
Rogue cops Eppolito and Caracappa "arrested" an unsuspecting Hydell and drove him to a private garage, where they met Frank Santoro. The three bound Hydell and threw him in the trunk. Santoro met Casso, Amuso, and Kaplan near a Toys R Us facility on Brooklyn's Flatbush Ave, where Santoro gave Kaplan the keys to the car with Hydell in the trunk. Kaplan passed the keys to Casso.

Casso took Hydell to the basement of a nearby friend's home and began to question and torture him. Finally, Hydell gave up the names of Mickey Boy Paradiso, Eddie Lino, and Bobby Boriello. Casso brought in Gambino powers Sammy Gravano, Joe "Butch" Corrao, and John "Handsome John" Giordano to learn what Casso now knew. Since Hydell was a Gambino Associate, Casso requested their blessing to kill the young hood. They agreed.

October 19, 1986
Casso shot Hydell many times with a silenced .22 semi-automatic, then threw him in the trunk one more time and drove it to meet Lucchese Soldier Patty Testa. The latter disposed of the body, and no one has ever found a trace of it.

October 1986
Long-time FBI informer James "Otto" Heidel told his handlers how Casso killed James Hydell.

October 1986
Lucchese Capo and Long Island garbage magnate Sal Avellino and seven other carters pled out, and the judge fined them and ordered community service.

November 19, 1986
According to turncoat Al D'Arco this is the date that convicted Lucchese Boss Anthony Corallo appointed Vic Amuso as Boss, Casso as Consigliere, and imprisoned Neil Migliore as Underboss.

December 1986
According to turncoat Al D'Arco, Amuso lured Capo Buddy Luongo to a private apartment and killed him. Amuso felt that Luongo had attempted to gain the Lucchese throne earlier in the year, and Amuso decided to stamp out his rival.

1987
Law officials in New Jersey estimated that the Lucchese Family had 100 members and 200 Associates.

January 1987
Once Judge Owen gave Anthony Corallo a 100-year sentence, Corallo sent word that Amuso was now the official Boss.

1987
Vic Amuso inducted Peter Chiodo in a room above a funeral parlor.

February 1987
FBI informer James "Otto," Heidel told his handler that Casso revealed that he had a detective source in the 63rd precinct.

August 1987
Capo Anthony Ciccone died of natural causes.

August 1987
James "Otto" Heidel participated in a robbery, forcing the FBI to drop him as a confidential informant. (CI) Heidel then dealt with the NYPD/FBI Joint Robbery Task Force.

After some suspicious incidents, Burton Kaplan began to suspect Heidel was an informant. Kaplan's concerns grew when Bonanno Soldier Tommy Pitera openly accused Heidel of being a rat in front of Kaplan. After expressing his concerns to Casso, the Underboss told Kaplan to consult his sources. They confirmed that Heidel was a confidential informant, so Casso ordered a hit.

September 3, 1987
Frank Santora, the link between the two rogue cops and Burton Kaplan, died on Bath Avenue in Brooklyn. It was his bad luck to have been walking with a Colombo Soldier who was in the middle of a shooting war to control that Family.

Anxious to continue to receive money from Casso, Lou Eppolito convinced Kaplan to continue their nefarious operations. Casso gave his approval.

October 8, 1987
Shortly after Heidel became a CI for the NYPD, Casso knew it.

November 4, 1987
Capo Sam Cavalieri died of natural causes.

November 11, 1987
Robert Bering pled guilty to the attempted murder of Anthony Casso, and the judge sentenced him to 15 years to life.

Note:
Between 1988 and approximately 1990, the New Jersey faction of the Family avoided meeting with the Lucchese Administration. For more details, please see the Chapter Jersey Boys.

1988
Amuso promoted Peter Chiodo to Capo.

1988
New Jersey banned Carmine Avellino from all their casinos.

May 1988
Boss Vic Amuso appointed Al D'Arco to Capo, replacing the recently deceased Paul Vario.

May 4, 1988
A jury found Neil Migliore guilty of bid-rigging and extortion in the construction industry. Later a judge sentenced him to 24 years and a fine of $266,000.

June 1, 1988
New Jersey banned Sal Avellino from their casinos.

Fall 1988
Police arrested Dominic Costa, a locksmith, on gun charges suspecting he was working with a robbery gang. Not wanting to do time, Costa agreed to become a CI for the NYPD. Unfortunately, that proved to be a dangerous decision.

October 10, 1988
Casso's cop sources passed along the news that Costa was an informant. Soon after, someone put six slugs in his head, but the locksmith lived.

October 25, 1988
Greek gambling figure Spyredon Velentzas wanted a former partner, Sorecho Nano, whacked-out for interfering in his gambling business. He approached Peter Chiodo, who sought and received Boss Vic Amuso's approval but insisted that Velentzas had to be in on the murder. Chiodo introduced Velentzas to Richie Pagliarulo to arrange the killing. Velentzas lured Nano to his travel agency, where Mike Spinelli killed him. When Chiodo rolled over in 1991, he revealed the details of this hit.

December 15, 1988
A grand jury indicted Peter Vario and two other officials of Local 66 of the Laborer's Union. However, the judge put off Vario's trial due to the death of a daughter. As a result, most of the other defendants ended up pleading guilty.

1988
James Bishop, secretary-treasurer of Painters District Council 9, hoped to be appointed a VP of the National Union. However, Underboss Anthony "Gaspipe" Casso vetoed the idea.

1989
A jury convicted Nicky Guido of second-degree assault in the attempted hit on Anthony Casso. His fellow shooter, Robert Bering, outlined the murder plot.

January 4, 1989
Lucchese New Jersey Soldier Michael Taccetta pled guilty to firearms and tax charges. The judge sentenced him to five years with a projected release date of July 1992.

February 6, 1989
After a failed attempt to kill Tom "Red" Gilmore on orders from Boss Vic Amuso, a hit team of Louie Daidone, Patrick Dellorusso, and Mike DeVito got it done.

February 28, 1989
Bonanno Associate Gus Farace killed undercover DEA Agent Everett Hatcher, bringing incredible pressure on all five Families.

1989
Amuso forced Acting Underboss Mariano Macaluso to retire and replaced him with Anthony Casso.

1989
Amuso inducted Soldier Joe DeFede in a ceremony in a basement in Canarsie, Brooklyn. After becoming a government witness, DeFede explained that he had been a 20 year Associate of the Colombo Family but switched over to the Lucchese Family after running into Vic Amuso.

March 31, 1989
New Jersey banned Carmine Avellino from their casinos.

May 13, 1989
Amuso and Casso had ordered Capo Mike Pappadio out of the garment center, where he had many interests. When Pappadio failed to heed the warnings, the two leaders told Al D'Arco to arrange his death.

Carmine Avellino lured Pappadio to a bagel shop where D'Arco and George Zappola killed the old Capo. They stuffed the victim into a body bag then into Zappola's trunk. Police never found Pappadio's body.

June 1989
Boss Vic "Little Vic" Amuso ordered Capo Peter Chiodo to force Jim Bishop, president of District Council 9, to resign in favor of Paul Kamen.
Bishop did step down but became an informer for the NYPD's Organized Crime Investigation Division. But, unfortunately, no one knew that outfit's

top guy was Kaplan's informant Steve Caracappa. Initially, the cops took Bishop up to Montreal, but he soon got lonely and insisted on moving home. That was a big mistake.

June 1989
Seventeen carters sued in an anti-trust suit agreed to pay more than three million in cash and services to dozens of Long Island communities that they had overcharged.

June 30, 1989
The Second Court of Appeals turned down Matthew Madonna's appeal of his civil contempt sentence. The result of this conviction and the judge's ruling meant Madonna's drug sentence was put on hold until the contempt term finished. The net effect was that Madonna's parole eligibility lengthened an additional 528 days.

August 11, 1989
At the request of Capo Sal Avellino, Amuso and Casso ordered a hit on independent garbage contractors Robert Kubecka and Donald Barstow. They cooperated with the government to rid Long Island of a Mafia-led garbage cartel.

September 13, 1989
Soldier John Petrucelli continued to hide fugitive Gus Farace despite being ordered to kill him by Boss Amuso. (See February 28, 1989). Al D'Arco ordered veteran Capo Mike Salerno to get the hit done. Finally, he sent Joey Cosentino and Anthony Magana to Petrucelli's apartment, where they gunned him down. Unfortunately for the killers, the police arrested them shortly after the murder.

September 1989
Amuso and Casso ordered Peter Chiodo to kill John Morrissey, Business Agent of Local 580 of the Architectural and Ornamental Ironworkers Union. Morrissey had been a critical player in the lucrative Window's Replacement scam, but Amuso feared he might roll over.

September 17, 1989
Chiodo lured Morrissey out to a housing development under construction in New Jersey. Tommy Carew accompanied them in an attempt to keep Morrissey relaxed. However, Richard Pagliarulo and Carew shot Morrissey to death in the model house. Mike DeSantis used a backhoe to bury the union leader outback.

Note:
Morrissey was not an informant.

September 19, 1989
Authorities returned the fugitive Capo Tony Acceturo to New Jersey from North Carolina, where they captured him in 1988. A judge gave him a jail term for contempt of a Grand Jury. Later he beat a race-fixing case, but a Florida jury convicted him of tax evasion.

November 10, 1989
Someone shot Joseph LaMorte as he exited his vehicle in front of his Pembroke Pines home in Florida. The shot wounded him in the side, but LaMorte could drive himself to the hospital. This hit attempt was part of Boss Amuso's plan to wipe out the New Jersey faction of the Lucchese Family.

November 17, 1989
After months on the run, a hit team finally killed Gus Farace, the murderer of a drug agent. Unfortunately, shooters James Galione and Louis Tuzzio also wounded Joe Sclafani, a Gambino Soldier riding with Farace. Gambino Boss John Gotti demanded revenge, so hitmen killed Tuzzio.

November 1989
The Lucchese Family inducted Louie DeSantis, Frank Pagliarulo, and two others.

February 4, 1990
Acting on orders of Amuso and Casso, a three-man hit team located Soldier Anthony DiLapi in California and killed him. Rather than attend a meeting in New York called by the two Lucchese leaders, Lapia had fled to Los Angeles to no avail. Joey D'Arco, George Conti, and George Zappolo composed the killing squad. Amuso told Al D'Arco that Lapi plotted with Buddy Luongo to seize power in the Lucchese Family back in 1986. Allegedly rogue cops Louie Eppolito and Caracappa provided the address for DiLapi.

February 11, 1990
The Manhattan DA issued a report that said the Lucchese Family controlled District Council 9 of the International Brotherhood of Painters and Allied Trades.

April 5, 1990
Thomas "Tommy Irish" Carew decided to roll over and reveal all to the FBI. Carew admitted he was involved in the hit on Sonny Morrissey back in 1989. In addition, Carew agreed to testify that Mike DeSantis, Richard Pagliarulo, and Frank Lastorino took part in the killing.

May 17, 1990
On orders from Amuso, Soldier Frank Pagliarulo killed Jim Bishop, former leader of District Council 9. The Lucchese leaders had ousted Bishop from his position and feared he would talk. In addition, rogue cops Eppolito and Caracappa told Casso (thru Kaplan) that Bishop was cooperating. Also in on the hit were D'Arco, Louie Daidone, George Zappolo, and Frank Lastorino.

Bishop's girlfriend told the investigating officers that Bishop was working with the Manhattan DA's office. Not long before, the hit officers had warned Bishop that they had a tape on which Lucchese guys were discussing whacking him out. Sometime later, Bishop's wife turned over a letter Bishop had written a year earlier. She was to open it if he died. Among the details was that Bishop met with Peter Chiodo, who warned him to resign from his District 9 position.

Police arrested Paul Kamen, the new leader of District Council 9, and Dan Reich, an employee of a paint firm. Reich paid Kamen $3,500 to ensure preferential treatment for his company.

May 27, 1990
Underboss Anthony Casso met Capo Al D'Arco and revealed he would join Boss Vic Amuso in hiding. Along with informing D'Arco that he would be the Acting Boss, Casso ordered the killing of veteran Capo Mike Salerno because a source had told Casso Salerno was a rat.

May 30, 1990
Authorities announced a massive indictment charging a variety of hoods with rigging $142 million in bids for replacement windows for the Housing Authority. Among those arrested were Chin Gigante, Boss of the Genovese Family, Peter Gotti, Acting Boss of the Gambino Family, Benny Aloi, Consigliere of the Colombo Family. But, unfortunately, the feds couldn't find union leader John Morrissey. (He was already in a grave.)

Through Burton Kaplan, the rogue cops informed Lucchese Boss Vic Amuso and Underboss Anthony Casso the takedowns were scheduled for the end of May, so the duo fled. Unfortunately, however, they didn't notify Capo Peter

Chiodo, whom the feds detained. The judge released the big man, but he began to worry for his safety.

The scheme was complicated, involving window manufacturing, installing the windows, rigging bids, and forcing legitimate companies to refrain from becoming involved. A key factor for the Lucchese Family was having control of Local 580 of the Architectural and Ornamental Ironworkers Union.

June 1990
On instructions from D'Arco, Joey Giampa and his brother allegedly lured Capo Mike Salerno to their auto repair shop, where they murdered him. They threw the body into the trunk of Salerno's Jaguar, where police found it a week later. In 1992, a jury acquitted the two Giampa brothers of this murder.

June 18, 1990
Capo Peter Chiodo suffered a heart attack and ended up in the hospital.

June 21, 1990
The feds announced a 153 count indictment of eight Painters Union leaders, four Lucchese members or Associates, and several painting contractors. Manhattan DA Robert Morgenthau told the press that there was "a mob tax on every major paint project in the city." The indictment said the extortion enterprise charged a tax of 10% on all significant painting contracts.

City and Labor Department agents had placed a camera and microphones in the offices of Painters Union District Council 9 in a two-year investigation. They also bugged the vehicle used to drive secretary-treasurer Paul Kamen around.

Among those charged were Capo Peter "Big Pete" Chiodo, Edward Capaldo, head of Painter's Local 1486, William Courtien, a representative at the headquarters of the Painters Union in Washington, Frank Arnold, a Lucchese Associate with Huber Painting Company, and Dan Reich a supervisor with Leeds Paint Company. Justice George Roberts released all those charged on bail.

August 1990
From hiding, Casso called D'Arco and ordered him to kill Bruno Facciola because he was a rat.

August 24, 1990
Bruno Facciola left home in a borrowed 1985 Mercury Sedan and picked up Louie Daidone. They drove to a garage in Brooklyn where Facciola was to

formally introduce Daidone to another made guy. At the location, Facciola sensed something was wrong and tried to run away at the last moment. Unfortunately, Daidone caught Facciola and dragged the victim into the garage, where they killed him.

August 30, 1990
Police found Facciola's body in the trunk of the 1985 Mercury after pedestrians complained of the smell.

September 25, 1990
Lucchese Capo Peter "Big Pete" Chiodo admitted threatening Painters Union District Council secretary-treasurer James Bishop so he would resign his position. This event took place in 1989 and involved Robert Morgan, a union mutt.

September 24, 1990
In the Witness Protection Program, Joseph Alonzo died of natural causes.

November 6, 1990
Rogue cops Steve Caracappa and Lou Eppolito gunned down Gambino Capo Eddie Lino on orders from Casso. They used a police light to pull Lino over on the service road next to the Belt Parkway, then Caracappa walked up and filled Lino full of holes. This hit was revenge for Lino's role in the attempt on Casso's life back in September of 1986. Casso paid the two cops $75,000 through Kaplan.

Note:
Some sources state that Caracappa was a friend of Tommy Bilotti, the Gambino Underboss gunned down by a John Gotti crew in 1985. This fact, if true, might have played a small role in Caracappa's decision to do the hit.

December 20, 1990
The US government sued to take control of Local 54 of the Hotel and Restaurant Employees Union.

1991
Capo Peter Chiodo made a plea deal to a New York State grand larceny charge then arranged a second guilty arrangement to settle his Window's federal counts. Amuso and Casso were infuriated and ordered his murder through D'Arco.

January 9, 1991
Boss Vic Amuso named Al D'Arco as his Acting Boss, with Anthony Baratta Acting Underboss and Steve Crea Acting Consigliere.

D'Arco organized a construction panel for the Lucchese Family. It consisted of Capo Dom Truscello, Capo (Acting Consigliere) Steve Crea and Soldier Danny Cutai. This panel's responsibilities were to settle any disputes with other Families over their many construction schemes.

February 5, 1991
Boss Vic Amuso ordered the killing of Associate Larry Taylor, who was seeking revenge for Bruno Facciola. Pat Dellarusso and Tom Anzeulotto gunned Taylor down when he arrived home. Al D'Arco, Frank Lastorino, and Louie Daidone were responsible for getting the hit done. The rogue cops had passed along a tape of Taylor and Al Visconti plotting against Casso.

March 26, 1991
Casso and Amuso put a contract on Al Visconti, a brother-in-law of Bruno Facciola whom they believed were plotting revenge. Al D'Arco was involved in the confusing murder planning, but it got done by a four-person hit team.

April 16, 1991
A judge sentenced District Council 9's former business agent Aaron Lefkowitz to a one to a three-year term for participating in extortion at the union. In the big June 1990 Painters Union indictment, Lefkowitz pled guilty to some counts.

April 1991
The Lucchese Family inducted Jay Giamp, Tom Anzeulotto, Rocco Vitulli, Patty Testa and Peter Del Cioppo.

April 13, 1991
Allegedly on information provided to Casso by rogue cops Eppolito and Caracappa, Frank Lastorino gunned down Gambino Capo Bobby Boriello in his Brooklyn driveway. This murder was further revenge for the attempt on Casso's life in September 1986.

April 19, 1991
A grand jury indicted New Jersey hoods Thomas Riccardi, Martin Taccetta, Anthony Acceturo, Michael Taccetta, and 49 others on racketeering, murder, and extortion charges.

May 8, 1991
On orders of Boss Vic Amuso, Lucchese shooters attacked Peter Chiodo at a Getty gas station at Fingerboard Road and Bay Street on Staten Island. Joe D'Arco (Al's son) and Frank Giacobbe pegged shots at the massive Chiodo, managing to hit him 12 times in a wild west shootout before the entire hit teams escaped in two vehicles. Chiodo survived and rolled over a few months later after considering his plight and hearing of threats against his family.

Early July 1991
Amuso and Casso decided that a four-person panel would run the Lucchese Family rather than Acting Boss Al D'Arco. The new group consisted of D'Arco, Frank Lastorino, Sal Avellino, and Anthony Barratta. In addition, Casso informed D'Arco that he would no longer control the rackets at JFK Airport. The result of this decision would be a significant loss in income for D'Arco. He was not happy, nor was the now-former Acting Underboss Steve Crea.

July 1991
Chiodo rolled over to the FBI and admitted four murders and two attempted murders. He also told them that Casso and Amuso had a source in the NYPD they called "The Crystal Ball."

July 29, 1991
The FBI finally tracked down fugitive Boss Vic Amuso in Scranton, PA. Amuso believed and continued to believe someone had set him up. When Casso hesitated to use his "Crystal Ball" to find the culprit, Amuso's suspicions fell on his Underboss. Amuso ordered all his men to have no contact with Casso from that point on.

August 1991
An appeals court overturned the conviction of Neil Migliore from May 1988.

September 11-13 1991
In front of Judge Raymond Dearie, Peter Chiodo initially had difficulty testifying in the Windows trial. He was weak and felt faint, probably due to his recent shooting and nerves. Nevertheless, Chiodo told everything he knew to the jury over the three days he was on the stand.

September 18, 1991
In later testimony, Al D'Arco claimed that Lastorino, Baratta, Mike DeSantis, and others tried to kill him in the Kimberley Hotel in NY. on this date.

Acting on orders from Underboss Casso, a crew killed architect Anthony Fava by gunshot and knife. Fava supervised the construction of an elaborate home for Casso, and the Underboss felt he knew too much of his business.

September 19, 1991
Police found the body of Casso architect Anthony Fava in the truck of a car.

September 20, 1991
The FBI warned D'Arco's parole officer that the mobster's life was in danger. The parole officer passed the bad news on to D'Arco.

September 21, 1991
Fearing for his life and family, D'Arco decided to become a government witness. He contacted the FBI and, among other things, admitted to extorting the Italian Bread Association and the Fruit and Produce Union at the Hunt's Point Market. D'Arco's revelation that Casso had access to the NYPD's top secrets was of critical importance. It took about 1000 pages for the FBI to copy down his information. (These papers are called 302's).

October 10, 1991
The news of D'Arco flipping contributed to Gambino Underboss Sammy Gravano's decision to become a cooperating witness. He had done a lot of business with D'Arco.

October 1991
The Lucchese Family held an induction ceremony in a house in Howard Beach, Queens. The new inductees were Frank Goia Jr, Thomas D'Ambrosia, Joe Tortorello, George Cappelo, and Jody Calabrese. Members present at the ceremony were Consigliere Frank Lastorino, Capos Sal Avellino, Anthony Barratta, and George Conte. There were about four other members there as well.

November 29, 1991
Michael Malena, a son-in-law of Capo Sal Avellino, torched the A-Tire Service. He pled guilty to this crime later.

December 18, 1991
Prosecution witness Nicholas Mitola was charged with the murder of an associate while in the Witness Program. He eventually got four and a half years plus five years for violating his parole.

1992
Lou Eppolito's book, "Mafia Cop: The Story of an Honest Cop Whose Family Was the Mob," was published. A picture in the book helped Anthony Casso identify Kaplan's police sources.

February 13, 1992
The feds indicted Amuso and Casso on federal racketeering charges, including nine murders.

1992
A grand jury indicted Ray Argentina, Louis Daidone, Alan Taglianetti, and Robert Mulinelli for committing a $1.2 million armored truck robbery in 1988.

March 10, 1992
Patricia Capozzoli, sister of Peter Chiodo, was shot outside her home. Members of the shooting crew were: Dino Basciano, Mike Spinelli, Robert Spinelli, Greg Cappelo, Jody Calabrese, and Joey D'Arco. Basciano admitted he was the shooter when he became a government witness years later.

March 1992
Someone attempted to murder Henry Motta.

April 1992
A grand jury brought down a superseding indictment. It included the Windows charges plus murder, murder conspiracy, and tax fraud charges against Boss Vic Amuso and Underboss Anthony Casso.

April 3, 1992
Someone fired a shotgun at Neil Migliore as he sat by the front window of Tesoro's Restaurant. An ambulance rushed him to the hospital in critical condition, but he recovered.

May 92
Amuso's trial began before Judge Eugene Nickerson.

May 1992
D'Arco began four days of testimony in the Amuso trial. Included was his account of buying an NJ property next to Tommy Riccardi and other attempts to kill him.

June 1, 1992
Amuso's defense attorney began cross-examining D'Arco.

June 15, 1992
A jury convicted Boss Vic Amuso of all 54 counts of an indictment, including nine murders before Judge Eugene Nickerson. According to prosecutor Charlie Rose, "Most of the members of the Lucchese Family are happy about Amuso's conviction."

Peter Savino and Peter Chiodo were key prosecution witnesses in the Windows phase of the trial. Then Chiodo and Al D'Arco buried Amuso on the murder counts.

August 17, 1992
The federal prosecutor in Brooklyn sought an order to keep Capo Sal Avellino away from the Private Sanitation Industry Association of Nassau/Suffolk Inc. He said Avellino, "Maintained control through bid-rigging, extortion, threats of labor unrest, and violence."

August 25, 1992
The Salem Sanitary Carting Corp and its former president, Capo Sal Avellino, agreed to pay $231,000 and perform 60 hours of community service in a deal with the federal government. They did not have to admit guilt of any kind. This settlement was part of a long process that began with a federal lawsuit in 1989. The feds recovered about $2.5 million, which they distributed to various Long Island communities gouged by the crooked carters.

1992
Fugitive Anthony Casso became Acting Boss of the Lucchese Family.

September 15, 1992
Michael Malena, a son-in-law of Sal Avellino, torched The Quality Fleet trucks in New Jersey. He later pled guilty to this crime.

October 9, 1992
Judge Nickerson sentenced Amuso to life plus a $250,000 fine.

December 2, 1992
Someone killed Patty Testa in his garage. Later, turncoat Frank Goia Jr explained that Casso ordered the hit for some reason.

1993
When Capo Joe DeFede went to collect protection money from Greek gamblers, two of them threatened his life at the point of a gun. So Boss Vic Amuso spoke to Greek gambling power Spyredon Velentzas who was in prison with him. Velentzas agreed to have his men apologize to DeFede. This sit-down took place at the All Nations Social Club in Gravesend, Brooklyn. Not sure what to expect DeFede had shooters standing by just in case. Everything went well.

January 4, 1993
Judge I Leo Glasser banned Sal Avellino from the carting business as requested by the feds.

January 13, 1993
An FBI Agent traced some calls to a cell phone located on a grid in northern NJ. So they checked around and figured out Casso was at 79 Waterloo Road, Budd Lake, the residence of long-time Casso friend Rosemarie Bilotti.

January 18, 1993
FBI Agent Robert J Lenchar obtained a warrant to arrest Casso and search the home he was hiding in.

January 19, 1993
The FBI busted down the door of Casso's hideout and took the stunned Boss into custody. During the residence search, the FBI found $340,000 in cash, money records, a list of proposed members for the Lucchese and Gambino Families, plus a list of the Lucchese crews and their Capos. The Agents also legally searched two Casso safety deposit boxes in two different banks in Brooklyn.

January 1993
Underboss Anthony Casso inducted Michael "Baldy Mike" Spinelli in a bathroom at the Manhattan Correctional Center. Informer Frank Goia told this tale when he rolled later.

February 2, 1993
Police found the frozen body of Frank Signorino in the truck of his vehicle. He was the uncle of Peter Chiodo.

April 10, 1993
Acting on a 72 count superseding indictment, the FBI arrested Sal Avellino and Frank Lastorino for multiple crimes. A partial list follows below.
Conspiracy to murder carters Kubecka and Barstow
Attempted murder of Capo Peter Chiodo
Conspiracy to murder NJ Capo Anthony Acceturo
Conspiracy to murder two other NJ crew members
The murder of Joseph LaMorte
The murder of architect Anthony Fava
Twelve other murders

September 1993
Frank Goia Jr went to prison.

1994
Sal Avellino admitted he helped plan the murders of Kubecka and Barstow, the cooperating Long Island garbage contractors.

1994
Greek gambling power Spyredon Velentzas told the New York Daily News that he paid $10,000 a month to the Lucchese Family to protect him from other hoods trying to muscle in on his operations.

February 4, 1994
Anthony DeSimone killed Louis Batlancio outside a Yonkers bar. Around noon an FBI Agent saw Lucchese Capo Anthony Santorelli throw two paper bags full of bloody clothes into a dumpster. DeSimone is the son of mobster Salvatore "Sally Bows" DeSimone.

February 8, 1994
Casso, Frank Lastorino, and Sal Avellino lost their appeal over the legitimacy of various searches conducted by the FBI as they tracked down Casso.

February 17, 1994
Judge Eugene Nickerson accepted Capo Sal Avellino's guilty plea to racketeering murder conspiracy and extortion conspiracy. The hood also settled a civil racketeering case by agreeing to give $550,000 to pay a compliance officer to monitor the Long Island carting industry. The judge sentenced Avellino to ten and a half years, followed by ten years of probation. Included

in the plea was Avellino's admission that he conspired to kill honest carters, Kubecka and Barstow. All things considered, Avellino got off lightly.

March 1, 1994
Casso decided to roll over. Before Judge Jack Weinstein, Casso admitted to endless charges, including complicity in 15 murders. In addition, Casso revealed that he had been using corrupt cops Lou Eppolito and Steve Caracappa for at least a decade. This information brought a stalled investigation of the two mutts back to life.

After a quick debriefing, the FBI flew him to the famous Valachi suite located in an army camp in Texas where prosecutors spend many days hearing his terrible stories.

Burton Kaplan's lawyer got the bad news and relayed it to Kaplan, who quickly headed out but not before warning some of his closest Associates and rogue cop Steve Caracappa. The next day Kaplan flew to San Diego.

April 20, 1994
The Second Court of Appeals affirmed Amuso's conviction on 54 counts on June 19, 1992.

1994
Amuso appointed Capo Joe DeFede as Acting Boss.

April 30, 1994
The Brooklyn US Attorney announced a consent decree between the court and several mobbed-up carting firms. The companies agreed to accept a compliance officer and three $1 million into a kitty to pay for this supervision over the next five years.

May 1994
Before Judge Eugene Nickerson, Richard Pagliarulo, Mike DeSantis, and Frank Lastorino pled guilty to union leader John Morrissey's killing in 1989. The prosecutor planned to use turncoats Al D'Arco, Tommy Carew, Peter Chiodo, and Corrado "Dino" Marino to prove his case.

Eventual Sentences:
Lastorino 18 years
DeSantis 21 years
Pagliarulo? years

July 4, 1994
Police arrested Cappelo on extortion charges. Later a jury convicted Cappelo, and he died behind bars in December 1997.

August 10, 1994
Police arrested Lucchese Associate Nicholas Stefanelli on drug conspiracy charges.

August 18, 1994
Steve Crea plead guilty to conspiracy to defraud the US government.

October 1994
A judge sent Soldier Thomas D'Ambrosia to prison. His release date was in October 1997.

1995
BOP officials released Matthew Madonna from his 1976 drug conviction sentence. Lucchese leaders inducted Madonna not too long afterward.

January 1995
The feds charged Carmine Avellino, Sal Avellino, Anthony "Bowat" Baratta, Frank Frederico, and Rocco Vitulli with the Barstow Kubecka murders.

1995
A judge sentenced Soldier George Conte to a lengthy prison term. He participated in the killing of union leader John Morrissey among other crimes.

May 3, 1995
A federal grand jury indicted DiNapoli for insurance fraud.

May 18, 1995
A New York State grand jury indicted Joe and Vince DiNapoli plus ten other people for participating in a racketeering enterprise. The state had set aside specific contracts for firms owned by minorities, but the DiNapoli's found a way around it. They placed a minority front man for their firms, thus allowing their bids for asbestos removal work.

June 1995
Frank Lastorino pled guilty to charges from his April 1993 indictment. Later a judge sentenced him to 18 years.

June 20, 1995
John "Johnny Boy" Petrucelli stabbed citizen Paul Cicero to death. Petrucelli sought a hood who shot his friend but came across Cicero first. Unfortunately, Cicero had nothing to do with the original fight.

December 9, 1995
Judge Sterling Johnson sentenced Steve Crea to nine months with three years of supervised release. In addition, Crea had to pay $22,230 in restitution and a $50 special assessment.

1996
DEA Agents arrested long time hood Bernard Kaplan on drug charges. Years later, he would become a crucial government witness.

1996
Neil Migliore signed a deal with the feds that called for a nine-year sentence and a $266,000 fine.

May 15, 1996
Casso testified before the Senate Governmental Affairs subcommittee.

July 1996
Carmine Avellino, Baratta, and Vitulli pled guilty to a series of crimes, including the murders of honest garbage contractors Barstow and Kubecka.

September 26, 1996
Nicholas Stefanelli pled guilty to a heroin conspiracy in New Jersey and a cocaine conspiracy in Florida.

November 7, 1996
Prison officials released Steve Crea from his nine-month sentence on December 8, 1995.

January 2, 1997
Judge Leonard Silverman ruled that a wrongful death suit launched by the Barstow/Kubecka families could proceed against New York City. Their claim accused the Organized Crime Task Force of failing to protect their men despite written and verbal promises.

May 4, 1997
Parole officials released Neil Migliore from prison.

June 25, 1997
A judge denied Steve Crea's request to change some conditions under his supervised release from his December 8, 1995 sentence.

July 15, 1997
D'Arco testified about the bomb plot that killed Gambino Underboss Frank DeCicco. However, the witness conceded he was not personally involved with Genovese Boss Vince Gigante in the plotting.

August 4, 1997
A Grand Jury indicted Capo Louis "Dukey" Demary and eleven others on gambling, murder, loansharking, and extortion charges.

August 8, 1997
Feds say Casso breached his cooperating agreement by poor behavior in prison, participating in criminal acts, and lying.

1997
James Galione and Mario Gallo pled guilty to killing Gus Farace.

August 26, 1997
Turncoat Associate Henry Hill appeared on the popular Geraldo Rivera show.

September 11, 1997
Steven Bisulca was shot five times but survived. He had been soliciting carting customers despite being warned by Lucchese Associate Frank Notarantonio. Notarantonio later pled guilty to extortion, including the shooting of Bisulca.

September 23, 1997
A grand jury indicted Bowat Baratta and 13 others for a large drug conspiracy. Later a judge sentenced Baratta to eight years.

1997
The feds sold Sal Avellino's carting business for twenty million as part of a consent agreement.

October 9, 1997
The Bureau of Prisons removed Anthony Casso from the Witness Protection program due to his many crimes in prison.

November 1997
A judge sentenced Jody Calabrese to prison.

December 26, 1997
Greg Cappelo died in prison.

March 98
A jury convicted NYPD officer Vincent Davis of tipping the Lucchese Family to an informer in their midst in north New Jersey. (He won release on an appeal in July 1999).

April 1998
A grand jury indicted Acting Boss Joe (Little Joe) DeFede and 11 others for controlling the garment industry. They promised labor peace in the delivery of goods in return for payoffs. After his arrest, Lucchese Capos accused DeFede of skimming off money for himself. DeFede appealed to the jailed Amuso for help but felt rejected. DeFede then began thinking of informing to protect himself and his family.

A special monitor appointed by the courts to clean up the garment district uncovered the extortion scheme. Among those charged was Michael Vuola, owner of AAA Garment Trucking Inc. The feds seized his company, three properties, and his big boat.

June 30, 1998
Judge Frederic Block ruled it was legal for the US Government to throw Anthony Casso out of the witness protection program.

July 9, 1998
A judge sentenced Casso to life for the murders of Kubecka and Barstow. Avellino and his brother Carmine had sought permission from Amuso and Casso to kill the two.

A Luchese crew headed by Anthony Baratta was assigned the job. Rocco Vitulli and Frank Frederico carried out the killing. Frederico disappeared later, and many believed he was dead; however, the feds caught him in 2003.

July 1998
A New Jersey court awarded $10.8 million to the families of Barstow and Kubecka. State officials had failed to protect the two victims despite knowing they were in danger due to their actions against the mob.

1998
A judge sentenced Burton Kaplan to 27 years for a drug conspiracy and tax fraud. He later rolled over on rogue cops Eppolito and Caracappa.

1998
Lucchese Associate Robert Spinelli completed a 71-month conspiracy to distribute marijuana conviction.

November 11, 1998
A jury found Soldier Mike Spinelli guilty of 6 counts of murder conspiracy, weapons charges, and tampering with a witness. These counts involved the attempted murder of Peter Chiodo's sister in 1992.

During the trial, Mike Spinelli took the stand and admitted to murder, assaults, extortions, and drug dealing but insisted he had nothing to do with the attempted murder of Peter Chiodo's sister. However, the gunman, Dino Basciano, testified to Spinelli's role.

The same jury convicted Robert Spinelli of one murder conspiracy count, two witness tampering charges, and one weapon count.

December 7, 1998
Acting Boss Joe DeFede pled guilty to garment center extortion.

January 7, 1999
Parole officials released Mariano Macaluso from prison. He had briefly been Acting Consigliere after the Commission trial jury convicted Consigliere Chris Furnari in 1986. They also released Capo Richard DeLuca on this date.

January 22, 1999
The Second Circuit Court of Appeals affirmed the District Court's decision not to change any conditions under Steve Crea's supervised release.

March 22, 1999
A judge sentenced Acting Boss Joe DeFede to five years.

June 1999
A judge sentenced Michael "Baldy Mike" Spinelli to 24 1/2 years for conspiracy to murder, assault using a dangerous weapon, and conspiracy to tamper with a witness. All these counts pertain to the attempted murder of Peter Chiodo's sister in 1992.

July 1999
A judge sentenced Robert Spinelli to ten years for conspiracy to murder, assault using a dangerous weapon, and conspiracy to tamper with a witness. All these counts pertain to the 1992 attempted murder of the sister of Peter Chiodo.

July 1999
Former NYPD officer Victor Davis won his appeal of illegally tipping the Lucchese Family to the presence of an informer.

July 14, 1999
A grand jury indicted Sal Avellino, his son Michael, a son-in-law Michael Malena, Frank Notarantonio, and others of racketeering, murder conspiracy, arson, extortion, and bribery. The feds claimed that Avellino conducted a 15-year reign of terror to control the carting business on Long Island. Among the charges were:
Arson attacks on 12 buildings
Murder of a rival
Shooting a salesperson of a rival company five times

The feds sought $50 million in damages from Avellino, who sold his two firms in 1997, and from Notarantonio and his three companies.

September 23, 1999
Turncoat Frank Goia Jr testified that Tony Francesehi told him that he and a cousin had killed police officer Ronald Stapleton on December 18, 1977.

November 4, 1999
Parole agents caught Acting Underboss Steve Crea in a violation. After a hearing, they jailed him for nine months until March 2000.

November 9, 1999
Anthony DeSimone turned himself in for the February 4, 1994 slaying of college student Louis Balancio.

The next chapter will continue summarizing the reign of Vic Amuso.

CHAPTER EIGHT

Boss Vic Amuso Continued

As the new century began, Vic Amuso continued to run the Lucchese Family from behind bars. How much control he maintained is challenging to measure, but there was general agreement the Family honored his Boss position. A summary of the significant events in that organization up to approximately 2021 follows.

2000
Louis Daidone allegedly became Acting Boss.

January 5, 2000
Former NYPD officer Victor Davis was on trial again for feeding information to the Lucchese Family.

January 15, 2000
Former Underboss Sal" Tom Mix" Santora died in prison.

April 3, 2000
Federal and state agents raided a bookmaking operation run by Nicholas Mitola, a man who was a government witness in the 1988 New Jersey trial of the Lucchese wing. A judge later sentenced Mitola to two years.

August 23, 2000
Former Boss Anthony "Tony Ducks" Corallo died in prison at 88.

September 6, 2000
Manhattan DA Robert Morgenthau announced a state grand jury indictment of 38 people, including Acting Boss Steve Crea Capos, Dom Truscello, and Joe Tangorra. Soldiers Joe Datello, Phil DeSimone, Tony Pezzullo, Joe Truncale, Phil DeSimone and Art Zambardi were also named.

The indictment charged Pezzullo, DeSimone, and Datello with running the Lucchese Family construction panel. Soldier Zambardi aided this group. The allegation was that the mobsters would bribe union leaders in the carpentry and brick unions to rig bids on projects plus extort companies for favorable treatment. The average mob tax was 5%.

The state indictment claimed that Steve Crea secretly ran Kent Building Systems, making modular classrooms for the Board of Education.

Manhattan DA Robert Morgenthau explained that Micheal Forde, president of the District Council of Carpenters, used false records from 1998 thru 1999.

On the same day, Mary Jo White, a Manhattan US Attorney, announced a federal indictment of six persons, including three Lucchese heavyweights. It charged Acting Boss Steve Crea, Capo Dom Truscello, Capo Joseph Tangorra, and three others with conspiring to commit extortion, wire fraud, and loansharking.

One count from the federal indictment alleged that Joseph Datello of the Lucchese construction panel inflated the bid for plasterboard at the Park Central Hotel in 1998. This act freed up $2 million for kickbacks to the Lucchese Family.

November 28, 2000
A grand jury handed down a racketeering indictment naming seven Lucchese members and Associates. Those charged: Capo Joseph Tangorra, Soldier Joseph Truncale, Capo Eugene Castelle, Lester Ellis, Robert Greenberg, John Castelluci, and Soldier Scott Gervasi. Among the many counts was the October 1988 murder of Victor Filocamo.

2001
Joseph "Big Joe" Giampa left prison a free man.

February 2, 2001
Joe DeFede secretly turned informer after being accused of stealing money from Amuso.

March 12, 2001
Frank Notarantonio pled guilty to various charges, including extortion in the carting industry in New Jersey. He also admitted to the September 11, 1997, shooting of Steve Bisulca.

November 15, 2001
Construction firm owners Joseph and Fred Scalamandre pled guilty to making payoffs to the Lucchese Family in return for favorable treatment by the unions. In addition, they agreed to pay five million in restitution.

2002
BOP officials released Ralph "Raffie" Cuomo.

March 19, 2002
This date marked the start of Nicholas Facciolo's trial for weapons possession in the 1990 shooting death of Ernest Abdul Mateen at the Brooklyn Terminal Market. A jury had convicted him of manslaughter, but he won an appeal.

2002
The good guys listened in as several moves made by Boss Amuso unfolded thanks to hidden bugs. First, Amuso transferred Soldier Vincent Salanardi from Capo Dom Truscello's crew to Acting Capo John Cerrella, filling in for Capo Domenico "Danny' Cutaia. Amuso also placed Soldier John Baudanza in another unit.

September 2, 2002
Feds announced that Acting Boss Joe DeFede had become a government informer. He pled guilty to murder, extortion, illegal gambling, and money laundering. In addition, DeFede admitted to extorting the famous Palm restaurant. The tax was $7,500 before Christmas and $7,500 just after New Year. Two Tony Roma eating establishments also had to pay up. Also, DeFede taxed three construction companies, Scalamandre, Martinelli, and Picone.

October 10, 2002
Judge Charles Briant sentenced former Acting Boss Al D'Arco to time served as the reward for his cooperation.

October 28, 2002
Former Acting Boss Joe DeFede testified in the trial of John Petrucelli for the murder of Paul Cicero. Petrucelli was a member of a street gang called the Tanglewood Boys. They got into a fight with other local mutts, and one of their guys got shot. Seeking revenge, Petrucelli couldn't find the shooter but came across Cicero, whom he stabbed.

November 4, 2002
A jury found John Petrucelli guilty of the murder of Paul Cicero. Back on September 13, 1989, shooters killed Petrucelli's father on orders of Boss Vic Amuso. The senior Petrucelli had been hiding Gus Farace, the killer of a DEA Agent, despite demands not to.

November 14, 2002
A Suffolk County Grand Jury indicted Acting Underboss Joe Caridi and 13 other Lucchese members or Associates. Suffolk County Assistant DA James Chalifoux said, "Joseph Caridi is the Tony Soprano of the Lucchese Family."

Note:
Sometime in 2002, Amuso promoted Caridi from Acting Underboss to Consigliere.

According to the state indictment, this bunch made up to $1.5 million through loansharking, illegal gambling, construction payoffs, restaurant extortion, and bid-rigging. The officials hit Caridi with the state charge of enterprise corruption, similar to the feds RICO charge. The judge released Caridi on $100,000 bail.

State and local police conducted 14 raids and seized more than $2 million in assets during the operation. In addition, they raided Louis Daidone's home but did not arrest him.

December 10, 2002
The feds announced a 36 count indictment, including Consigliere Joe Caridi, Capo John "Johnny Sideburns" Cerrella, Acting Capo Vince Mancione, Soldiers Vince "Vinnie Baldy" Salanardi, Carm Profeta, and John Vanasco. Among the charges were drug dealing, extortion, gambling, and perjury.

Magistrate Cheryl Pollak refused bail for Caridi until a hearing later in the week. At that time, the officials denied Caridi's release till trial.

One of the main counts was the extortion of the Hudson and McCoy Fish House in Freeport. This facility opened in 2000 with John Gotti Associate Lewis Kasman as an investor. The owners felt Kasman was looting the place and allegedly turned to the Lucchese Family for protection.

Using Capo John "Johnny Sideburns" Cerrella and Soldier Vincent "Vinnie Baldy" Salanardi, Cardi took charge chasing Kasman out. Cardi's crew raked in from $7,000 to $10,000 each night from the restaurant's outdoor bar.

December 11, 2002
Lawyer Frankie Gangemi had arranged a plea deal for conning 20 clients out of more than $6 million. However, the feds discovered evidence during their investigation of the Caridi crew that involved Gangemi. From wiretaps, the feds learned that Gangemi had contacted Vincent "Vinny Baldy" Salanardi to intimidate witnesses against him. The feds turned this information to the state, scuppering Gangemi's sweet plea deal.

December 19, 2002
A grand jury handed down a two-count indictment charging Acting Boss Louis "Louie Bagels" Daidone with loansharking. Judge Richard Berman released Daidone on $1 million bail. Future FBI head James Comey was the US Attorney in this case.

December 30, 2002
Mariano Macaluso died of natural causes at 90

January 27, 2003
The FBI arrested Frank Frederico for the carters' murders of Kubecka and Barstow on August 10, 1989. The veteran Soldier went missing in March 1992 when a Grand Jury subpoenaed him to provide DNA samples.

March 14, 2003
A federal grand jury charged Acting Boss Louis "Louie Bagels" Daidone with racketeering, involving the killing of Soldier Bruno Facciola (August 1990) and Tom "Red" Gilmore (February 1989). The judge refused bail for the hood. US Attorney James Comey noted that previous Acting Bosses had been

jailed and said, "Others who aspire to that position would be well advised to take note of the fates of their predecessors."

Note:
Murder is a state offense. However, the feds can include murder in a RICO (racketeering) charge. For example, the feds must prove that the person carried out at least two serious crimes for the benefit of the enterprise, in this case, the Mafia Family.

March 19, 2003
Before Judge Steven Gold, Consigliere Joe Caridi admitted to the federal charge of the extortion of the Hudson and McCoy restaurant in Freeport, NY. Cardi also admitted to running gambling out of his house and not paying income tax for at least five years. Additionally, he agreed to forfeit $400,000. Caridi's projected release date was November 28, 2009.

Note:
This plea deal took care of state charges of loansharking and gambling.

September 22, 2003
After completing a parole violation sentence BOP officials released Matthew Madonna.

October 1, 2003
Before Judge Ronald Ellis, Underboss Steve Crea admitted to shaking down Scalamandre Construction.

Capo Dominic "Crazy Dom" Truscello pled guilty to extorting Commercial Brick Construction Company to give him a no-show job in a separate proceeding.

December 10, 2003
The Second Court of Appeals vacated the conviction and sentence of Robert Spinelli for his role in the attempted murder of Peter Chiodo's sister.

2004
Long-time hood Kaplan agreed to roll over to the DEA. At this point, he had completed eight of his 27-year drug sentence and was anxious to be with his family. Fortunately, he had a lot of secrets to spill, which would gain his freedom.

2004
Prison officials released Patrick "Patty" Dellorusso.

January 13, 2004
Former Acting Boss Al D'Arco testified in the trial of Acting Boss Louis Daidone. He said Underboss Anthony Casso ordered the death of Soldier Bruno Facciolo and to use Daidone to get it done. Daidone later told D'Arco that he held Facciola down while another guy shot him. D'Arco also testified that Casso ordered Daidone to kill Thomas Gilmore in 1989.

January 4, 2004
Judge Ronald Ellis sentenced Steve Crea to 34 months for extorting payments from the Scalamandre Construction Company.

January 23, 2004
A jury convicted Louis "Louie Bagels" Daidone of racketeering, loansharking, and murder. They found him guilty of killing Bruno Facciolo in 1990 and Thomas "Red" Gilmore in 1989. Turncoat Al D'Arco was a key prosecution witness testifying that Underboss Anthony Casso ordered him to use Daidone in the two hits. Frank Gioia, another turncoat, said that Daidone told him of his involvement in the Facciolo murder. Judge Richard Berman presided over the trial.

February 24, 2004
Prison officials released Carmine Avellino.

March 8, 2004
A judge sentenced Acting Underboss Steve Crea from two to six years for pleading guilty to enterprise corruption and restraint of trade. These state charges would run concurrent to the federal sentence given in January.

March 11, 2004
Steve Crea began serving a 34-month sentence.

March 16, 2004
A federal judge rejected Frank Frederico's plea deal over the carters' murder in 1989.

March 23, 2004
A federal judge accepted Frank Frederico's plea deal, which gave him a fifteen-year sentence for his part in the murder of carters Kubecka and Barstow. Frederico was 76. He also admitted lying that an FBI nurse tortured him while taking a DNA sample.

March 9, 2005
A grand jury indicted former cops Eppolito and Caracappa for eight murders, conspiracy to murder, attempted murder, obstruction of justice, kidnapping conspiracy, witness tampering, bribery, money laundering, and drug trafficking. Detective William Oldham of the NYPD and DEA agents arrested them in Las Vegas.

April 1, 2005
The body of diamond dealer Isadore Greenwald is dug up from a garage on Nostrand Avenue in Brooklyn.

September 29, 2005
Authorities freed Barry Gibbs from a murder conviction after serving nineteen years in prison. However, allegedly rogue cop Louie Eppolito forced a witness to testify against Gibbs falsely.

December 8, 2005
BOP officials released Martin Taccetta from New Jersey prison on orders of the court. However, later he lost his appeal and returned to do his life sentence.

2006
BOP authorities released Steve Crea after doing 30 months in prison.

March 15, 2006
New Jersey banned Danny Cutaia from its casinos.

August 2006
BOP officials released Vincent Mancione.

October 13, 2006
BOP officials released Capo Salvatore Avellino.

2007
Someone killed Soldier Frank Lagano in the parking lot of a diner he owned in East Brunswick, NJ. Turncoat Al D'Arco had identified Lagano as a one-time member of his crew.

April 17, 2007
A grand jury charged John Baudanza, Capo Joe Baudanza, and his brother Carmine with various gambling and other offenses.

Aug 2007
Boss Vic Amuso demoted Nicky Scarfo Jr to Soldier and replaced him as Capo with Ralph Perna.

October 2007
The Lucchese Family inducted Capo Ralph Perna's sons Joe and John in Toms River.

October 20, 2007
District Court Judge Raymond Dearie denied Mike and Robert Spinelli a new trial.

December 18, 2007
The police arrested Joe DiNapoli, Matthew Madonna, Capo Ralph Perna, and Soldier Alfonso Cataldo on gambling and other charges.

December 2007
A judge sentenced Capo Joe Baudanza, his brother Carmine Baudanza, and Carmine's son John Baudanza to prison. The latter received seven years.

2008
BOP officials released Frank Lastorino.

May 28, 2008
BOP officials released Castella.

2008
Authorities arrested Capo Danny Cutaia, Soldier Michael Carcione, John Baudanza, Sal Cutaia, and others on loansharking and gambling charges.

September 10, 2008
BOP officials released Capo John Capra from prison.

December 21, 2008
One time Consigliere Frank Lastorino won parole after doing 14 years for various crimes.

December 31, 2008
The Second Court of Appeals confirmed Mike Spinelli's racketeering convictions but remanded him for a sentence reduction.

2009
Boss Vic Amuso appointed Capo Matthew Madonna as Acting Boss replacing the Lucchese panel.

July 30, 2009
An appeal court reinstated Martin Taccetta's life sentence.

October 1, 2009
The Good Guys arrested Capo Andrew DeSimone of the Bronx for bribery and gambling. Also nabbed were Soldiers Dominic Capelli and Anthony Croce, along with about 30 others.

October 1, 2009
The Manhattan DA announced an indictment that charged Acting Boss Matthew Madonna, Consigliere Joe DiNapoli, and Acting Capo Anthony Croce with running many schemes—also indicted were six former inspectors for New York's Department of Buildings. They had the power to extort bribes.

Among the schemes were:
Overlooking safety violations
Speeding up the granting of permits
Voiding previous violations
Lifting stop-work orders
Speeding up inspections
Gambling
Loansharking
Gun trafficking
Extortion

October 1, 2009
The feds charged 12 Lucchese hoods and seven other men with gambling, loansharking, and extortion. In addition, acting Capo Andrew DeSimone and Soldier Dominic "Nicky Pepsi," Capelli faced allegations of paying $222,000

in bribes to an NYPD Detective and a Sergeant to protect gambling spots. The problem for the hoods was that this was a sting operation; the cops were good guys.

October 25, 2009
A judge sentenced Capo Danny Cutaia to three years for bank fraud.

November 27, 2009
Prison officials released Soldier John Cerrella.

November 2009
Police arrested Soldier Joe Datello on gambling charges. (see Ap 2010)

January 2010
Capo Dom Cutaia began a three-year sentence for bank fraud.

April 2010
Soldier Joe Datello pled guilty to gambling charges. (See May 2010.)

May 13, 2010
The feds arrested thirty-four members and Associates of the Lucchese Family, including Joe DiNapoli and Matthew Madonna, two ruling panel members.

May 2010
A judge sentenced Soldier Joe Datello to 1¾ to 3½ yrs. for illegal gambling.

June 22, 2010
A judge sentenced Capo Anthony Croce for loansharking. He had pled guilty.

June 28, 2010
Matthew Madonna pled guilty to a variety of charges from his October 2009 indictment for loansharking, extortion, gambling, and bribery of building inspectors.

July 15, 2012
Former Acting Boss and turncoat Joe DeFede died in Florida.

September 25, 2012
Prison officials released Bowat Baratta.

October 13, 2012
Former union power Frank Manzo died.

April 2013
Acting Boss Matthew Madonna inducted Joe Pennesi and two others.

September 30, 2013
Prison officials released Soldier Dominick Capelli from his 2009 conviction.

March 2014
Prison officials released George Conte. He was involved in the California killing of Anthony DiLapi.

George "Georgie Neck" Zapolla won his freedom as well.

May 13, 2014
A grand jury accused Carmine Avellino of extortion for collecting $100,000 from victims using or threatening violence.

July 4, 2014
A jury convicted Soldier Nicky Scarfo Jr in a massive fraud scheme. He and others looted a company of many millions.

January 29, 2015
New York City finally attempted to atone for the incredible wrongs committed by rogue policemen Lou Eppolito and Steve Caracappa.
They awarded innocent victim Nicky Guido's aged mother five million dollars. The money wouldn't bring her adored son back, but it was better than nothing.

Feb 2015
Martin Taccetta lost the appeal of his life sentence,

June 17, 2015
Matthew Madonna, Martin Taccetta, and John Mangrella each pled out to gambling charges.

July 28, 2015
A judge sentenced Soldier Nicky Scarfo Jr to 30 years for a lucrative stock scam.

September 30, 2015
A judge sentenced Matthew Madonna to five years, Martin Taccetta and John Mangrella to eight years each. On June 17, 2015, the three hoods pled guilty to a May 2010 indictment.

May 31, 2017
A massive federal indictment charged Acting Boss Matthew Madonna, Underboss Steve Crea Sr, Consigliere Joe DiNapoli, and many others. Madonna, Crea Sr, and Crea Jr (a Capo) faced the Michael Meldish murder count. Others accused in that included Joe Datello, Paul Cassano, and Terrence Caldwell. The counts included conspiracy, extortion, loansharking, and labor racketeering.

The judge ruled no bail for Steve Crea Jr and others.

2017
Amuso sent out a coded letter ordering that Acting Boss Matthew "Matty" Madonna step down in favor of Mike DeSantis.

2017
Mike DeSantis Acting Boss
Patty Dellorusso Acting Underboss
Andrew DeSimone Acting Consigliere
Seven Crews

May 2017
Sal "Sammy Meatballs" Aparo died.

June 17, 2018
A judge sentenced Lucchese Capo John Castellucci to 37 months plus a $150,000 fine for loansharking.

August 2018
Dom Cutaia died.

August 2018
Judge Cathy Seibel released Steve Crea Jr on bail. The authorities had him locked up since the indictment of May 31, 2017. Judge Seibel's main reason for the release was her publicly stated skepticism over the honesty of the prosecution's main witness.

September 24, 2018
Joseph Datello pled guilty to the attempted murder of a federal witness against Underboss Steve Crea, drug trafficking, extortion, and collecting loanshark debts.

October 1, 2018
Soldier John Pennisi finally decided it was too dangerous to continue in the life, so he rolled over to the FBI.

October 26, 2018
Someone killed Lucchese Associate Vincent Zito in his home. Gambino Associate Anthony Pandrella, a good friend of Zito, was the main suspect.

2019
Vincent Bruno admitted to attempted murder and racketeering conspiracy. The judge gave him 15 years for his involvement in the Crea insult revenge plot from 2012.

Paul Cassano Jr admitted to conspiracy to commit assault with a deadly weapon during the 2012 Crea insult revenge plot. The judge handed down a 12-18 month sentence.

May 21, 2019
A jury convicted Boobsie Castelle of racketeering for operating an illegal gambling business. Turncoat Soldier John Pennisi was an effective prosecution witness. Later a judge sentenced Castelle to 77 months.

August 20, 2019
Judge Cathy Seibel took the guilty plea of Steve Crea Jr.
He admitted to:
Conspiring to kill and assault a victim to maintain his position in a criminal enterprise.
Committing the crimes of illegal gambling and extortion.
Directing others to use threats of violence to gain control of illegal gambling machines in the Bronx.

The conspiracy to kill charge came from an incident in 2012 at a Lucchese social club. Bonanno Associate Carl Ulzhemer insulted Underboss Steve Crea, who was furious. Crea ordered Crea Jr to seek revenge. The son hired two thugs, Paul Cassano Jr and Vincent Bruno, to kill Ulzhemer. Fortunately, they couldn't find him.

November 15, 2019
A jury convicted Acting Capo Matthew Madonna, Underboss Steve Crea, Soldier Christopher Londonio, and Associate Terrence Caldwell of the November 2013 murder of gangster Michael Meldish. The theory was that Meldish owed Madonna money and refused to pay. Other accounts state that Meldish insulted Steve Crea. Whatever the reason, Meldish ended up dead.

January 23, 2020
Judge Cathy Seibel sentenced Steven Crea Jr to 13 years after the gangster pled guilty to charges in August 2019. He received:
Five years for racketeering (gambling and extortion)
Five years for conspiracy to murder Carl Ulzhemer
Three years for conspiracy to commit assault (on some gambling rivals).

February 19, 2020
Judge Ron Abrams sentenced witness David Evangelista to time served for two bank robberies in 2018. But, importantly, he said it would be too risky to send the turncoat to prison.

Prosecutors explained that Evangelista was a critical witness in the Meldish murder trial of Underboss Steve Crea, Chris Londonio, and Matthew Madonna. Evangelista testified that Soldier Chris Londonio explained that Meldish insulted Madonna, who responded by issuing a hit order. He went on to say that Steve Crea Sr and Jr ordered him to kill Meldish.

April 16, 2020
Parole officials released Castelle from prison due to the danger of the virus. He would appeal his May 2019 sentence.

May 5, 2020
Judge Raymond Dearie released Mike Spinelli from prison due to the Covid dangers. However, at some point, Spinelli would return to jail for resentencing.

July 27, 2020
Judge Cathy Seibel sentenced former Acting Boss Matthew Madonna to life for racketeering conspiracy. The jury found him guilty of ordering the hit on Michael Meldish for failure to repay a debt. Madonna protested, "I am innocent. I had absolutely nothing to do with the tragic death of Michael Meldish. I conspired with no one."

Judge Seibel sent Soldier Chris Londonio away for life. The jury found him guilty of luring his friend Meldish out and driving to a prearranged spot where Terrence Caldwell gunned him down.

A jury found Terrence Caldwell guilty of killing Michael Meldish. Accordingly, Judge Seibel hit him with a life sentence.

August 26, 2020
Judge Cathy Seibel sentenced Joseph DiNapoli to 52 months and a fine of $250,000. DiNapoli would appeal.

August 27, 2020
Judge Seibel sentenced Lucchese Underboss Steve Crea to life in prison. She also ordered him to forfeit $1 million. The prosecutors wanted another million, but she rejected that.

Note:
The forfeiture order is controversial. First, Crea made a legal loan of approximately $1 million to contractor Randolph Silverstein. Then Silverstein earned up to $1 million in interest by illegally overbilling at a construction site. The feds felt that all this money was subject to forfeiture under the RICO act. Ultimately Judge Seibel forced Crea to give up the loan principal and not the interest.

November 2020
Lawyers for Anthony Casso filed an emergency application for the First Step program in Judge Frederick Block's court. A very unsophisticated explanation of the program would be that officials designed it to free aging ill convicts if they met specific qualifications. Fortunately, the judge did not free Casso.

February 18, 2021
Joseph DiNapoli agreed to plead guilty to one count of conspiracy to participate in the affairs of an enterprise through a pattern of racketeering activities. His penalty would be between 37-46 months with a fine of $15,000 to $150,000.

Unfortunately for DiNapoli, the probation people decided that the sentence calculations were inaccurate and that the old gangster deserved a harsher sentence. Accordingly, Judge Seibel handed down a penalty of 52 months and a fine of $250,000.

DiNapoli went to the Second Court of Appeals, which affirmed his sentence and fine.

September 8, 2021
Judge Cathy Seibel denied the latest in appeals by Joseph DiNapoli to vacate, set aside or correct his sentence of 52 months.

It is impossible to predict the future, but it is a good bet the Lucchese Family will keep trucking for years to come.

CHAPTER NINE

Capo Paul Vario

Paul Vario was a long-time Capo in the Lucchese Family. He first came to fame when the NYPD bugged his construction trailer and caught all kinds of incriminating conversations. Later the book Wiseguys and the movie Goodfellas brought him lasting fame, although the film used a pseudonym. What follows is a summary of his long life in La Cosa Nostra.

DOB
July 10, 1914
NYC

DOD
May 3, 1988
Fort Worth Federal Prison

First Wife
Vita
Second Wife
Phyllis

Sons
Peter
Paul Jr
Leonard-died 1972

Residences
132 Island Parkway, Island Park, NY.
Circa 1970

1957
Paul Vario planned to burn a man who owed him money with a mixture of lye and another substance. Unfortunately for Vario, the concoction blew up in his face requiring a visit to a Mob doctor.

April 1969
Vario refused to testify before a grand jury investigating organized crime on Long Island three times.

1970
Boss Carmine Tramunti may have elevated Vario to either Acting Underboss or Underboss this year.

January 29, 1970
After five days of testimony, a jury convicted Paul Vario of criminal contempt for refusing to testify before a grand jury investigating organized crime on Long Island. Assistant DA Dominick Minerva asked Judge Harold Spitzer to deny bail. The judge agreed and remanded Vario to Nassau County Jail until sentencing.

April 7, 1972
Detectives working for DA Eugene Gold placed bugs in the construction trailer on a Canarsie junkyard lot controlled by Vario. They would record criminal conversations for the next six months.

April 19, 1972
DA Gold's bug in Vario's trailer taped Vario telling bookie Frank Heitman to flee to Florida rather than testify in an investigation of the Nassau County Jail. This tape would lead to charges against Vario and others later.

June 10, 1972
Friends dropped Leonard Vario off at a hospital and drove away, leaving the severely burned Vario lying there. He refused to talk to the police. Coincidentally a factory burned down nearby. After a long battle, Leonard died.

June 13, 1972
DA Gold's bug in Vario's trailer caught the Mob Capo discussing a recent hijacking with three hoods. They had turned over the trailer load of goods to another crew, but the police confiscated the cargo. Vario ruled that the second crew had to pay the first group despite the cops ending up with the load. This tape would bite Vario later.

June 1972
DA Gold announced the indictment of Vario and 24 guards from the Nassau County Jail. They were accused of perjury and bringing contraband into the facility.

September 26, 1972
Justice Stark dismissed the indictment of Vario and various Nassau County correctional officers accused of bribery and bringing contraband into the jail at Mineola.

September 27. 1972
Justice Thomas M Stark dismissed tampering with a witness charge against Vario and another man. Assistant DA Martin Walsh asked for an adjournment, but the justice said the delay would infringe on the defendant's right to a speedy trial. The cops had taped Vario telling a witness to travel to Florida rather than testify in the prosecution of the corrupt correctional officers.

October 10, 1972
Hoods attacked two TV camera operators and a police officer at the funeral of Leonard Vario at St Fortunata Church in East New York.
(Leonard was the son of Paul Vario).

October 25, 1972
DA Gold announced the indictment of Vario and three other hoods for hijacking a trailer load of women's slacks.

October 1972
Police officers raided Vario's construction trailer.

November 1, 1972
DA Eugene Gold announced an indictment involving tampering with a witness. The DA had been conducting an investigation into corruption at the jail in Mineola when a trailer bug caught Vario advising a witness to flee to Florida.

November 21, 1972
DA Gold announced another indictment based on Vario's Canarsie-based trailer bugs. It charged Vario and three other men with grand larceny, conspiracy, and presenting a false insurance claim. One of the men claimed someone stole his 30' boat called the Playpen from a marina. Later, police found the boat half-submerged and stripped. He put in an insurance claim and received $7,147. DA Gold's bug caught the whole conspiracy on a tape resulting in the indictment.

December 6, 1972
A grand jury indicted Vario and two friends with bribing two cops.
Police had arrested four female relatives of a Vario acquaintance. One detective came to Vario's bugged trailer soliciting a bribe for him and his partner to get the case dropped. On the day of the trial of the women, the witness against them failed to show up. The indictment charged Vario and his two friends with bribery, rewarding official misconduct, and giving unlawful gratuities.

December 1972
Police charged Vario with drunk driving, which was a breach of his parole. This incident resulted in a six-month jail term.

February 9, 1973
A jury convicted Vario of tax fraud.

April 6, 1973
Judge Jacob Mishler sentenced Vario to two three-year terms to be served concurrently for his tax fraud. Vario was in prison doing a six-month parole violation bit at this time.

May 1, 1973
Prison officials released Vario after completing his six-month parole violation term from December 1972.

September 12, 1973
The Second Circuit Court of Appeals affirmed Vario's tax conviction, and he went off to prison.

1973
The best evidence suggests that the Lucchese leadership demoted Vario from Underboss to Capo around this time.

1978
Capo Paul Vario approved the attempt to commit a major robbery at the Lufthansa Airlines facility at JFK Airport.

December 11, 1978
A group of thieves robbed the Lufthansa warehouse at JFK of approximately $5.8 million in cash and jewelry. Below is a rough summary of how this famous event happened. In addition, the book "Wiseguys (1985)" by Nick Pileggi and the film "Goodfellas (1990)" by Martin Scorcese do a terrific job of revealing the lifestyle of the mutts involved in this and other capers.

Lufthansa employee Louis Werner owed bookie Marty Krugman a lot of money. He explained to Krugman how Lufthansa stored millions in currency in their warehouse under less than serious protection.

Krugman explained the situation to Lucchese Associate Henry Hill.

Hill outlined a plan to rob Lufthansa to legendary Lucchese Associate Jimmy Burke, who made a great living hijacking trucks at JFK Airport.

Burke organized six hoods who went to JFK Airport and took the Lufthansa warehouse employees hostage. They looted the place of many boxes of valuables and drove away in a van and their car. The good guys never recovered any of the money or jewelry.

Ironically only Lufthansa employee Louis Werner served prison time for the heist. His ex-wife and another Lufthansa employee ratted him out. Werner had no cards to play. His only contact with the gang was bookie Marty Krugman, whom the team murdered.

More than ten people associated in some way with the robbery ended up dead. The victims ranged from a mutt who failed to dispose of the van used in the theft to bookie Marty Krugman to members of the robbery team. It was not a pretty picture, and this violence scared Henry Hill.

In 1980 Henry Hill's out-of-control life came to a brief halt when the good guys arrested him on drug charges. Fearing a lengthy prison sentence and the wrath of Capo Paul Vario and the fears of Jimmy Burke, Hill rolled over and testified against many. Hill helped convict Burke of a college basketball point-shaving scheme, but it was a murder conviction that finished Burke. He died behind bars.

June 22, 1983
The authorities charged Paul Vario and nightclub impresario Philipe Basile with providing Lucchese Associate Henry Hill with a no-show job. This move permitted Hill to be free of prison. In addition, Basile's people falsified pay vouchers to indicate Hill went to work at the business when he didn't. Hill ratted the two out when he rolled over.

February 9, 1984
A jury convicted Paul Vario and Philipe Basile of defrauding the federal government by providing Henry Hill with a no-show job.

April 3, 1984
A judge sentenced Capo Paul Vario to four years and a $10,000 fine for a no-show job scheme for Henry Hill.

February 21, 1985
The feds announced a massive 23 counts indictment naming 11 defendants, including Vario and Lucchese Underboss Sal Santoro. The hoods used the power of Teamsters locals 295 and 851 to extort three freight companies and used insider information on one of them to make a killing on Wall Street with the extorted money. Magistrate Simon Chrein released Santoro on $150,000 bail, but Vario was in prison doing time for another conviction.

October 8, 1986
Judge Joseph McLaughlin accepted the plea deals of Vario, Frank Manzo (president of Local 295), and three others from the February 21, 1985 indictment. Ed McDonald of the Organized Crime Task Force said, "We are very pleased we have convicted significant organized crime figures and labor racketeers."

December 10, 1986
Judge McLaughlin sentenced Paul Vario to a six-year term and a $25,000 fine for his racketeering at JFK Airport. Vario had five months left on a previous conviction to serve.

May 3, 1988
Vario died of lung cancer in the Fort Worth Medical Prison.

CHAPTER TEN

Capo John Dioguardi

John Ignazio Dioguardi
Dioguardi was an earner for the Lucchese Family from the 1930s to well into the 1970s. His skills ran from organizing labor unions which permitted him to extort businesses to stock fraud. Along the way, he made millions of dollars but faced countless legal problems along with years of bad press. On the low-end, Dioguardi allegedly conspired to blind labor writer Vincent Riesel in the 1950s. His mutts stole millions of dollars from unsuspecting investors in his various stock schemes. It is hard to estimate how much money Dioguardi spent on lawyers during his lifetime. His death behind bars seemed very fitting for many of his victims.

DOB
April 29, 1914
NYC

DOD
January 12, 1979

Description
5'8"
165 Lbs
Brown eyes

Black hair
Dark complexion

January 8, 1958
Norma Adams of the Daily News described the long incarcerated Dioguardi with the following phrases.
Pasty complexion
Grey suit hung loosely on him
His collar seemed three sizes too big
Shallow faced little man

Residence
109 Freeport Ave
Point Lookout, LI

Wife
Ann Chrostek

Daughter
Rose

Sons
Dominick
Thomas

Note:
The two sons became members of La Cosa Nostra.

Father
Dominick

Mother
Rose Plumeri

Dioguardi Businesses
Mizrach Provisions
Tel Aviv Provisions
JARD Products
They produced restaurant napkins with advertising on them.

Dioguardi Timeline

1929 approx.
Dio worked at the Empire Yeast Company, delivering yeast.

August 3, 1932
Police arrested Dioguardi for coercion.

October 13, 1932
A judge dismissed the coercion charge.

May 10, 1933
Police charged Dioguardi with felonious assault, coercion, and conspiracy.

September 4, 1934
Judge Freschi dismissed the charges.

May 26, 1936
Police charged Dioguardi with vagrancy.

March 27, 1936
Magistrate Perlman dismissed the charge.

March 19, 1937
Police charged Dioguardi with extortion.

May 4, 1937
Judge McCook of the Superior Court dismissed the extortion charges.

May 4, 1937
Police charged Dioguardi and James Plumeri with extortion, conspiracy, and assault.

July 26, 1937
After the prosecution presented its case, Dioguardi and Plumeri pled guilty. They admitted to conspiracy, malicious mischief, extortion, and second-degree assault. Judge McCook sentenced Dioguardi to three to five years.

October 30, 1944
Authorities charged Dioguardi with conspiracy to violate state tax laws in Newark, NJ. They dropped the charges later.

1950
The United Auto Workers appointed Dioguardi as their regional director. The allowed him 12 charters for locals in the garment center. This action gave Dioguardi the power to demand money from employers who wished to remain union-free.

1951
Dioguardi used his AFL-UAW Local 102 to organize New York cab drivers. It was a perfect vehicle to extort cab company owners.

October 19, 1952
Thomas Dioguardi, John's brother, married Rosemary Livorsi at St Ignatius Roman Catholic Church. Six hundred guests attended the reception at the Hotel Commodore.

February 10, 1953
Dave Beck, President of the Teamsters, announced a nationwide drive to organize taxi drivers. He appointed Thomas Hickey, a Teamster VP from the New York area, as leader of the charge. Beck also added that while they would welcome the cab drivers in Dioguardi's UAW Local 102, they did not want Dioguardi involved.

April 27, 1953
US Attorney Frank Hogan charged Dioguardi with tax fraud from 1950 and 1951. Dioguardi sold his Allentown, PA dress company for $12,000 but took another $11,200 under the table. Secretly Dioguardi guaranteed the new owner that he would not have a union for that hidden payment. The gangster didn't declare that income in his taxes, plus he didn't report part of his salary from UAW Local 102 in the fall of 1951.

May 22, 1953
The Executive Committee of the AFL directed the United Auto Workers to revoke the charter of Dioguardi's Local 102. He had been calling dozens of small strikes disrupting New York City. The stated purpose of these actions was to grow the local membership, but they were also a perfect tool for extortion. The parent AFL Union ordered Dioguardi to end the strike due to unfavorable publicity.

1954
Dioguardi worked to help Teamster power Jimmy Hoffa become union president.

March 26, 1954
Magistrate Haddock sentenced Dioguardi to 60 days in the New York City Work House for his tax fraud conviction.

August 23, 1954
The President of the United Auto Workers Union stripped Dioguardi of all titles and commissions in the union. In addition, he banned the gangster from the organization and revoked the charters of Dioguardi's six UAW locals in New York. Authorities had put pressure on the UAW for some time to expel Dioguardi and end his extortions using union power.

Dioguardi's six UAW locals (214, 224, 225, 227, 228, and 355) never passed on the dues they collected to the national office. Instead, he just pocketed the money.

November 29, 1955 - December 15, 1955
Teamster power Jimmy Hoffa permitted Dioguardi to charter seven paper locals. (They only existed on paper and had no actual members.) The plan was for Dioguardi to work with Teamster leader John J O'Rourke to oust the New York Joint Council leader Martin T Lacey. In turn, this would give Hoffa strength for a presidential run for the Joint Council controlled many delegates who elected the President of the Union.

A long, complicated legal and political battle ensued from the contest.
The paper locals became the focal point for the media and the McClellan Committee. Eventually, Lacey stepped away, leaving O'Rouke in charge of the Joint Council. Dioguardi's paper locals disappeared.

April 5, 1956
Low-life hood Abraham Telvi threw acid in the face of Victor Riesel, which blinded the activist reporter. Riesel and an assistant had left Lindy's restaurant around 2:30 AM and were walking to their vehicle when the attack occurred. His companion rushed Riesel back to the restaurant; others rushed him to St Clare's Hospital. In addition, a witness stated that Gondolfo "Sheikie" Miranti followed Riesel out of Lindy's. This identification would eventually help break the case. A special rackets Grand Jury had scheduled an appearance by Riesel for a few days later.

The motive behind the attack may have been Riesel's relentless attacks on corrupt unions and his upcoming appearance before the New York Crime Commission.

April 17, 1956
Police place Leo Telvi in protective custody as a material witness to the Riesel attack.

May 3, 1956
Dioguardi appeared before a special rackets grand jury but did not bring the papers they had requested, nor would he speak. Assistant DA Aloysius J Melis brought Dio before Judge Mitchell D Schwitzer. The Judge informed Dioguardi that he had no right to the 5th amendment protection in this case. He ordered Dioguardi to testify the next day.

At the time, Dioguardi listed his employment at Equitable Research Associates of 250 W 57th St. It was supposed to be a labor consulting outfit, but it was a vehicle for extortion. The grand jury wanted to see this firm's papers.

District Attorney Frank Hogan described Dioguardi and his two fellow defendants as "Underworld forces making an effort to capture control of New York's 125,000 Teamsters."

May 7, 1956
Police charged Dioguardi with a traffic violation in Mineola, Nassau County.

July 28, 1956
Someone found Abe Telvi, shot in the back of the head in front of 282 Mulberry St.

August 17, 1956
Police arrested Miranti in the Riesel case along with Leo Telvi.

August 28, 1956
The FBI arrested John and Tom Dioguardi, Dominick Bando, Charles Carlino, and Charles Turso in the Victor Riesel case.

August 29, 1956
The authorities arraigned John Dioguardi, Tom Dioguardi, and three others in the Riesel case. Commissioner Earle Bishop set bail at $100,000 for three of the men. The bail for Tom Dioguardi was $75,000.

September 7, 1956
A federal grand jury indicted John Dioguardi and six others in the Riesel case.

September 17, 1956
Federal Judge Sylvester Ryan set the Riesel trial date for October 15, 1956.

September 27, 1956
The Second Circuit US Court of Appeals refused to intervene in the District Judge's refusal to lower Dioguardi's $100,000 bail.

October 10, 1956
Commissioner Earle Bishop released Dioguardi on $100,000 bail posted by the Public Service Mutual Insurance Company. Lawyer Noah Braunstein represented Dioguardi.

October 16, 1956
Dioguardi appeared in Federal Court before Judge David Edelstein. He requested that the Judge dismiss the indictment and move the case out of New York. Judge Edelstein rejected both motions. Judge John W Clancy set November 9 for the trial.

October 18, 1956
Matthew Brandenburg, the lawyer for Gondolfo Miranti, filed a motion in Federal Court hoping to suppress the statements Miranti made to FBI Agents, US Attorney Staff, and before the Grand Jury. Miranti had a long list of actions the FBI Agents and Prison staff took to make him talk.

November 2, 1956
The US Attorney's Office asked Federal Judge Frederick Van Pelt Bryan to delay the Riesel trial. The feds wanted the case broken up into two separate trials.

November 7, 1956
Judge Van Pelt Bryan agreed to split the case into two federal trials. Miranti, Bando, and Telvi would go first.

November 14, 1956
The trial of defendants Miranti, Brando, and Vincent Telvi began with Federal Judge William Herlands presiding.

November 15, 1956.
Witness Joseph Carlino told the court that Abe Telvi was "Tricked, lied to, and swindled" into blinding Riesel. He said the tricksters were "The boys uptown." They did not tell Telvi who the victim was to be and only gave him a total of $1,175. He, Leo Telvi, and Telvi's girlfriend, fled to the home of George Moore in Ambridge, PA. However, Abe Telvi returned to New York and demanded more money. Someone killed him shortly after that.

November 27, 1956
Before Judge William B Herlands, FBI Agent John R Anderson testified about Miranti's confession. He said that Miranti began to fear Dioguardi et al. would kill him in August. According to Miranti, John Dioguardi first handed over $50 for the Riesel attack then paid $500 afterward. Someone read the transcript of Miranti's testimony before a grand jury on September 6, 1956. Judge Herlands would rule later about the admissibility of the confession.

November 28, 1956
Judge William B Herlands decided to allow Carlino's confession into evidence. He ruled that the authorities protected Carlino's rights despite Carlino's last-minute claims of coercion.

December 6, 1956
The jury convicted Miranti, Bando, and Vincent Telvi of conspiring in aiding Abe Telvi to flee charges in the Riesel federal case.

December 6, 1956
Judge Herlands sentenced Gondolfo Miranti to five years and a $10,000 fine for conspiracy in the Riesel case. He gave Domenico Bando five years and Leo Telvi two. Prison authorities would credit Telvi four months for the time he was in prison waiting for trial.

December 10, 1956
Judge Herlands postponed the federal trial of Dioguardi, Charles Tuso, Theodore Riji, and Charles Carlino. He explained that it was best to calm the public before proceeding: the Judge set April 24, 1957, as the new date.

January 21, 1957
Before Judge Mullen, Miranti pled guilty to conspiracy and maiming Riesel. He warned that he would not testify against anyone. This event was a state trial.

January 25, 1957
Judge John A Mullen accepted Bando's guilty plea for second-degree assault. These were state charges.

February 21, 1957
Federal Judge Mullen sentenced Miranti to seven and a half to 15 years and a $10,000 fine. He also gave the hood one year in New York City jail for conspiracy to maim. To top things off, Judge Mullen said Miranti was "unfit to associate with decent people." Finally, the Judge hit Bando with a two and a half to a five-year term in state prison.

May 20, 1957
Miranti refused to testify in the Rio/Riesel case. As a result, the Judge sentenced him to five years for contempt.

May 22, 1957
A judge suspended the pending federal trial of Dioguardi and two others for assaulting Riesel. The witnesses refused to testify.

June 17, 1957
A federal grand jury indicted Dioguardi for evading taxes and conspiracy to evade taxes. However, the feds did not open the indictment until August 15, 1957.

June 19, 1957
The trial of Dioguardi and two former union officials began in NYC. The government alleged the three men shook down Kings Electroplating and Kings Automobile Plating for $30,000 to avoid union problems.

June 25, 1957
Judge John A Mullen granted parole from the end of each day's court until 10 PM for defendants Dioguardi, Sam Goldstein, and Mac Chester.
The release would permit the men to confer with their lawyers.

July 28, 1957
A jury found Dioguardi and two others guilty of bribery and conspiracy. Judge Mullen did not allow bail and sent the men back to the Tombs Prison.

August 8, 1957
On parole from the Tombs Prison, Dioguardi appeared before the McClellan Committee but took the 5th 140 times. First, the authorities played a series

of tape recordings that showed Dioguardi and Teamster leader Jimmy Hoffa were allies. Next, the tapes showed that Dioguardi lied when he said he left the labor union business in 1951. Later outside the hearing room, photographers were hounding Dioguardi. Then, finally, a picture captured the scowling Dioguardi in a fighting pose with a cigarette dangling from his mouth. This photograph became a classic.

August 15, 1957
US Attorney Paul W Williams opened an indictment charging Dio and Theodore Ray with evading taxes and conspiracy to evade taxes.

August 22, 1957
Before Federal Judge William B Herlands, Dioguardi and Theodore Ray pled innocent to evading taxes and conspiring to evade taxes. The Judge denied bail for Dioguardi, for he was in jail awaiting sentencing on a conspiracy and bribery case.

January 8, 1958
Judge John A Mullen sentenced Dioguardi to 15 to 30 years and Teamster leader John McNamara to five to ten years for extortion. The feds charged that they received $4700 from Tower Crossmas Stationary Corp and Atlas Stationery by threatening strikes.

June 23, 1959
The New York State Appellate Division set aside the convictions of John Dioguardi and Teamster leader John J McNamara. The authorities had convicted the two of extortion and sentenced Dioguardi to 15 to 30 years and McNamara to five to ten years. Dioguardi was in Auburn Prison serving his time.

June 24, 1959
In Syracuse, the feds arrested Dioguardi after his release from Auburn Prison. They brought Dioguardi before Commissioner Edward Conan, who released the hood on $35,000 bail. Dioguardi had tax problems.

April 7, 1960
Federal Judge Edward Weinfeld found Dioguardi and Theodore Ray guilty of conspiracy and income tax fraud. They extorted money from garment firms and a garment trade association.

July 8, 1960
The US Supreme Court overturned the decision of the Appellate Division of New York Supreme Court to throw out the convictions of Dioguardi and McNamara from January 8, 1958. Instead, the court ordered the reinstatement of the indictment and a new trial date.

1963
BOP officials released Dioguardi.

November 11, 1967
A jury convicted Dioguardi, Theodore Ray, and another defendant of bankruptcy fraud. The allegation was that Dioguardi and others took over Consumer Kosher Provisions. After the business began failing, Dioguardi attempted a merger with another firm, but that move didn't work. So instead, he and his buddies incorporated First National Kosher Provisions and secretly moved about $30,000 of meat products from Consumers to First National. The resultant bankruptcy left investors with significant losses.

Judge Walter R Mansfield set the three defendants' bail at $50,000 while they appealed.

Later the Second Circuit Court of Appeals upheld the verdict, and the US Supreme Court refused to hear an appeal.

December 11, 1967
Judge Walter R Mansfield sentenced John Dioguardi to a five-year term and a fine of $10,000 for his bankruptcy fraud conviction. He gave lesser time to the other two convicted. The judge raised Dioguardi's bail to $100,000 while he appealed.

March 16, 1968
Dioguardi was among 1000 guests at the annual Humanity Club Dinner at the Waldorf-Astoria. Some other mobsters were in attendance. Interestingly, most had something to do with the rackets at JFK Airport.

February 26, 1969
Dioguardi appeared before the State Investigations Committee but refused to answer 14 questions. An official read a report by Nassau County DA William Cohn. It summarized the Dioguardi bankruptcy conviction of November 11, 1967, and explained the growth of Dioguardi's kosher meat empire.

DA Cohen explained that Dioguardi formed the New York Kosher Corporation from the ashes of a previous failed company. Dioguardi and his men convinced significant supermarket chains to carry his products using the threat of union problems. As a result, according to Cohen, New York Kosher "completely dominated" the low-priced kosher meat product market in New York.

April 29, 1969
Assistant US Attorney Robert B Fiske Jr told Judge Weinfeld, "For the protection of society as a whole, a substantial sentence should be imposed on Dioguardi." Then Judge Weinfeld sentenced Dioguardi to four years and a $5,000 fine for his April 7, 1960, conviction. The Judge described the hood as a man unfit for rehabilitation and a persistent evader of taxes. Next, Weinfeld hit Theodore Ray with a 15-month term. Finally, he revoked the men's' bail and sent them off to prison.

October 2, 1970
Dioguardi turned himself into Federal Court Judge Edward C McLean to begin serving a five-year sentence for concealing assets of Consumer Kosher Provisions.

November 19, 1970
A grand jury indicted Dioguardi and 15 other men in a stock fraud case.

January 13, 1971
A grand jury indicted Robert T Carson, an aide to US Senator Hiram Fong Hav, with four counts of conspiracy. Someone promised Carson $100,000 if he could derail an SEC probe of Dioguardi and Carmine Tramunti. An undercover FBI Agent recorded much of the plot.

Later, the grand jury said that even after the above indictment, Dioguardi and Tramunti offered $100,000 to Deputy Attorney General Richard Kleindienst to end the probe. Kleindienst rejected the bribe.

May 27, 1971
US Attorney Whitney North Seymour Jr. announced a 40 count indictment alleging manipulation of the stock of Belmont Franchising Corp between October 1969 and May 1970. The nine defendants fraudulently ran the stock up from $5 to $45 before it collapsed. Dioguardi and Carmine Tramunti were among the defendants. Dioguardi and Michael Hellerman ran the second phase of the scheme.

June 11, 1971
Dioguardi pled innocent to stock fraud charges in Federal Court. Eventually, Dioguardi won a severance due to ill health.

May 1972
The Parole Commission denied Dioguardi freedom from his five-year sentence. Instead, they ruled he had to do the full term.

May 15, 1972
Federal Judge Lawrence W Pierce had to dismiss 100 potential jurors after accidentally using the potentially prejudicial term "extortion" as he instructed the jurors.

August 2, 1972
The United States Parole Board declined to release Dioguardi.

January 26, 1973
A jury convicted Dioguardi and Louis Ostrer of bank fraud. The jury found Ostrer guilty of 11 of 17 counts and Dioguardi guilty of 4 of 19 counts.

March 20, 1973
Jay Goldberg, Dioguardi's lawyer, requested a hearing in Federal Court. A female juror in Dioguardi's trial had sent him a strange letter in prison. Dioguardi's position was that the court needed to give her a competency hearing. He hoped that she would be found mentally incompetent, thus questioning the legitimacy of his conviction. US Attorney Andrew Shaffer opposed having a hearing.

April 12, 1973
Federal Judge David Edelstein sentenced Dioguardi to nine years and a $30,000 fine for a 1969-1970 stock fraud. He ordered that Dioguardi begin serving the term next year when he finished a previous five-year bit. Ostrer received three years and a $55,000 fine.

April 24, 1973
US Attorney Whitney North Seymour Jr announced an indictment of 13 men involved in fraud with At Your Service Leasing Corp. Dioguardi was among those accused, along with Acting Boss Vinny Aloi.

The government accused the men of selling 135,000 inflated At Your Service Leasing Corp shares to unsuspecting buyers. The firm had been acting at a loss since its founding in 1965.

May 1973
The Parole Commission re-opened Dioguardi's case but finally denied his application.

July 18, 1973
Chief Judge David Edelstein of the District Court in SNDY denied Dioguardi and Ostrer a new trial. A jury had convicted the two on January 26, 1973, of bank fraud.

November 1973
The Parole Commission re-evaluated its rules and then modified eligibility for parole conditions.

December 22, 1973
The jury found Dioguardi, Acting Boss Vinny Aloi, and others guilty of a $1.5 million stock fraud. The case involved shares in At Your Service Leasing Corp.

January 4, 1974
The Second Circuit Court of Appeals affirmed Dioguardi's April 12, 1973 bank fraud conviction and rejected a request for a new trial.

February 5, 1974
Judge Knapp sentenced Dioguardi to 10 years to be served concurrently (at the same time) as his last nine years bit. This sentence was for his December 22, 1973 stock fraud conviction involving At Your Service Leasing Corp.

August 1975
The Parole Commission rejected Dioguardi's application.

August 1977
The Parole Commission turned Dioguardi down.

January 1978
Judge Knapp heard a motion from Dioguardi that he and Judge Edelstein were not aware of the new 1973 parole guidelines when they sentenced him. Judge Knapp rejected the move.

November 15, 1978
The Second Circuit Court of Appeals cited a US Supreme Court ruling that only the Parole Commission decides to grant parole. Furthermore, the question of parole should not be a part of sentencing.

January 12, 1979
Dioguardi died in Lewisburg Prison.

January 16, 1979
Dioguardi's family held his funeral at St Theresa's Catholic Church in the Bronx.

Dioguardi Headlines
During his lifetime of crime, Dioguardi attracted a lot of media attention. Some samples of headlines are listed below.

May 4, 1956
Dio Defies Labor Rackets Probe
Faces Judge Today

May 9, 1956
Dio Is Quizzed by Court
Told He Must Talk

October 30, 1956
Dio and Pal Indicted
in 11 G Labor Shake

March 7, 1957
Dio Is Awakened
To Take Subpoena

August 9, 1957
TV: Repetitive Script; Du Mont Tally Machine
Kept Busy as Dio Invoked Fifth Amendment at Hearing

June 24, 1959
Dio and Pal Beat Rap on Appeal
Case 'Unproved'

March 31, 1960
Firm Paid Out $500 to Dio

April 8, 1960
Dio and Ray Guilty of Conspiracy,
Tax Rap

July 9, 1960
Court Rules Dio Must Be Retried
Upset Appellate Division, 4 to 3
Earlier Conviction for Labor Extortion
And Conspiracy Was Thrown Out

October 3, 1970
Dio Begins Prison Term

March 21, 1973
Dio, in Unusual Argument,
Makes Bid for New Trial

Letter to Dio May Spring Him

May 31, 1973
Dioguardi is Denied Parole

January 16, 1979
John (Johnny Dio) Dioguardi, 61,
A Leader in Organized Crime, Dies

Valachi Mentions Dioguardi

Valachi was a partner in the Prospect Dress and Negligee Company in the Bronx. He assured his fellow owner that there wouldn't be any labor problems, for he has talked to union power Johnny Dioguardi. Prospect operated with non-union workers to save money for the owners.

One day union organizers entered the shop and shut down the main power switch. They had no idea that Valachi was mob-connected.
The partner was terrified that the organizers would call the union, causing all kinds of problems. So Valachi called his buddy Johny Dioguardi who supposedly ended the dispute.

However, the two union organizers returned and asked questions about the workers' pay scale. Valachi chased them out with a pistol.

A laughing Dioguardi called an hour later and said, "That's the way to handle them. They said there was a wild man up there, and they were lucky to get out alive. Don't worry, and they won't be back."

Valachi wrote that Boss Vito Genovese had put a hit on him, thinking Valachi was an informer. The two hoods were in Atlanta Prison at the time.

Valachi noticed John Dioguardi quietly conferring with a Valachi enemy. Later, Dioguardi tried to lure Valachi into a trap in the shower area, where Dioguardi handed out the clean clothes. He commented to Valachi that he hadn't seen him in the shower area for a few days. Then he told Valachi to come in the next day and obtain a clean uniform. The terrified Valachi didn't go near the place.

CHAPTER ELEVEN

Consigliere Vincent Rao

Vincent Rao was the long-time Consigliere to Boss Tommy Lucchese. His father had been a successful entrepreneur, and Rao probably inherited some of his wealth. But, as seen in the list below, Rao also had many business interests that provided legitimate income.

Although there is no evidence of his participation in the many Mafia upheavals during his reign, it is safe to assume he would have thrown in his two cents in most cases. For example, he probably backed Lucchese in the dethroning of Costello and Anastasia in 1957. Similarly, he would have been behind Lucchese and Gambino as they attempted to maneuver Joe Bonanno out of his position as Boss in 1964.

What follows is a summary of the many legal challenges Rao faced. Records exist, providing a reasonably accurate description of the events.

Vincent John Rao

DOB
June 21, 1898
Palermo, Sicily

DOD
September 25, 1988
Florida

Descriptions
5'5"
180 lbs
Brown eyes
Black-grey hair

Norma Abrams of the Daily News described Rao as Pudgy and aging in a May 4, 1969 article.

Wife
Carmelina Alberti

Two daughters, one married to hood Joseph Vento

Residences
East 108th St, NYC
Circa 1910

231 E 107th, NYC
Circa 1918

235 E 107th St, NYC
Circa 1930

19 E 80th St, NYC
Circa 1940

Businesses
Five Borough Hoisting
1343 Gun Hill, Bronx

Regal Wine and Liquor Store
2006 3rd Ave

Rao Realty

Rao Parking
Vin-Sons Painting Inc.
309 E 167th Street, Bronx

Marcy-Rao Fuel Oil Company

B&C Realty
1775 Lexington

Residences

225 East 107th in New York
Circa 1931

192 Dunwoodie Street, Yonkers

1910
The US Census found Rao living with his parents on East 108th Street. The card listed his father's name as Tony and his mother as Laboria.

1926
The Five Boro Hoisting Company began operating this year. Later Rao became involved.

1930
The US Census listed Rao as living in his own house at 235 E 107th St.

1931
Rao worked for the Automint Vending Company as a bondsman. This company would convince shopkeepers to take a slot machine. Customers would put in a nickel and get a packet of mints. Occasionally the machine would spit out a handful of nickels or slugs. The winner would redeem the slugs for merchandise in the store. The law labeled this as gambling and thus illegal.

During this period, the Appellate Division investigated the lower courts for corruption. Not surprisingly, the operation of slot machines played a big part in these matters. Rao testified before Judge Samuel Seabury and described his work.

Rao said that he was one of several people with the same duties. First, they would wait in an office until a call came in from a shopkeeper who the police had raided. Then, Rao would race to the police station and post bond from a wad of cash he'd carry for this purpose. Later Rao would appear in court with the shopkeeper making sure the right lawyer represented him.

Automint had a lawyer on call for such matters. He testified that he handled between 175 and 200 Automint cases each year. The judge would usually dismiss the case if the shopkeeper hadn't redeemed slugs. However, if he redeemed slugs, the lawyer would plead the shopkeeper guilty in Sessions Court. A fine of $25 was the usual result.

There were many slot machine operators in New York during this era. A police investigation estimated that these entities gained a net profit of $20,000,000 a year!

1940
The 1940 US census found Rao living in a rented house at 19 E 80th Street. Rao claimed to be a manager.

February 5, 1942
Rao registered for the draft.

1951
According to an FBI report, Tommy Lucchese appointed Vincent Rao as his Consigliere.

1951
The Westchester Lathing Corporation came into existence with Anthony "Little Augie Pisano" Carfano and his brother. Vincent Rao was a stockholder.

1952
Before the New York State Crime Commission, Rao admitted to knowing Frank Costello, Jack Dragna (LA Boss), Willie Moretti, and Tommy Lucchese. Additionally, the Commission put Rao's five arrests since 1919 with no convictions into the record.

June 24, 1955
Rao and his wife depart NYC by ship.

July 30, 1955
Rao and his wife arrived in NYC aboard the Cristoforo Colombo, which departed from Naples.

November 14, 1957
New York State Troopers stopped and identified Rao at the National Meeting of La Cosa Nostra at Apalachin, New York.

December 20, 1957
Rao appeared before the Joint Legislative Committee and took the 5th 44 times.

March 31, 1959
Media reports said Rao was missing and might be dead. No one had seen him after an appearance before a federal grand jury. The Daily News described him as "A king-maker in East Harlem politics." The story included that Rao's late father was a wealthy contractor and East Harlem realty investor.

May 7, 1959
At the office of lawyer Eli Levy, Rao accepted a seven-month-old subpoena from the New York State Investigative Committee. Corporal Edward Lent of the New York State Police told Rao that he should appear at the committee offices on May 11, at 10:30 AM.

June 10, 1959
New York State Investigative Committee grilled Rao about his presence at the infamous November 14, 1957, Mafia gathering in Apalachin, New York. Rao said the late Sal Tornabe asked him to visit a friend. So they and Joseph Rosato drove up in Rao's 1956 Caddy and found about 25 men there and perhaps six to eight vehicles. The mobster claimed he didn't know anyone there.

July 20, 1959
In his appearance before the Investigative Committee, Rao was often testy. For example, when asked about his relationship with the late Boss of Los Angeles, Jack Dragna, he started yelling.

1960
The FBI listed Rao as the Lucchese Family Consigliere.

1961
The Liquor Authority revoked the license for Regal Wine and Liquor Corp because of Rao's criminal record. However, he tried to slide out from that claim by saying his son-in-law was the owner. Rao went on to say that he had lent the previous owner $70,000, but the guy repaid the loan. The grand jury didn't believe Rao and interpreted the $70,000 loan as imaginary.

February 1964
Authorities impaneled a grand jury to investigate narcotics and organized crime, including the Lucchese Family.

February 14, 1964
Rao appeared before the grand jury but did not testify.

April 24, 1964
Rao appeared before the grand jury but did not testify.

May 8, 1964
Rao appeared before the grand jury but did not testify.

January 12, 1965
Rao refused to testify four times before a federal grand jury. Judge Charles Tenni then granted Rao immunity and ordered him to appear again on January 15.

January 21, 1965
The US Attorney made an application to the court to grant immunity to Rao. The judge granted this request and ordered Rao to testify before the grand jury.

January 22, 1965
Rao testified that he had gone to Apalachin with Sal Tornabe and Joseph Rosato. He further elaborated that he had never told a different story to law enforcement officers. The government countered and said Rao had previously stated he traveled to Apalachin alone.

March 17, 1965
The feds indicted Rao for lying before a federal grand jury investigating the Lucchese Family, drugs, and organized crime. US Attorney Robert Morgenthau explained that they attempted to trace funds used to buy narcotics. Later, they released Rao on a $25,000 bond.

March 24, 1965
Before Judge Ben Cooper, Rao pled innocent to lying before a federal grand jury. Then Cooper continued Rao on his existing $25,000 bail.

November 17, 1967
A jury found Rao guilty of count five of the perjury charges before a grand jury probing narcotics and organized crime. The jury convicted Rao of lying

when he denied having an interest in or regularly visited Trinchi's Restaurant at 1144 Yonkers Ave in Yonkers. The Bureau of Narcotics had the place under surveillance early in 1965.

The jury could not reach a verdict on counts one, two, and three. Judge Herlands dismissed count four related to his explanation of how he got to Apalachin during the trial.

Assistant US Attorney Andrew M Lawler asked for bail of $100,000, which Judge William Herlands agreed to.

A lengthy series of appeals followed.

Date Uncertain
The Court of Appeals confirmed Rao's conviction.

December 12, 1967
The probation department submitted a pre-sentence report on Rao to Judge Herlands. It mentioned Rao's high rank in the Mafia.

December 28, 1967
Authorities remanded Rao into custody. He had been on bail.

January 4, 1968
Authorities granted Rao bail after seven days in custody.

October 14, 1968
The US Supreme Court refused to hear Rao's appeal of his perjury conviction.

November 6, 1968
After the Supreme Court refused to hear his appeal, authorities remanded Rao into custody. At a later date, the Supreme Court denied a rehearing for Rao.

1969
The FBI listed Rao as the Lucchese Family Consigliere.

February 5, 1969
The Bureau of Prisons submitted a report on Rao to Judge Herlands. It mentioned Rao's high rank in the Mafia.

March 4, 1969
Judge William B Herlands sentenced Rao to five years and a $2,000 fine for lying to a Federal Grand Jury investigating narcotics and organized crime. He explained that he did not consider charges that Rao was an influential Mafia member when he set the sentence. However, the Judge credited Rao with 125 days he had already served.

Judge Herlands put Rao's present medical condition into the record.
He had: obesity, ulcers, arthritis, bronchitis, and many sclerotic conditions.

Herlands permitted Rao to speak, and the mobster went on a ten-minute outburst proclaiming his innocence. Finally, Rao said, "All I done is good. If it's organized crime or not, I don't know. I am not connected to anyone. I'm personally prejudiced against people in narcotics. I wouldn't care if you gave them life."

1971
Parole officials released Rao from prison. He lived quietly in Yonkers.

1973
Rao resigned as Consigliere.

September 25, 1988
Rao died in Florida

CHAPTER TWELVE

Unions

For many decades the Lucchese Family was deeply involved with a wide variety of union locals. Below is a small sampling of their activities that came to light. Unfortunately, the list of extortions, payoffs, bid-rigging, and hundreds of other schemes is too long to document thoroughly. Hopefully, the summaries below will give the reader a sense of the immensity of the union problem.

Corruption and Racketeering in the New York City Construction Industry

Interim Report by the New York State Organized Crime Task Force

CHARACTERISTICS OF THE LABOR MARKET CONTRIBUTING TO RACKETEERING SUSCEPTIBILITY

Why construction unions are powerful.

They have a monopoly on skilled workers in NYC

The unions control apprentice training

Political support for unions has been strong

All major construction projects are unionized

Most contractors sign a pre-hire contract
with a union committing them to use their
workers

Why construction unions are susceptible to racketeer domination.

Construction depends on the availability, reliability, and competency of labor

There was no effective means of policing internal union affairs

The history of labor racketeering demonstrated organized labor's unwillingness or inability to keep its own house clean.

In the construction industry, union internationals typically delegate to union local's autonomy over their internal affairs.

Once racketeers infiltrate a union; it is very difficult to wrest control away from them. They can use threats of violence, violence, and loss of work assignments to cow dissidents.

CHARACTERISTICS OF THE COLLECTING BARGAINING PROCESS CONTRIBUTING TO RACKETEERING SUSCEPTIBILITY

Collective bargaining in the construction industry is marked by numerous specialty unions, each with exclusive jurisdiction over discrete tasks or functions. Thus, there are separate unions for electricians, carpenters, plumbers, boilermakers, glaziers, etc. The large number of specialty unions, each fiercely protecting its exclusive jurisdiction, creates the potential for constant disputes between contractors and unions or among unions over which labor group will perform a specific work task.

The contractor who tries to hire from one union where two or three might be required inevitably faces job actions or strikes. The result is the industry is filled with inefficiencies and featherbedding. The existence of so much inefficiency provides a strong incentive either to pay off union officials not to press their jurisdictional claims or to reach out to racketeers who can dictate accommodations between competing unions.

Another important feature of the construction industry's collective bargaining structure is the imbalance between the strong unions and weak employer - associations. Employer associations are associations of contractors in the same trade who band together for purposes of collective bargaining. All members of the association are represented by the same negotiator and agree to be bound by the agreement that the negotiations produce.

However, the various associations are often divided by conflict of interest. For example, one association might not object to a union demand, for it doesn't affect them. But a second association might be faced with increased costs if that article is included in the bargaining. Secondly, associations are often weak due to the members' lack of participation or interest.

HIGH COST OF DELAY

The high cost of delay is a key contributor to racketeering susceptibility for two reasons.

It creates incentives for builders to pay bribes to ensure the construction proceeds expeditiously and without disruption.

It increases the leverage racketeers have for extorting money with threats to cause disruption and delay.

Some examples of union power from Operating Engineers Locals 14 and 15.

A two-member crew from each local union must operate hydraulic cranes that only need one operator.

A compressor operator's sole responsibility is to start the compressor in the morning and turn it off at night.

Several operating engineers must be assigned to pumps easily staffed by a single person.

Electrician Union Local 3 rules:

Superintendents, who have no actual duties, supervisory or otherwise, are required to be on the job.

Stand-by electricians must be present whenever any trade has four workers working overtime under temporary lights.

Mason Tenders Local 59 required:

Gatemen must be hired on large projects in order to open the entrance gate in the morning. Security guards could easily open the gate but were not allowed to.

JFK Airport

James B Jacobs's excellent book, "Gotham Unbound," provided the background on the following superficial explanation of the Lucchese Family's union connections at JFK Airport.

Cargo Example:
An American company has United Airlines fly a container of its product into JFK. Employees of United Airlines unload the container and take it to Don's Freight Forwarding warehouse on the airport grounds. Bill's trucking company picks up the container and takes it to a Walmart in Albany.

All the truck drivers coming in and out of JFK have to be members of Teamster Local 295 controlled by the Lucchese Family. So too do the lift truck operators, the mechanics, and assorted other workers. All this movement of cargo requires a great deal of paperwork. The Lucchese Family also controls all the clerical help and dispatchers through Local 851.

A few of many benefits to the Lucchese Family

Union Salaries
Locals 295 and 851 have some administrators pulling down good salaries.

The leaders of the Lucchese Family hand out these positions to members or Associates.

Union Fees
Each member of these locals pays a weekly fee to help pay the cost of running the local and its benefits. But unfortunately, there are many ways to use this money illegally. One example would be to deposit a large sum in a friendly bank with the expectation that a kickback would result.

Trucking Cartel
The Lucchese Family formed the Metropolitan Import Truckmen's Association, an alliance of trucking companies permitted to do business at the airport. Each trucking outfit would pay fees for this privilege. In addition, some hoods owned trucking companies and were guaranteed work. An example would be Lucchese Associate Frank Manzo, who owned LVF Air Cargo Inc. and LVF Airport Service Inc. Because the Luccheses controlled the union locals, they also held power over the trucking companies making them toe the line. The Association set prices ensuring hefty profits for its members and kickbacks to the bad guys.

Freight Forwarding Companies
To ensure, they don't have union problems and that their cargo moves in and out of the airport quickly, these companies often pay under the table for this privilege. They could not independently choose a trucking company but had to use one approved by Local 295. Lead agents decided the driver assignments and other employee responsibilities. They were union members and not employed by the Freight companies.

Hijacking
Some people at the airport provided tips on valuable cargos to truck hijackers. The Lucchese Family had a crew specializing in this work headed by Associate Henry Hill. The excellent movie "Goodfellas" focuses on this crew. Even a young John Gotti and his team got in on the action.

Criminal Examples from Jacob's Book

Between September 1980 and September 1982, Lucchese union powers forced Union Air Transport to pay for the use of a specific warehouse and transportation service.

The same Lucchese union powers threatened to organize the workers at Pandair unless they paid off.

There were countless other methods for making money by controlling the unions at the airport.

Early History of Local 295

In 1956 Corallo and Dioguardi formed this local with the backing of Teamster VP Jimmy Hoffa. Not only would it bring great riches to the Lucchese Family, but it was part of Hoffa's strategy to control Teamster's Joint Council 16. They put Harry Davidoff in charge, and he did whatever the Lucchese Family wanted for many decades to come.

Some Lucchese Members or Associates Involved at JFK

Harry Davidoff, VP of Local 851
Frank Calise, president of Local 295
Frank Manzo, the top Lucchese guy at JFK, truck company owner
Anthony Calagna, president of Local 295
Mark Davidoff, secretary-treasurer of Local 851

Cleaning up JFK

Professor Jacobs and his associates provided the best explanation of the fed's cleanup efforts at JFK in the early 1990s. These moves were part of a massive effort to reform the Teamsters Union, beginning with a 1988 Civil Racketeering suit. My summary below will be a pale comparison to Jacob's outline.

March 1991
Judge Eugene Nickerson banned Harry Davidoff and Frank Calise from Locals 295 and 851. Also, they were not permitted to contact persons involved with those locals. Finally, the judge ordered the two to repay $961,400 that they had extorted from freight forwarding companies.

April 1992
After determining that the trustee appointed by the Teamsters could not clean out Local 295, Judge Nickerson appointed respected lawyer Thomas Puccio as the permanent trustee with broad powers.

October 1994
Judge Nickerson appointed Ron DePetris, a former federal prosecutor, to supervise Local 851. His primary responsibility was to root out corruption. DePetris removed six of the fifty shop stewards and disciplined sixteen lead agents. Curt Ostrander, the temporary trustee, appointed by the Teamsters, would run the daily operations of the local. Their jobs would end when an honest election for the Local 851 positions took place.

The summary above does not do justice to the long and complicated process of removing the Lucchese Family's control at JFK. The key was a federal RICO case against the Teamster leadership and civil RICO suits directed at Locals 295 and 851. Unfortunately, these efforts did not rid JFK Airport of all crime but devastated the Lucchese Family's long-time grip on the gold mine.

Painting Unions

For decades the Mafia controlled the six locals and District Council 9 of the Painters Union. As a result, there were many opportunities for making money.

Union Salaries
The administrative positions of the locals and District Council 9 drew hefty salaries along with health benefits and often a vehicle. Either Soldiers or Associates filled these slots. Often the secretaries etc., were related to mobsters.

Shakedowns
The union would expect any painting company which won a contract to kickback 10%. In turn, they often used cheaper non-union labor or paid less into the benefits folder.

Cartel
Painting contractors approved by the Mafia became members of an association. Of course, they paid dues that went right into the hoods' hands. The association would fix the prices on the thousands of painting contracts available, assuring the companies' good profits and kickbacks to the bad guys.

Painting Supplies
To get in on the big contracts painting supply outfits would make payoffs to ensure they got a slice of the pie.

1973
After a long battle, the Lucchese Family succeeded in unseating a reforming president of District Council 9. They placed Jim Bishop in the top position, and he did their will for decades. Along the way, he made a lot of money for himself. However, the power wheel continued to turn.

In 1986 the feds managed to convict the entire leadership of the Lucchese Family in the Commission Case. The new administration wanted to place their own man as president of District Council 9, so they removed Bishop. Although he retained control of one local, he was not a happy man. Knowing that a massive investigation was happening, the Lucchese leadership began to fear Bishop might cooperate. He was.

May 17, 1990
Bishop backed his beige Lincoln out of a Whitestone parking lot when hitman George Zappola fired three slugs into him at close range with a .38 Berretta. Prosecutor Mike Cherkasky responded, "The Lucchese crime family murdered Jim Bishop." He was correct. Later, Lucchese turncoat, Al D'Arco, explained that Underboss Anthony Casso believed Bishop was cooperating with the good guys and ordered him killed.

June 21, 1990
DA Robert Morgenthau announced a 153 count indictment charging that the International Brotherhood of Painters and Allied Trades District Council 9 had rigged "Virtually every single paint contract in the city for the last 12 years." Among those accused were Antonio "Gaspipe" Casso, Lucchese Family Underboss, and Capo Peter Chiodo. The indictment portrayed the Lucchese Family as," the secret power in the city's multi-million-dollar painting industry."

Every contract had a hidden 10% tax. The painting contractor would expect to win jobs for this money, sometimes use non-union labor, pay less in benefits, etc. Like their methods in other industries, the union/Mafia formed a cartel of painting contractors who dominated the market in return for payoffs.

The good guys had hidden cameras and microphones in the offices of District Council 9, the administrative umbrella for six locals. The evidence was so overwhelming most of the defendants pled guilty, including president Paul Kamen. The feds put the union into receivership.

June 21, 1990
The feds announced a 153 count indictment of eight Painters Union leaders, four Lucchese members or Associates, and several painting contractors. Manhattan DA Robert Morgenthau told the press that there was "a mob tax on every major paint project in the city." The indictment said the extortion enterprise charged a tax of 10% on all significant painting contracts.

Among those charged were Capo Peter "Big Pete" Chiodo, Edward Capaldo, head of Painter's Local 1486, William Courtien, a representative at the headquarters of the Painters Union in Washington, Frank Arnold, a Lucchese Associate with Huber Painting Company, and Dan Reich a supervisor with Leeds Paint Company. Justice George Roberts released all those charged on bail.

Concrete

Capo Neil Migliore represented the Lucchese Family's construction interest. One of his prime responsibilities was to ensure Lucchese-backed concrete firms got their share of the work leading to kickbacks to the mob.

1991
When former Acting Boss Al D'Arco rolled over, he revealed a payoff scheme he ran with the Quadrozzi Concrete Company. The owner would give cash to the Lucchese Family to ensure his firm received lucrative contracts and had no union problems with Teamster's Local 285. In addition, D'Arco occasionally collected debts for the firm and promoted its products. D'Arco said that by 1991 the monthly payoffs were around $20,000 with two additional lump sum payments of $125,000.

Interestingly D'Arco claimed that Quadrozzi purchased two concrete companies that the feds had seized in the Commission Case aftermath in the late 1980s. The Manhattan US Attorney vouched for the legitimacy of Quadrozzi Concrete, enabling the sale.

Note:
"Mob Boss," the excellent book on Al D'Arco and the Lucchese Family by Jerry Capeci and Tom Robbins, provided much of the information above.

Garment District

April 1998
A Grand Jury indicted Acting Boss Joe (Little Joe) DeFede and 11 others for controlling the garment industry. They promised labor peace in the delivery of goods in return for payoffs. After his arrest, Lucchese Capos accused DeFede of skimming off money for himself. DeFede appealed to the jailed Amuso for help but felt rejected. DeFede then began thinking of informing to protect himself and his family.

A special monitor appointed by the courts to clean up the garment district uncovered the extortion scheme. Among those charged was Michael Vuola, owner of AAA Garment Trucking Inc. The feds seized his company, three properties, and his big boat. Within the year, most of those charged pled out.

Lucchese Construction Panel

September 6, 2000
Manhattan DA Robert Morgenthau announced state grand jury indictment of 38 people, including Acting Boss Steve Crea Capos, Dom Truscello, and Joe Tangorra. Soldiers Joe Datello, Phil DeSimone, Tony Pezzullo, Joe Truncale, Phil DeSimone and Art Zambardi are also named.

The indictment charged Pezzullo, DeSimone, and Datello with running the Lucchese Family construction panel. Soldier Zambardi aided this group. The allegation was that the mobsters would bribe union leaders in the carpentry and brick unions to rig bids on projects plus extort companies for favorable treatment.

On the same day, Mary Jo White, a Manhattan US Attorney, announced a federal indictment of six persons, including three Lucchese heavyweights. It charged Acting Boss Steve Crea, Capo Dom Truscello, Capo Joseph Tangorra, and three others with conspiring to commit extortion, wire fraud, and loansharking.

One count from the federal indictment alleged that Joseph Datello of the Lucchese construction panel inflated the bid for plasterboard at the Park Central Hotel in 1998. This act freed up $2 million for kickbacks to the Lucchese Family.

November 15, 2001
Joseph and Fred Scalamandre, owners of a construction company, pled guilty to payoffs to the Lucchese family and agreed to pay $5 million in restitution.

Construction Indictment

April 20, 1989
Peter Vario held various positions in Local 66 of the General Building Laborers, a part of the Laborers International Union. First, he was an organizer, then the VP, and finally the Funds Administrator. He worked with the local from 1978 until 1989.

The feds brought down a superseding indictment on April 20, 1989, charging Vario, the local business manager, his assistant, and contractor Silvestro Spilebotte. I've outlined the counts below:

Count One:
The defendants conspired to conduct the affairs of Local 66 through a pattern of racketeering activities. (RICO conspiracy).

The defendants committed 68 acts of racketeering in the furtherance of the conspiracy.

Included in those 69 acts was the solicitation and receiving of payoffs from concrete contractors. They would pay to avoid living up to collective bargaining agreements.

The feds threw in an obstruction of justice charge as well.

Counts Two through Fourteen
These were payoffs received from various concrete contractors.

If the concrete contractors resisted paying off the union, they would threaten a strike or order one. In addition, the defendants could use their contacts with concrete suppliers to slow down or halt deliveries to the contractor.

All the defendants but Vario pled guilty. A jury found him guilty of all 14 counts, with Judge Mishler sentencing Vario to 46 months on each count but ran the terms concurrently. The judge added a fine of $50,000 and ordered three years of supervised release. Vario appealed on several grounds.

The Second Court of Appeals affirmed Vario's conviction and sentence.

Other Union Local influenced by the Lucchese Family.

Local 282 of the Teamsters Union, one of the most powerful construction unions in New York and Long Island, used to be under the control of the Lucchese Family. They operated through President John O'Rourke, who dominated the local from 1931 to 1965.

Lucchese Soldiers Luigi "Louis Bean" Foceri and Frank Bellino controlled Laborers Local 20 of the Cement and Concrete Workers Union for years. The bomb that blew up Gambino Underboss Frank DeCicco in 1986 also injured Bellino.

In the 1980s, Lucchese Capo John Capo controlled Laborers Local 29 of the Blasters and Drill Runners Union.

Gerald Corallo, son of Anthony Corallo, served as President of Teamsters Local 239. In addition, he sat on the board of Teamster Joint Council 16.

In 1985 an unidentified, knowledgeable union member told the President's Commission on Organized Crime that the Lucchese Family controlled the following locals in New York.

Laborers Locals 1298 and 66
Capo Paul Vario

Laborers Local 731
Consigliere Chris Furnari

Laborers Local 18A
Capo Vinnie DiNapoli

Blaster's Local 29
Soldier Sam Cavalieri

Legitimate Businesses

Capo Neil Migliore of the Lucchese Family was a salesperson for Port Dock and Stone. They were a major supplier of stone for the concrete producers.

Migliore represented the interests of Northberry Concrete, a member of the concrete club.

Union racketeering continues but not near the level before the feds got serious about cleaning up the locals.

CHAPTER THIRTEEN

The New Jersey Crew

Unfortunately, I have not been able to find prime evidence of the origins of the Lucchese Family's New Jersey branch. There is a lot of information on the seven other Families which operate in that state, but it is not until the 1950's that members of the Lucchese Family come into public view. This caution does not mean there is no material in existence about these guys. However, what follows is a summary of what I know of this interesting branch of the Lucchese Family. I have left tons of information out not to overwhelm the reader more than I already have.

October 23, 1902
Settimo "Big Sam" Accardi was born in Vita, Sicily.

1927
Settimo Accardi entered the US from Italy by way of Cherbourg, France.

1936
Settimo Accardi married Teresa Menio.

January 22, 1945
Settimo Accardi received his naturalization papers. However, he failed to mention an indictment for an illegal still and lied about working at the Josephine Dress Company and the American Button Company. These lies

would come back to haunt him later. His residence was 188 Franklin Street, Bloomfield, NJ.

1951
Accardi pled guilty to operating an illegal still in NYC. He paid a $3,000 fine and did nearly one year in jail. His residence was 188 Franklin Street, Bloomfield, NJ.

July 1952
The IRS was after Accardi for failure to pay $159,363 in back taxes from the operation of his illegal NYC still.

November 6, 1952
US Attorney Grover C Richman filed a petition seeking the revocation of Accardi's naturalization due to lying and omissions when the government granted him citizenship.

June 14, 1955
The Immigration Department entered an order of deportation against Accardi. Special inquiry officer Lennox F Kanzler served the order on Accardi's lawyer in Washington.

August 1955
A federal grand jury indicted Accardi and eight others for a drug conspiracy. Reporters asked the deported Lucky Luciano for his opinion on the arrests since he knew some of those detained. About Accardi Luciano said, "I haven't seen or heard of 'Big Sam' in ten years."

August 18, 1955
A judge released Accardi on a $75,000 bond from his drug conspiracy arrest. In addition, newspaper reports from the time mentioned that Accardi was already out on bail of $10,000 and $7,500 from two other separate charges.

September 28, 1955
Accardi must have decided that he wouldn't have much of a chance in court, so he fled to Italy. The officials confiscated his three bails totaling $92,500.

1956
Anthony Accetturo did ten days in the slammer for attempted robbery in Essex County, New Jersey.

June 20, 1956
Weehawken, NJ, police arrested Salvatore LoProto for some unknown reason. His booking information said he was 5'8" with dark brown hair, blue eyes, and a fair complexion.

1958
An informant told the FBI that Settimo Accardi, Bonanno Soldier Anthony Riela, and Lamandra were partners in illegal alcohol and drug dealing.

November 30, 1959
Police arrested Capo Salvatore Lo Proto at 110 St and 1st Ave in New York. They found a piece of paper in his pocket with 13 numbers bets listed.

December 11, 1959
Authorities named Salvatore Lo Proto in a criminal information filed in Special Sessions court in New Jersey that charged him with collecting numbers bets. Then, the magistrate released LoProto on $500 bail.

1959
Authorities charged Accetturo with break and entry plus attempted larceny. They dismissed the case.

1959
A New Jersey jury convicted Accetturo of possession of illegal lottery tickets. The judge sentenced him to two years' probation.

1960
A judge dismissed a resisting arrest charge against Accetturo.

1960
The US issued a presidential warrant seeking the return of fugitive Settimo Accardi from Turin, Italy.

September 1960
A July 1, 1967 report in the Buffalo Courier-Express gave details of an Italian Tribunal holding hearing in NYC. Buffalo Boss Stefano Magaddino reportedly refused to pay Settimo Accardi for five kg of heroin worth $100,000. Magaddino considered Toronto his territory, and Accardi had no business operating there without approval.

1962
Police arrested Soldier Peter Martello for interstate gambling. He was dealing in a monte game.

1963
A judge dismissed interfering with a police officer charge against Accetturo.

July 1963
Spring Valley Foods Inc. of 711 Springfield Ave in Newark went bankrupt. It had been operated by Lucchese members Anthony "Ham" Delasco and Vito Pizzolato.

October 1963
A judge sentenced Delasco to one year for tax evasion.

October 1963
An informer told the FBI that Salvatore LoProto's nickname was "Sally the Blond."

1963
The FBI named the following individuals as members of the Lucchese New Jersey faction:
Capo Salvatore John Lo Proto
Soldier Vito La Salla
Soldier Peter Martella
Soldier Leonard Pizzolato
Soldier Vito Pizzolato

November 28, 1963
Settimo Accardi returned to the US after the Italian government deported him. Judge John M Cannella set bail at $500,000.

1964
Lucchese member Anthony "Ham" Dolasco died.

February 13, 1964
Salvatore Lo Proto refused to testify before a special federal grand jury investigating the Lucchese Family. Unfortunately, he was just one of many who did the same. They listed LoProto's address as 77 Baldwin Terrance, Wayne, NJ.

February 1964
Two FBI informers said that Lo Proto was spooked his appearance before the special federal grand jury. Consequently, he dropped out of the operation of a numbers game in New York. One of the informers told his FBI handler that LoProto was involved in the garbage business in NJ.

July 20, 1964
A jury found Settimo Accardi guilty of drug conspiracy and jumping bail.

August 24, 1964
Judge John M Cannella sentenced Accardi to 15 years in prison plus a $16,000 fine for drug conspiracy and bail jumping.

August 30, 1964
Parade Magazine was a Sunday newspaper magazine printed in various papers all over the United States. A man named Lloyd Shearer wrote a column called, "Walter Scott's Personality Parade," that had an estimate 50,000,000 readers. On this date Shearer mentioned Settimo Accardi informing his fans that the good guys recently convicted the gangster of a drug conspiracy.

1966
Accetturo beat two separate charges of break and entry and arson.

November 7, 1966
After the cruise ship Olympia docked, the feds arrested Soldier Peter Martella and 24 other persons. Martella worked in the gambling operation being run on the ship, supposedly for charity.

January 1967
A grand jury indicted Martella for illegal gambling on the cruise ship Olympia.

October 14, 1967
Gunmen entered Peter "Flat Nose" Martella's 309 Club on Lafayette Street, Newark, NJ, and gunned down Martella, Nicholas Colucci, and Pasquale Colucci. The killers shot each victim at very close range as there were powder burns on the entry holes.

October 16, 1967
Newark police arrested some hoods and held them as material witnesses to the Martella hit. Locked up were; Joseph "Scoops" Licata, Candita Truepa,

Frank Colleo, George Colleo, Ferris Solomon, Anthony Giordano, and Donald Cross. Frank Colleo co-owned the 309 Club with Martella.

At the time, police speculated Martella may have owed money, but that was just a guess. We can also GUESS that since Martella was a made guy, Boss Tommy Lucchese must have signed off on his murder.

October 18, 1967
An Essex County grand jury began hearings into the Martella shooting. I am not aware of any indictment, but that may indicate a lack of thorough research on my part.

1971
Capo Anthony Accetturo fled to Florida to avoid a New Jersey State Commission of Investigation subpoena. A judge had sentenced several prominent hoods to jail terms for refusing to testify before that body.

September 28, 1971
A Florida grand jury indicted Accetturo for interstate transportation to commit extortion. Robert Hollister claimed Accetturo tried to extort $15,000 from his business and went to the FBI. The judge held the hood in Dade County Jail pending a bail hearing. A jury eventually convicted Accetturo, but the judge gave him probation.

1972
A New Jersey jury convicted Angelo and Michael Taccetta of gambling.

1973
The government accused Accetturo of extorting excessive interest on a loan he provided for Herbert Gross, a future informant. Unfortunately for the prosecution, the defense attorneys found hidden bugs in their office during the trial. The FBI denied any responsibility, but Acceturo went free.

November 12, 1974
A jury acquitted Accetturo and future murder victim Vincent Craparotta S. of loansharking and extortion.

February 11, 1975
WCKT-TV in Miami did a series of exposes on Organized Crime. They described Acceturo as "The most closely watched underworld figure in Florida." Included on the show was a film clip showing Accetturo outside

his Hollywood, Florida home with hoods Angelo Taccetta, his son Martin and nephew Michael Taccetta.

November 1975
A grand jury indicted Accetturo, Gambino Capo Joe Paterno, Joseph Covello, Michael Contino, shooting victim Michael Angelo, and alleged shooter Ciro Caruso for conspiring to give false testimony. They also charged Caruso with assault to kill.

Ciro Caruso shot Michael Angelo in 1972. The authorities brought Angelo before a grand jury, where he denied knowing who assaulted him. Allegedly Accetturo, Joseph Covello, and Gambino Capo Joe Paterno arranged this perjury.

Authorities held Accetturo and Covello on $25,000 bail and flew them to Newark.

January 1976
A New Jersey grand jury subpoenaed Accetturo for allegedly giving evasive answers to the panel.

February 26, 1976
Judge Lacey ordered Accetturo to appear before a New Jersey federal grand jury on March 11 unless Accetturo could prove he was ill.

May 3, 1976
The New Jersey Commission of Investigation and an Essex County grand jury wanted to talk to Capo Anthony Accetturo. The latter resided in Florida, claiming he was too ill to return to New Jersey. Judge Frederick Lacey ordered a new psychiatric exam for Acceturo but said the doctor had to do it in New Jersey.

June 22, 1976
Judge Lacey ruled that Accetturo did not need to appear in NJ as long as he presented himself to a Florida grand jury. He quashed the subpoena from the Newark Strike Force. He said, "There can be little doubt that Accetturo is suffering from a mental deficit of some kind." Judge Lacey had read reports from Florida doctors who examined Accetturo.

1977
The Florida Organized Crime Control Council listed Accetturo as a Gambino Family Associate. However, the information was incorrect; he was a Capo in the Lucchese Family.

August 9, 1977
Acceturo appeared before a Florida grand jury investigating Accetturo and alleged threats, extortions, and beatings.

December 3, 1977
The one-time New Jersey Capo for the Lucchese Family, Settimo Accardi, passed away in Newark, NJ.

1978
Before a Florida judge, Accetturo and three other men pled guilty to conspiracy to extort money from a Miami Beach hotel owner. The judge hit Accetturo with a four-month sentence.

August 12, 1980
A Florida grand jury charged Accetturo and one other with fixing horse races at Calder Race Track in 1975. A judge released him on $450,000 bail.

June 12, 1984
Soldier Thomas Riccardi beat Lucchese Associate Vincent Craparotta Sr to death with a golf club at the victim's Ocean County Auto Sales on Route 9, in Dover, New Jersey. Craparotta had been resisting efforts of the Lucchese New Jersey faction to extort a Joke Poker manufacturing company owned by the victim's nephews.

August 19, 1985
A New Jersey grand jury indicted 22 alleged members and Associates of the Lucchese Family. Among the charges were racketeering, extortion, illegal gambling, and drug dealing.

Magistrate G Donald Haneke released Michael Taccetta on $350,000 bail. Michael Perna posted $200,000 while Thomas Riccardi had to ante up $50,000 for his freedom. Lead defendant Anthony Accetturo continued on $450,000 bail posted in an earlier Florida case.

October 18, 1985
Judge Ackerman revoked the bails of Accetturo, Perna, Riccardi, and Michael Taccetta after the prosecutor argued they were a danger to society due to threats. However, the judge granted a stay while the men appealed.

October 24, 1985
The Third Circuit Court of Appeals denied a continuation of Judge Ackerman's stay.

October 25, 1985
The four defendants surrendered to authorities, including Accetturo, in Florida.

March 3, 1986
Judge Ackerman ordered the release of defendants Anthony Accetturo, Michael Taccetta, Thomas Riccardi, and Michael Perna. Since October 25, 1985, they had been in jail after the prosecutor successfully argued the judge should revoke their bails.

November 1986
The massive RICO trial of the New Jersey crew of the Lucchese Family began. The grand jury indicted the 20 plus defendants for racketeering, loansharking, illegal gambling, credit card fraud, and drug dealing.

1987
Law officials in New Jersey estimated that the Lucchese Family had 100 members and 200 Associates.

1988
Commissioner James Zazali of the State Commission of Investigation testified before congress that Joseph Abate, Anthony Accetturo, and Michael Taccetta were Lucchese Family Capos in New Jersey.

1988
According to the later testimony of former Acting Boss Al D'Arco, the New Jersey faction was falling behind in the tribute payments, which caused concern to new Boss Vic Amuso and Underboss Anthony Casso. As a result, they labeled the New Jersey Capo, Anthony Accetturo, and Anthony Jr as rats.

Amuso ordered the New Jersey members to attend a meeting at the Walnut Bar in Canarsie, but once they arrived, fear took over, and they all left. Amuso and Casso responded by ordering a hit on all of them.

February 24, 1988
Capo Anthony Accetturo asked Judge J Harold Ackerman for severance in the big 20 person New Jersey crew trial due to the terminal illness of his lawyer.

February 25, 1988
Judge Ackerman appointed a New Jersey lawyer and a Florida lawyer to defend Accetturo rather than sever him.

February 29, 1988
Judge Ackerman held New Jersey lawyer Matthew Boylan and his firm in contempt for refusing to defend Accetturo. He set a fine of $2,500 a day for Boylan and $10,000 a day for his firm until they complied.

March 9, 1988
The Third Circuit Court of Appeals upheld Judge Ackerman's order that lawyer Boylan defends Accetturo. However, they stayed his contempt finds. In addition, the Court overturned Ackerman's ruling that a Florida lawyer assists with Accetturo's defense.

April 5, 1988
Justice William Brennan of the US Supreme Court rejected an emergency request to suspend Judge Ackerman's orders about Accetturo's lawyer.

August 26, 1988
After nearly two years, 40,000 pages of transcripts, $3 million in public defender costs, the jury acquitted all twenty defendants in the trial of the New Jersey crew of the Lucchese Family. Later the good guys learned the Lucchese men bribed a juror.

December 1988
Underboss Anthony Casso tried to lure Anthony Accetturo and his son to a meeting at Tommy "Tommy Irish" Carew's parent's place. But, neither Accetturo made the trip from Florida, not trusting Casso.

Casso sent Peter Chiodo to Florida with $50,000 for a Cuban hitman in response to the snub. Unfortunately for Casso, the killer was not able to find Accetturo.

December 1988, just before Christmas.
Amuso and Casso invited three New Jersey Soldiers to the Walnut Bar in New York. Unfortunately, none showed, so the slighted leaders issued a kill order.

January 1989
Boss Amuso sent Chiodo to Florida in another attempt to find Anthony Accetturo. He checked out Accetturo's Florida home and a hotel to no avail.

January 4, 1989
Lucchese New Jersey Soldier Michael Taccetta pled guilty to firearms and tax charges. The judge sentenced him to five years with a projected release date of July 1992.

January 1989
New Jersey members Michael Perna and Lenny Pizzolato met with Amuso and Casso. However, things got heated when Pizzolato objected to Amuso's choice as the new Capo in New Jersey.

1989
Amuso designated Peter Chiodo as the new Capo of the New Jersey crew. That did not go over well with the New Jersey members, and they hesitated before entering a meeting at a Holiday Inn in New Jersey. Fear or caution took over once again, and they fled. Amuso responded with another "whack 'em all" order.

D'Arco claimed he and another man scoped out the home of Thomas Riccardi and the residence of Michael Taccetta, but nothing came of their efforts.

1989
According to D'Arco, cooler heads prevailed, and Soldiers Martin Taccetta, Michael Perna, and other members attended a meeting with Casso and Amuso at the Helmsley Place Hotel in New York. The New Jersey faction pledge their loyalty to their Boss.

Fall 1989
The rogue cops sent word to Casso through Kaplan. They felt Accetturo was in North Carolina. So Casso sent Accetturo there, but he had no luck finding the target. Then Chiodo proceeded to Florida, but he still couldn't find the elusive Accetturo.

September 19, 1989
Authorities returned the fugitive Capo Tony Accetturo to New Jersey from North Carolina, where they captured him in 1988. A judge gave him a jail term for contempt of a grand jury. Later he beat a race-fixing case, but a Florida jury convicted him of tax evasion.

November 11, 1989
Acting on orders from Underboss Casso, two Lucchese guys tried to kill Joe LaMorte but only wounded him. They told Chiodo the details.

July 1990
The New Jersey faction killed Associate John Redman because they feared he'd become an informant. But, in August 1993, police found his body after Anthony Accetturo and Thomas Riccardi became government witnesses.

September 1990 to September 1993
In September 1993, Michael Perna admitted he participated in conspiracies to murder the following people to take over the New Jersey crew.
Anthony Accetturo
Thomas Riccardi
Joseph Riccardi
Dan Riccardi
Dan Miano,
Anthony Accetturo Jr.
Nicholas Stefanelli
Anthony Cuozzo

April 19, 1991
A grand jury indicted New Jersey hoods Thomas Riccardi, Martin Taccetta, Anthony Accetturo, Michael Taccetta, and 49 others on racketeering, murder, and extortion charges.

October 3, 1992
Police arrested Soldier Michael Perna for illegal gambling.

November 12, 1992
A grand jury brought down a two-count indictment charging Soldier Thomas Riccardi and three Associates with conspiracy and gun possession offenses. A raid on Riccardi's home in April of 1991 provided much of the evidence.

December 29, 1992
A federal grand jury indicted Michael Perna and eight others on 84 counts involving a kickback scheme and the Newark Department of Sanitation.

January 26, 1993
A grand jury indicted Michael Perna for illegal gambling and related activities.

March 18, 1993
A grand jury indicted Martin Taccetta, Capo Mike Taccetta, Associate Ralph Perna, and Ron Librizzi. The indictment charged them for bribing a citizen to claim he was at a murder scene, but Martin Taccetta wasn't.

June 15, 1993
Former Philadelphia Underboss Phil Leonetti testified at a trial of the central New Jersey powers of the Lucchese Family. Allegedly the NJ crew attempted to extort control over SMS Manufort Inc., a manufacturer of Joke Poker machines. The company owners claimed they "belonged" to a Philadelphia member named Charles Costello. Martin Taccetta contacted Leonetti to discover the truth of the claim.

According to Leonetti, Martin Taccetta told him that Riccardi beat Vincent Craparotta Sr to death with a golf club. The victim was not cooperating in the shakedown of the company. Taccetta described Riccardi's relationship to Craparotta as "he hated this guy, so he gave it all he had" (swinging a golf club).

July 26, 1993
Before Judge Joseph Irenas, Michael Perna pled guilty to illegal gambling and related activities.

August 13, 1993
A Toms River NJ jury made the following decisions:

Soldier Thomas Riccardi guilty of the murder of Associate Vincent Craparotta Sr.
Soldier Martin Taccetta was not guilty of the murder.
Associate Michael Ryan was not guilty of the murder.

They found Thomas Riccardi, Martin Taccetta, Michael Taccetta, and Anthony Accetturo guilty of racketeering and extortion for their attempts to take over SMS Manufort Inc. This company made Joker Poker machines.

Note:
The jury found Martin guilty of counts 1, 2, 5, and 6.
The jury found Michael guilty of counts 1, 5, and 6.
These details are essential in the sentencing and appeal phases.

September 8, 1993
Thomas Riccardi, Dan Riccardi, and William Corea pled guilty to a federal conspiracy charge involving the Newark Sanitation Department kickbacks.

September 1993
Thomas Riccardi agreed to cooperate with the feds in return for leniency. (See April 12, 1996). He eventually received a twenty-year state sentence and a ten-year federal term. He would be eligible for parole in 2003.

September 10, 1993
Acting on information from turncoat Thomas Riccardi the good guys dug up the body of John Redman. He has been missing since 1990.

September 20, 1993
Michael Taccetta and Michael Perna pled guilty to federal racketeering charges before Judge Alfred J Lechner Jr.

Perna admitted to a series of crimes in furtherance of the affairs of the Lucchese Family. (RICO)
He was a Lucchese Soldier.
He extorted an air freight company for ten years.
He ran an illegal gambling business.
He was involved with jury tampering in the trial of Decavalcante Family Boss John Riggi.
He was involved with some murder conspiracies, including six murders.
Richard Demary 1976
Greg Minichino October 1977
Pat Morran August 1980
Ray? December 1980
Black Numbers Writer 1982 or 1983
John Redman July 1990

September 24, 1993
Judge Joseph Irenas sentenced Michael Perna to five years for his illegal gambling conviction.

October 19, 1993
Judge Manuel Greenburg sentenced Martin Taccetta to life for the attempted extortion of a Joker Poker manufacturing company. In addition, he would have to serve 30 years before parole eligibility.

A judge sentenced Capo Michael Taccetta and Soldier Michael Perna to a maximum of 25 years with parole possible after 12 1/2 years. The two hoods had admitted to extortion, illegal gambling, loansharking, bribery, drug dealing, jury tampering, and ten murders.

Note:
Sentencing details for those interested.
Martin
Counts 1&2, life with the possibility of parole after 30 years.
Count 5, ten years with parole possibility after five years. He will serve this term after (consecutively) Counts 1&2
Count 6, ten years with parole possible after five years. He will serve this sentence simultaneously as Count 5 (concurrent) but after Counts 1&2 (consecutively)

Michael
Count 1, twenty years with parole possibility after ten years.
Count 5, ten years with parole possibility after five years. He will serve this sentence consecutively with Count 1.
Count 6, ten years with parole possibility after five years. He will serve this sentence consecutively with Count 5.

March 2, 1994
The New York Times reporter Selywn Rabb interviewed former Lucchese Capo Anthony Accetturo on why he became a government witness. Accetturo said it wasn't the loss of income but his Bosses having no honor that caused his going over to the good guys. Speaking of Amuso and Casso Accetturo said, "All they want to do is kill, kill, get what you can even if you didn't earn it."

July 22, 1994
Judge Alfred J Lechner sentenced Michael Taccetta to 25 years and a $100,000 fine. In a plea deal, Taccetta admitted to nine murders plus bribing a juror in an extensive New Jersey organized crime case from 1991.

July 25, 1994
Judge Alfred J Lechner sentenced Michael Perna to five years for a gambling conviction and 20 years for his RICO guilty verdict. The two terms were to run consecutively.

August 10, 1994
A judge sentenced Michael Taccetta to forty years for his August 1993 extortion conviction in New Jersey. He must serve about twenty years before being eligible for parole on August 13, 2013. The judge gave Michael Perna 25 1/2 years with parole eligibility set at 12 1/2 years. A jury convicted the two men of racketeering and racketeering conspiracy.

September 30, 1994
Michael Taccetta decided to appeal his August 13, 1993 state conviction.

December 15, 1994
Judge Manuel Greenburg sentenced Anthony Accetturo to twenty years and a $400,000 fine on state racketeering charges.

1995
"The Boys from New Jersey, How the Mob Beat the Feds," by reporter Robert Rudolph went on sale. It detailed the New Jersey crew's two-year trial that ended with not guilty verdicts for everyone.

June 28, 1995
The Third Circuit Court of Appeals affirmed Michael Perna's five and 20-year sentences to run consecutively.

July 27, 1995
Deputy Attorney General William R Gicking of New Jersey announced the indictment of 12 men seeking to establish rackets in New Jersey. Fortunately, the plot was doomed from the start, for the state authorities succeeded in placing an undercover agent in the crew, plus they had an informer. The charges included racketeering, loansharking, extortion, felonious assault, gambling, and drug dealing. One of those indicted was Capo Joe Indelicato of the Bonanno Family.

August 7, 1995
A jury convicted seven Lucchese men of attempting to re-establish rackets in New Jersey.

Note:
This case was not the same group arrested on July 27.

October 2, 1995
The US Supreme Court refused to hear Michael Perna's appeal of his two sentences running consecutively.

April 12, 1996
A judge sentenced Thomas Riccardi to ten years in federal prison. This term was his reward after cooperating with the government.

May 23, 1997
The Appellate Division of New Jersey's Superior Court rejected the appeals of Martin and Michael Taccetta over their 1983 convictions and the subsequent lengthy sentences.

July 21, 1997
Judge Alfred J Lechner denied Michael Perna's writ of habeas corpus.

2004
The New Jersey Commission of Investigation named Robert Caravaggio as a Lucchese Capo.

November 2007
Investigators watched as a group of hoods congregated at the Toms River home of Capo Ralph Perna. New York Lucchese heavyweights Joe DiNapoli and Matthew Madonna attending the induction of Joseph and John Perna, sons of Ralph. The good guys had a bug in Joseph's vehicle and heard him talking about the ceremony. Joseph used this vehicle to bring Madonna over to meetings in NJ; thus, the investigators gathered a lot of evidence.

Note:
Perna family tree:
Old-time Lucchese New Jersey mobster Joseph Perna had two sons, Michael and Ralph. We have talked about Michael a great deal above.
By 2007, Ralph Perna was the New Jersey Lucchese Capo. He had two sons, John and Joseph.

July 6, 2010
A Morris County grand jury indicted Joseph Perna and 31 other men on 34 counts. The charges included money laundering, extortion, drug dealing, assault, tax evasion, and internet sports betting.

Spring 2015
Thomas Manzo, a part-owner of the Brownstone Restaurant, hired John Perna to beat the husband of Manzo's ex-wife.

June 17, 2015
Judge Salem Vincent accepted guilty pleas from six Lucchese men charged with a racketeering enterprise of running a very lucrative illegal betting operation. Those involved were; Soldier Ralph Perna, Associates Joe and John Perna, Capo Matthew Madonna, Soldier Martin Taccetta, and Soldier John Mangrella.

July 2015
John Perna beat the husband of Thomas Manzo's ex-wife.

August 2015
The Brownstone Restaurant in Patterson, NJ, hosted the lavish wedding reception of John Perna's daughter. He received an exceptionally cut-rate bill for the affair. This gift was in return for the beating he performed for Thomas Manzo.

September 30, 2015
Judge Salem Vincent sentenced Capo Matthew Madonna to five years for his gambling guilty plea, and Soldier Martin Taccetta received eight years.

October 29, 2015
Judge Salem Vincent sentenced Soldier John Mangreallo to eight years for his RICO gambling guilty plea from June 17, 2015.

January 6, 2016
Judge Salem Vincent handed out sentences for the six Lucchese mobsters who pled guilty to RICO gambling on June 17, 2015.
Ralph Perna 8 years
Joe Perna 10 years
John Perna 10 years

July 1, 2020
John Perna pled guilty to beating the husband of Thomas Manzo's ex-wife. In return, Perna received an exceptionally cut-rate wedding reception at Manza's Brownstone Restaurant in Patterson, NJ.

July 7, 1921
A judge sentenced Michael Perna to 2 1/2 years and $18,000 in restitution for his guilty plea to beating the husband of Thomas Manzo's ex-wife.

The Lucchese Family continues to operate in New Jersey. The names and faces continually change, but there is always someone willing to step up with the hopes of avoiding an early death or prison.

CHAPTER FOURTEEN

Frankie Carbo Boxing Czar

Carbo became famous due to his connection to the boxing world. Over the years, there were many attempts to clean up the sport, and the media would provide regular coverage. Carbo was usually part of the story. I offer a brief outline of his known Mafia activities below.

DOB
August 10, 1904
Agrigento, Sicily

DOD
November 9, 1976
Miami Beach

Residences

528 Timpson Place
Bronx, NY
Circa 1920

299 Freeman Ave
Long Island City, Queens
Circa 1931

52-36 62nd Street
Maspeth, Queens
Circa 1936

400 E 219th Street
New York City
Circa 1947

970 Northeast 111th Street
Miami Beach
Circa 1970

Descriptions

Daily News, 1959
Natty appearance

Frank Holman 1960
Daily News Reporter
Neatly trimmed wavy white hair
Big dark eyes
Sharp blue suit
Lean, sallow face

April 24, 1920
Carbo robbed the $272 payroll of the Messenger Company at 432 Austin Place in the Bronx. Bystanders chased Carbo down the street and caught him with the money. Authorities charged him as a juvenile delinquent and sent him to the Children's Society.

1920?
Police arrested Carbo in the Arnold Rothstein murder investigation but soon released him.

1928
A Judge gave Carbo a two to four-year sentence for the first-degree manslaughter of a Bronx cab driver in a pool room. Carbo served 23 months.

September 3, 1931

Police arrested Carbo at the Hotel Cambridge at 60 W 68th Street. They suspected him of being involved in the murder of Philadelphia bootlegger kingpin Micky Duffy. A witness claimed to have seen Carbo around the Ambassador Hotel in Atlantic City, where someone whacked Duffy.

In West Side Court, Magistrate Louis Brodsky refused bail for Carbo and his girlfriend. Eventually, authorities dropped charges against Carbo after he provided a rock-solid alibi for his whereabouts at the time of the hit.

April 12, 1933

Someone killed beer barons, Max Hassel and Max Greenberg.

October 23, 1935

Hoods shot Dutch Shultz in the Palace Chop House in Newark, New Jersey. He died the next day in the hospital. Police questioned Carbo in this case, but he was not involved.

January 18, 1936

Police arrested Frankie Carbo in the Elizabeth Cartaret Hotel in Elizabeth, NJ, to face the Hassel and Greenberg murders. In addition, the authorities ruled there would be no bail. Nothing came of these charges.

November 22, 1939

East coast mobster Harry "Big Greenie" Greenberg" died in his vehicle when a gunman fired on him. Greenberg was on the run from a New York murder indictment and had worried his fellow defendants by demanding money. Lepke Buchalter and Mendy Weiss responded by sending hitman Al Tannenbaum to Los Angeles with two guns.

Champ Segal picked Tannenbaum up at the LA Airport and took him to Bugsy Siegel's residence. After several days of scouting out the murder plan, Siegel finally ordered Tanenbaum to follow him and Carbo in his vehicle.

When the group arrived at Greenberg's residence, Carbo exited Siegel's vehicle and hid in the bushes. Greenberg soon drove up when Carbo jumped out and fired up the victim still seated in his car, killing him. The group raced off to meet up with Champ Segal. The latter drove Tannenbaum to San Francisco, taking a plane back to New York.

Tannenbaum would tell his story to two grand juries and the Carbo/Siegel trial jury.

November 24, 1939
Police found the Greenberg hit car with two weapons in it. One was a .45 semi-automatic with a full clip. The other was a .38 revolver with five empty shells.

August 16, 1940
DA Burton Fitts announced the arrest of Ben Siegel for the Greenburg murder.

August 20, 1940
A county grand jury in Los Angeles indicted Frank Carbo, Ben "Bugsy" Siegel, Champ Segal, Lepke Buchalter, and Mendy Weiss for the 1939 murder of Harry "Big Greenie" Greenberg. Famous New York gunmen Abe Reles and Al Tannenbaum testified about the murder plot. After several missteps, the DA dropped this indictment in favor of another from September of 1941.

November 19, 1940
A civil suit filed by the widow of Harry Greenberg demanded $105,350 from Carbo, Siegel, and others. It claimed these men formed a conspiracy to kill Greenberg.

December 11, 1940
DA Dockeiler announced the dismissal of the murder case against Ben Siegel. The co-defendants were not available, and a court ruling in New York prevented DA William O'Dwyer from bringing critical witnesses to LA.

August 18, 1941
Carbo surrendered to LA police officials seeking him after the Greenberg indictment from 1940.

August 19, 1941
Officials arraigned Carbo before Judge Benjamin Scheinman on charges from the 1940 Greenberg indictment.

September 23, 1941
A Los Angeles County grand jury indicted Ben "Bugsy" Siegel" and Frankie Carbo for the 1939 murder of Harry "Big Greenie" Greenberg.

September 24, 1941
Officials arraigned Carbo before Judge Edward Brand on the new Greenberg indictment. He was still in prison after surrendering on the first Greenberg indictment.

October 27, 1941
Judge A A Scott set the Carbo/Siegel trial date for January 19, 1942.

January 13, 1942
Turncoat killer Allie Tannenbaum began his trip to Los Angeles to testify in the Carbo trial.

February 11, 1942
Carbo's ex-girlfriend, Sally Sweets, testified that she was in Seattle with Carbo on November 22, 1939, when someone killed Greenburg in LA.

February 12, 1942
On the advice of his attorney Jerry Geisler, Carbo decided not to take the stand in his defense.

February 20, 1942
Judge A A Scott declared a mistrial when the jury in the Frank Carbo case could not reach a verdict on his guilt in the 1939 Harry Greenberg murder. After the prosecution finished its presentation, the judge dismissed charges against co-defendant Bugsy Siegel. LA never retried Carbo.

March 24, 1942
At the request of Los Angeles County DA Arthur Veitch, Superior Court Judge Edward R Brand dismissed the Carbo charges.

June 3, 1947
At the request of DA Frank Hogan, the New Haven Connecticut police detained Carbo with a subpoena for the New York grand jury investigating boxing.

November 20, 1947
The DA wanted to question Carbo about the LaMotta/Fox fight. A spokesman told the press that Carbo refused to talk without a lawyer present and refused to sign a waiver of immunity for the grand jury.

November 22, 1947
Police arrested Carbo and five other men for disorderly conduct. The bar owner asked the group to leave at closing time, but they refused and damaged the joint. In Weekend Court, Magistrate Henri Schwab released the men after the bar owner declined to press charges.

July 24, 1958
A grand jury indicted Carbo for illegally being involved with the International Boxing Club (IBC) and acting as an unlicensed boxing manager. His criminal record prevented Carbo from legally working in these capacities. In the morning, Judge William Strouse denied bail, but later Judge Benjamin Dzick permitted Carbo's release on a $25,000 bond.

May 30, 1959
Police in Camden, NJ, arrested Carbo, who had been on the move for ten months.

April 6, 1959
Carbo agreed to return to NYC voluntarily.

August 7, 1959
Authorities transported Carbo from Camden, NJ, for a New York Court appearance. Before Assistant District Attorney John Bonomi, Carbo pled not guilty to acting as an undercover boxing manager and conspiracy to do the same. Bonomi tried to convince Judge Gerald P Culkin to hold Carbo for another 48 hours, but he refused. Bonomi set bail at $100,000, which the Citizens Casualty Company posted.

October 5, 1959
Two US Marshall's served Carbo with federal tax papers alleging Carbo owed about $1 million in taxes, penalties, and interest.

Judge Mullen supervised the selection of a jury for the Carbo trial. He then sent Carbo back to prison.

October 30, 1959
After opening arguments, Carbo agreed to plead guilty to three of ten charges. Judge Mullen then sent Carbo back to Rikers Island to await sentencing.

December 8, 1960
Before Senator Kefauver's Anti-Trust subcommittee, former boxing power James Norris changed his tune in private testimony. He finally admitted working closely with Carbo and even employed Carbo's wife in his organization. Norris explained his International Boxing Club was failing, so he turned to Carbo, who had about 35 years of experience in boxing.

December 14, 1960
US Marshalls transported Carbo from prison at Rikers Island to Senator Kefauver's Anti-Trust subcommittee. He took the 5th about 30 times.

May 30, 1961
A jury convicted Carbo, Blinky Palermo, Joe Sica, Louis Tom Dragna, and Truman Gibson Jr of trying to cut in on the earnings of boxer Don Jordan. The government proved that the men threatened Jordan's manager and a Hollywood fight promoter.

December 2, 1961
Federal Judge George Boldt denied Carbo and the four other defendants a new trial. Instead, he sentenced Carbo to 25 years and a $10,000 fine. Los Angeles Soldier Joe Sica received 20 years and a $10,000 fine. Judge Boldt denied bail for both men.

Judge Boldt handed Palermo a 15-year fine and $10,000 but freed him on $100,000 bail. Dragna and Gibson received five-year sentences; however, the judge suspended Gibson's term.

March 30, 1962
Judge Gregory F Noonan ruled that Carbo owed the feds $1,100,940 in back taxes, penalties, and interest.

1976
BOP officials released Carbo from Marion Prison in Illinois.

November 9, 1976
Carbo died in Miami Beach.

New York Daily News Obituary

Carbo Dies, 72---Ring Figure
Miami Beach (Special) Frank Carbo, 72, one-time underworld figure with ties to pro boxing, died Tuesday of diabetes.

The Harlem-born Cardo was sentenced to 25 years in 1961 for extortion and conspiracy involving an attempt to muscle in on the earnings of former welterweight champion Don Jordan and spent most of his remaining years in federal prisons. He was paroled within the last year from Marion, Ill. prison and spent his remaining life in this resort area.

Carbo, who operated on the periphery of the underworld during the heyday of the late Mike Jacobs of the Twentieth Century Sporting Club and the late James J Norris of the International Boxing Club, was alleged to control the middleweight division during the mid and late Thirties. At that time, he was also alleged to be the go-between for the managers of Freddie Steele, Al Hostak, Solly Kreiger, and Babe Risko and prominent promoters throughout the country.

Despite his underworld connections, Carbo was well-liked by the show business crowd and was instrumental in touting Dean Martin and Jerry Lewis to night club owner Angel Lopes, who headlined them at his old Havana-Madrid club on Broadway.

CHAPTER FIFTEEN

Two Lucchese Drug Dealers

Nov 1952
Lucchese gave his opinion on drug dealers. "Any man who got a family should die before he goes into any of that kind of business."

November 14, 1952
Before the Kefauver Committee Bureau of Narcotics Agents, George White and Joseph Amato labeled Lucchese as a drug kingpin. They explained that the informer Eugene Giannini stated that Lucchese had overall control of four narcotics zones in New York. However, the gangster operated some garment district businesses as a cover.

What follows is an examination of the lives of two of Lucchese's Mafia members to see if his statement was smoke and mirrors or the truth.

John Ormento
DOB
August 1, 1912
NYC

DOD
1974

Descriptions
5'10"
240 lbs
Black hair
Brown eyes
Heavy build

Norma Adams of the New York Daily News
Described Ormento as a "Hulking, pot-bellied man."

Wife
Carmela Forte

Son
Thomas married Patricia, a daughter of Frank Livorsi.

Daughter
Connie

Businesses
O&S Trucking in NYC
Long Island Garment Truck Company in NYC

1937
Ormento served three years on a federal narcotics conviction.

1941
Ormento served eight years on a federal narcotics conviction.

1951
Lucchese appointed Ormento as Capo to replace the incarcerate Eddie Coco.

January 18, 1952
Bureau of Narcotic agents arrested Ormento on conspiracy to import narcotics. He would serve a four year term.

January 27, 1955
An FBI informer stated that Ormento met Dallas Boss Joe Civello, and Carmine Pellegrino at Idlewild (JFK) Airport on this date.

November 14, 1957
New York State Troopers identified more than 50 mobsters who attended the National Meeting of La Cosa Nostra at Boss Joe Barbara's Apalachin estate. Troopers recorded Ormento as being present.

November 13, 1957
Nassau authorities brought Ormento in for questioning. They released him without charges but ordered the Mafioso to leave their county.

December 13/14, 1957
The New York State Joint Legislative Committee members, sitting in Albany, peppered Ormento with 165 questions. He took the 5th each time.

February 6, 1958
Ormento refused to testify before the Tioga County grand jury.

June 1958
Ormento fled a month before a big drug indictment. This action suggests someone tipped him off.

July 8, 1958
The feds indicted Ormento and 37 others in a giant drug conspiracy. Fellow defendants included Boss Vito Genovese, Lucchese Capo Salvatore Santoro, Lucchese Soldiers Joe and Charles Di Palermo, and future Genovese Boss Vincent Gigante.

March 24, 1959
Before the New York State Investigative Committee, Mrs. Marguerite Russell gave testimony involving Ormento at Apalachin. She said that on the morning of November 14, she arrived to find three men in the house other than the Barbaras. According to her, one was called "Big John," the nickname of Ormento.

March 30, 1959
Agents arrested fugitive Ormento at 1466 Gun Hill Road in the Bronx. He had been living in a 3rd-floor apartment.

March 31, 1959
At the request of US Attorney Arthur H Christy, Judge Edmund L Palmieri set Ormento's bail at $150,000. Christy described Ormento as "One of the most persistent violators known to drug agents."

April 3, 1959
A jury convicted Lucchese Capo Salvatore Santoro, Vito Genovese, and others for a big drug conspiracy. Ormento avoided this trial by going into hiding.

April 1, 1959
Officials arranged for Ormento to plead before Judge Edmund L Palmieri. Ormento claimed his innocence, and the Judge continued him on a $150,000 bond. Commissioner Earle Bishop accepted Ormento's bond backed by a bond company.

April 6, 1959
Judge Thomas F Murphy reduced Ormento's bail to $100,000.

May 21, 1959
A grand jury indicted Ormento and 26 other Mafioso with conspiracy to obstruct justice. They had not given satisfactory answers as to why they were at the Apalachin estate of Joe Barbara on November 14, 1957.

December 18, 1959
A jury convicted Ormento and 19 others for conspiracy to obscure the reason for the November 14, 1957, Mafia meeting at Apalachin.

January 13, 1960
Federal Judge Irving Kaufman sentenced Ormento (and others) to five years and a $10,000 fine on the Apalachin matter. However, he allowed the gangster to continue on his previously posted $100,000 bail in another case but tacked on $1,500.

April 27, 1960
Vito Genovese and eight convicted drug dealers appealed to the US Supreme Court. One of their points was that Nelson Canteloupes, a key turncoat witness, had recanted part of his damaging testimony.

Solicitor General J Lee Rankin asked the court to refuse to review the gangsters' conviction. He stated that a Federal grand jury in New York was looking into an alleged attempt to convince Canteloupes to change his testimony using bribery and coercion.

A New York report claimed that Ormento met Canteloupes at his Bronx luncheonette and arranged a meeting for the witness with three lawyers.

The lawyers offered Canteloupes $3,000 immediately and $27,000 later if he recanted his testimony. However, Canteloupes soon had second thoughts and went to the police. The law quickly put Ormento, the three lawyers, and Canteloupes before a grand jury.

Note
Genovese and the others lost their appeal to the Supreme Court.

May 6, 1960
The feds indicted Ormento and 28 others in a vast drug conspiracy. He pled innocent before Federal Judge John FX McGohey. The judge set bail at $7,500 after considering that Ormento had already posted $101,500 in another case.

July 11, 1960
Federal Judge Edmund L Pal set September 12, 1960, for the drug trial of Ormento and 21 other hoods.

November 21, 1960
The drug trial of Ormento and others began before Judge Richard H Levert.

November 28, 1960
The US Court of Appeals reversed the convictions of Ormento and 19 other hoods. A jury had convicted them of a conspiracy to obscure the reason for the November 14, 1957, Apalachin meeting.

December 6, 1960
During the Ormento drug trial, witness Edward L Smith described a May 1958 meeting between himself, Ormento, and hood Tony Mirra. Ormento, "Cracked Tony Mirra in the face," knocking him to the ground. Smith didn't know what the problem was.

Comment
Mira was a legendary tough guy. For him to allow Ormento to deck him indicates their relative stature in La Cosa Nostra. Mira was clearly on a lower rung.

January 30, 1961
Judge Levet remanded Ormento and others to jail rather than let them continue on bail.

February 8, 1961
The Second Court of Appeals confirmed the remand order of Judge Levet.

April 12, 1961
Police found jury foreman Harry Appel, 68, in an abandoned building with injuries to his head and spine. As a result, the judge postponed the drug trial.

May 15, 1961
The injured jury foreman was unable to continue. That reduced the original twelve-person jury and four alternates down to 11 people. Judge Richard H Levert declared a mistrial. He made it clear he believed the Appel injury was a continuation of the defendants' multiple attempts to gain a mistrial. According to media reports, Ormento gave a big grin to his supporters in the audience.

September 5, 1961
Judge John M Cashion set the Ormento trial for September 25, 1961.

April 3, 1962
The retrial of Ormento and 13 other defendants began before Judge Lloyd F MacMahon.

June 25, 1962
After a three-month trial, a jury convicted Ormento and 11 others of a drug conspiracy.

June 26, 1962
Judge Lloyd F MacMahon sentenced Ormento and 11 others for contempt during their drug trial. His opinion that their outrageous behavior was an attempt to gain a mistrial. Ormento received a 60-day sentence, and the judge said he used language "Of such vile and obscene nature that the court will not repeat it."

July 10, 1962
Judge MacMahon sentenced Ormento to 40 years and a $20,000 fine for his drug conviction. He said Ormento was "Incurable cancer on society." He handed out stiff sentences to the other defendants.

July 20, 1962
The Second Court of Appeals affirmed Ormento's contempt sentence from June 26, 1962.

January 30, 1963
An Appeal Court upheld Judge Lloyd MacMahon's decision not to rule a mistrial in the Ormento case.

June 13, 1963
The US Court of Appeals upheld the convictions of Ormento and his eight co-defendants.

January 1, 1964
Prison officials transferred Ormento from Lewisburg to Leavenworth penitentiary.

October 21, 1971
The US Supreme Court rejected Ormento's challenge that Judge Lloyd MacMahon had a bias against him at the 1962 trial.

1974
Ormento died. Presumably in prison.

Note:
The FBI listed Ormento as a Capo from 1951 to at least 1969.

Joseph "Joe Beck" Di Palermo

This guy is unbelievable. He was in trouble from an early age up until he croaked. It would be funny, except Di Palermo peddled so much heroin the devastation that resulted would be incalculable. Moreover, his Mafia career makes a mockery of the "honor" of La Cosa Nostra and its mythical ban on drug dealing. What follows is a long, tedious recital of his transgressions.

DOB
June 8, 1907
NYC

DOD
October 25, 1992
Danbury, Fairfield Connecticut

Wife
Mary Cattone

Description

Bureau of Narcotics
5'6"
120 lbs
Brown eyes
Light brown balding hair
Wears glasses

Daily News July 1958
Skinny, consumptive-looking

Daily News
Wispy, gnome-like

Residences

259 Elizabeth St Manhattan
1910

240 Elizabeth St Manhattan
1940

November 20, 1925
Police arrested Di Palermo for selling narcotics. I don't know the outcome of that case.

February 16, 1928
Police arrested Di Palermo for possessing a dangerous weapon, a knife.

March 2, 1928
Officials released Di Palermo on this date. Whether he did a short sentence or a jury found him not guilty is unclear.

October 7, 1930
Di Palermo married Maria Cattone in NYC.

February 7, 1937
Agents arrested Di Palermo for transporting illegal liquor.

March 11, 1937
The court fined Di Palermo $250 for transporting illegal liquor.

October 1, 1941
Police arrested Di Palermo for homicide.

December 12, 1941
A grand jury indicted Di Palermo for manslaughter. I don't know the outcome of this case.

August 25, 1943
A jury convicted him of conspiracy to operate a still, and the judge handed down a one-year sentence with a $100 fine. They also found him guilty of violating revenue laws; however, the year sentence would run consecutive to the first one.

June 29, 1944
A jury convicted him of possession of a still. This time the judge gave him two years in Atlanta prison.

July 10, 1944
Marshalls took Di Palermo to Atlanta.

May 5, 1945
Marshalls took Di Palermo to the medical prison in Springfield, Illinois.

September 18, 1945
Marshalls took Di Palermo to Leavenworth prison in Kansas.

June 23, 1949
Di Palermo flew into Boston on Pan Am from Lisbon, Portugal. His final destination was NYC on another flight. So a reasonable guess would be that Di Palermo was in Europe cooking up a drug deal.

April 3, 1950
Agents arrested Di Palermo for drug dealing.

April 30, 1950
Police charged Di Palermo with possessing counterfeit American Express checks.

September 20, 1950
A judge sentenced Di Palermo to seven years for the conviction of possessing counterfeit American Express checks.

March 1, 1955
BOP officials gave Di Palermo his conditional release from Atlanta prison.

September 11, 1957
Treasury agents searched for Di Palermo on drug charges.

November 6, 1957
Agents raided a home hoping to catch fugitive Bobby Basile. They failed but arrested people for harboring a fugitive. Eventually, all six were convicted. Later a grand jury indicted Di Palermo for hiding Basile.

November 18, 1957
Drug Agents arrested Mrs. Jean Capece, the girlfriend of Joe Di Palermo. After questioning, Assistant DA Joseph Kottler took her into court and asked for bail of $50,000 as a material witness. The judge agreed.
Assistant DA Aaron Kode announced that he would bring Capece before a grand jury in an attempt to find Di Palermo, who remained in hiding.

July 3, 1958
Drug agents arrested Di Palermo in NYC. After a month-long stakeout, they caught Di Palermo at E Fourth St and Second Ave. Judge Edelstein set bail at $75,000. George H Gaffney, the district supervisor of the Federal Narcotics Bureau, commented, "He is an extremely important figure, one of the most notorious and persistent narcotics traffickers we have yet encountered."

July 8, 1958
Judge Hyman Barshay upped Di Palermo's bail another $100,000. This change was due to Di Palermo facing an indictment for harboring a fugitive.

July 11, 1958
Di Palermo appeared in court on the federal drug indictment. He told Judge William B Herlands that he had no money for his defense and requested that a lawyer be appointed. The judge ruled he would consider this request later. (The judge turned it down).

July 21, 1958
Federal Judge Richard H Levet postponed Di Palermo's pleading to two separate drug indictments until July 23.

July 23, 1958
Di Palermo pled not guilty to a narcotics conspiracy that involved Boss Vito Genovese and 35 others. Federal Judge Richard H Levet assigned Di Palermo's plea date to a second drug conspiracy for July 25, 1958. A jury convicted Harry "Nate Rosen" Stromberg and 17 others of that conspiracy while Di Palermo was on the lamb.

January 1959
The vast drug trial involving Di Palermo, Vito Genovese, and assorted defendants began.

April 3, 1959
A jury convicted Di Palermo and his brother Peter on conspiracy to violate federal narcotics law. Many others also went down, including Boss Vito Genovese and future Bosses Vincent "Chin" Gigante and Natale Evola of the Bonanno Family.

April 17, 1959
Judge Alex Bicks sentenced Di Palermo to 15 years and a $20,000 fine for his drug conviction. However, the judge refused to continue Di Palermo on his $75,000 bail due to his long record. After rhyming off some of Di Palermo's rap sheet, Judge Bicks said, "The risk is too substantial to warrant bail." To this ruling, Di Palermo responded, "I've been here every day of the trial. I could have laid you ten to one, I'd be convicted, but I came in just the same."

June 21, 1962
In the mistaken belief that he was Joe Di Palermo, Joe Valachi battered inmate John Saupp to death. Valachi feared Vito Genovese had ordered his death and lashed out at his perceived killer in desperation. This action led to Valachi becoming the most famous Mafia turncoat in history.

August 8, 1963
According to Joe Valachi debriefing on this date, at some point, Di Palermo asked Vito Genovese for permission to whack some narcotics agents framing him and his friends. Genovese ranted about a particular agent responsible for his conviction and said something would be done about the agents. Valachi and the other two hoods were in Atlanta prison on narcotics convictions.

An Outline of Di Palermo's Last Drug Conviction

April 15, 1977
DEA informant Vincent Marchese met with George Gillette at Marchese's home. Gillette explained he had a friend who manufactured Quaaludes but could not get any chemicals. Marchese agreed to find the needed materials.

Marchese contacted the DEA, who agreed to find a source for the chemicals. They did so and informed Marchese. In turn, Marchese told Gillette that he had a source for the chemicals, and the price would be $10,000. Gillette's friend agreed to the deal.

January 23, 1977
Marchese and Gillette picked up the chemicals from the manufacturer and took them to a secrete NJ warehouse.

Mid-September 1977
The caretaker of an isolated house in Staten Island negotiated with three men over renting the place. Two men did the dealing but returned to their vehicle, where a third man stood. Later, the caretaker would identify this man as Joe Di Palermo in court.

October 1977
DEA Agents followed George Gillette from the NJ warehouse into New York on two separate occasions, where he met with Di Palermo.

October 31, 1977
DEA agents watched as Gillette and Marchese used a Ryder truck to move the chemicals from the NJ warehouse to the home of Salvatore Lombardi. Later that night, Lombardi trucked the substance to the Staten Island location at 135 Ellis Ave.

One of the conspirators hired Allan Kassebaum, a chemist, to make the Quaaludes.

November 14, 1977
DEA Agents raided the Staten Island home and arrested Kassebaum. They picked up Di Palermo, Marchese, and Lombardi later.

March 13, 1978
US Attorney David Trager and DEA regional director John Fallon announced an indictment of Di Palermo, George Gillette, Salvatore Lombardi, Allan R Kassebaum, and others for a drug conspiracy.
Assistant US Attorney Richard Abbleby said that Di Palermo selected the site for the dope lab and the warehouse in NJ where they stored the drugs.

US Magistrate John Cade released the trio on $25,000 personal recognizance bonds. Drug agents had arrested Kassebaum in November of 1977 when they raided his drug lab.

June 9, 1978
A grand jury indicted Joe Di Palermo, Peter Di Palermo, and two others for bribing a probation officer. James Gannon, chief of pretrial services for the probation office, admitted to taking payments in return for good parole reports. The Di Palermo group paid Gannon to help out one of their buddies.

1979
A jury convicted Joe Di Palermo, George Gillette, Salvatore Lombardi, and Allan Kassebaum for conspiracy to manufacture and possession with intent to distribute Quaaludes. Judge Edward R Neather sentenced the men. (I don't know the terms)

August 21, 1979
The Second Court of Appeals affirmed Di Palermo's drug conviction. A jury found him guilty of conspiracy to manufacture and possession with intent to distribute Quaaludes.

July 20, 1988
Parole officials released Joe Di Palermo from his drug sentence.

October 28, 1992
Di Palermo died in Danbury, Fairfield, Connecticut.

CHAPTER SIXTEEN

Capo Eddie Coco

Ettore "Eddie Coco

Eddie Coco was a long-time Lucchese mobster who spent much of his time in Florida. As a young man, he was very active in the boxing rackets that the Mafia dominated. This activity made his name well known. In the early 1950s, he made the headlines in Miami for killing a black man. Then, late in life, the good guys jammed him up on a bingo scam up in Baltimore. An outline of his Mafia life follows.

DOB
July 12, 1908
Palermo, Sicily

DOD
December 26, 1991
NYC

Description
Pudgy fight manager

July 28, 1922
Coco arrived in New York aboard the Providence. He indicated that his father Antonio resided in the US.

1921
Coco and his wife divorced. She left with their two kids.

1931
Coco did 30 days for vagrancy.

July 9, 1934
Coco completed his Declaration of Intention form indicating that he was a grocery salesman living at 1831 Edison Ave in the Bronx. The document gave his statistics as 5'4", 145 lbs, brown hair, brown eyes, and a medium complexion.

1939
Coco did 30 days for petty theft.

1943
The Illinois State Athletic Commission interviewed famous boxer Rocky Graziano, about his connection to Eddie Coco. He said that Coco became his manager in the 1930s and took 11% of his purses until they broke off the arrangement in 1943.

February 1, 1951
Coco and his girlfriend returned to the Shore Apartments at 6881 Bay Drive, Normandy Isle. A black man, Johnny B Smith, asked Coco to pay for a car wash he did for Coco. The hood ignored the man and walked into his unit. A short time later, Coco came out and shot Smith. He then proceeded to get up close to Smith and emptied his .32 into the innocent victim. Coco went back into his apartment and fell asleep.

When the cops came, Smith was dead. So they searched around Coco's apartment and found some .32 casings and the gun in a garbage can outback. Strangely the casings never made it to the police station. Then an idiot fired the wrong bullet caliber in the .32 ruining its rifling. The fix was on.

February 6, 1951
Justice of the Peace Kenneth Oka held Coco over for a grand jury.

March 30, 1951
The grand jury indicted Coco for first-degree murder.

June 10, 1951
Circuit Court Judge Grady L Crawford denied the pleas of defense lawyers Albert Hubbard and Bernard Frank for a delay in the trial.

June 12, 1951
The jury found Coco guilty of second-degree murder.

Not long afterward, famous boxing promoter James Norris wrote a letter saying, "I have known Eddie Coco for a period of about ten years. In my association with him, I have always found him to be a man of his word, well-liked and highly respected by his many friends." Media accounts of Norris's support of Coco pointed out that authorities arrested the hood for felonious assault, vagrancy, robbery, petty theft, and rape over the years.

June 17, 1951
Judge Crawford sentenced Coco to life but released him on a $25,000 bond pending appeal.

October 9, 1951
Judge Stanley Milledge ruled that Coco had to pay $50,000 damages to the widow of victim Smith.

1953
Joe Valachi wrote that Genovese Boss Vito Genovese ordered a hit on Lucchese Soldier Dominic "The Gap" Petrilli because he was an informer. According to what Valachi heard, Eddie Coco drove the hit car while Anthony Lo Pinto, Joe Bendinelli, and Anthony Castaldi were involved somehow.

January 20, 1953
The Florida State Supreme Court granted Coco a new trial because of an error made by the judge.

March 19, 1953
Judge Ben C Willard threw out the second-degree murder charge on technical grounds. County Solicitor John D Marsh filed new murder charges.

June 9, 1953
The County solicitor's office revealed that some of the Coco evidence was missing (The shell casing from the murder scene).

September 21, 1953
Judge Willard delayed the Coco trial at the request of defense attorneys Pat Whitaker and Robert Taylor.

October 30, 1953
The jury convicted Coco of second-degree murder.

November 12, 1953
Judge Willard sentenced Coco to life imprisonment but released him on a $25,000 appeal bond.

1955
Newspaper accounts claimed that Coco ran the biggest crap game in New York.

February 25, 1955
The Florida State Supreme Court upheld Coco's sentence. However, Coco appealed for a new hearing.

March 8, 1955
The Florida State Supreme Court granted two weeks to appeal.

March 26, 1955
The Florida State Supreme Court agreed to hear ground for a new hearing.

April 27, 1955
The Florida State Supreme Court refused to grant a new hearing for Coco. As a result, defense lawyers Louis Carbonaro and Joseph Carbonaro announced an appeal to the US Supreme Court.

May 5, 1955
Coco surrendered after losing his last appeal.

October 10, 1955
The US Supreme Court refused to hear Coco's appeal.

January 29, 1966
The US Parole Commission released Coco. However, in 1968 a top official for the State of Florida told the Miami Herald, "Someone goofed in granting the parole. We apparently weren't aware at that time of his Mafia connections."

July 13, 1967
Boss Tommy Lucchese died of natural causes.

August 28, 1967
Coco gave the following details to the FBI during an interview. They had renewed interest in the thug because an informant indicated that Coco might be in the running for Boss to replace Lucchese.

He lives well thanks to the generosity of his family and his wife's family.

Famous boxing promoter Jack Norris contributed to his murder defense in the 1950s.

He met Norris in New York while doing boxing promotions in the late 1930s.

His brothers are no longer involved in the numbers rackets in Harlem.

He relies on others' generosity to provide tickets to Miami boxing.

He does not own a piece of boxer Tony Venture.

FBI surveillance of Coco provided the following information.

Employed at Ace Delivery Service in Miami.
Associated with hoods, Ralph Sorrentino and Joseph Indelicato.
Coco arrives at Ace Delivery at 9 AM most mornings.
He spends his afternoons at the Fifth Ave Gym, where he supervises the training of boxer Tony Ventura.
Coco leaves for home around 5 PM and spends most evenings at home.

June 13, 1972
A grand jury indicted Coco, Louis Nash, and another man for conspiracy to extort and extortion related to loansharking. At the time, Florida had Coco on life parole.

August 1972
A jury convicted Coco of two counts of conspiracy to extort and four counts of extortion. They also convicted Louis Nash on similar charges.

September 11, 1972
The Florida Parole Commission publicly discussed whether they should revoke Coco's parole. However, their officials picked him up a few days previously.

October 18, 1972
Judge Peter Fay sentenced Coco to 15 years and a $60,000 fine for his extortion convictions. He gave Louis Nash 10 years and a $5,000 fine. Florida revoked Coco's parole, and authorities returned him to prison. Coco and his fellow defendant indicated they would appeal.

July 6, 1973
The Fifth Circuit Court of Appeals upheld the convictions of Coco and Nash.

July 30, 1973
The Fifth Circuit Court of Appeals denied a rehearing request from Coco and Nash.

August 8, 1973
The Fifth Circuit Court of Appeals denied a rehearing request from Coco and Nash.

1974
The Fifth Circuit Court of Appeals affirmed the denial of the District Court to vacate Coco's sentence.

October 29, 1976
The Fifth Circuit Court of Appeals affirmed the denial of the District Court to vacate Coco's sentence.

March 13, 1978
An appeal court confirmed Coco's conviction.

?????
BOP officials released Coco from prison.

October 27, 1990
The feds indicted a bunch of hoods, including Coco, for money laundering. They used Bingo World on Belle Grove Road in Brooklyn Park, Maryland, to launder money from criminal rackets.

The hoods sought Coco's permission to operate in Maryland. Baltimore used to have a Gambino Family crew, so I am not sure why the conspirators checked with a Lucchese Family member. They would give Coco a piece of the action for his OK.

One of the conspirators solicited Coco's help in firebombing the rival Forty-Niners Bingo Hall in 1988.

1991
The feds arrested Coco and the other Bingo World accused.

November 22, 1991
Federal Judge Frederick N Smalkin approved a delay in the Bingo World trial because two defendants were involved in a massive money laundering case in Florida. He rescheduled the trial for October 28, 1991.

December 26, 1991
Ettore "Eddie" Coco died in NYC

Coco Headlines

Slayer Eddie Coco "Honorable" Man To Ring Bigwigs.
Miami Herald November 6, 1954

It's Take Helps Coco Fight a Murder Rap
NY Daily News January 14, 1955

How Does Eddie Coco Do It?
Miami News May 12, 1955

Eddie Coco To Be a Mafia Boss?
Miami Herald January 14, 1968

Jail-Time For Eddie Coco
Miami Herald September 8, 1972

CHAPTER SEVENTEEN

Underboss Salvatore Santoro

Salvatore "Tom Mix" Santoro

Despite the myth that La Cosa Nostra banned such activity, Salvatore Santoro was a Lucchese drug dealer. He had three heroin convictions, including a twenty-year prison term from 1959. When they released him in 1978, Santoro returned to the Mafia life and soon rose to be Underboss during Anthony Corallo's reign. But, unfortunately, it did not end well.

Note:
Santoro had the Tom Mix nickname due to his resemblance to an old Hollywood cowboy star.

DOB
November 18, 1915

DOD
June 25, 2000
In prison

Description
5'9"
200 lbs

Black hair
Brown eyes
Stout build

Wife
Mary Zangaglia

Known Address

136 Long View Ave, Leona, NJ.
Circa 1958

1930
The US Census takers found the young Santoro living at 42 Macy Ave in Brooklyn.

October 26, 1940
Santoro registered for the draft. They described him as 5'9", 200 lbs, black hair, black eyes, and a dark complexion.

1942/43
The feds indicted and convicted Santoro, Ormento, and Joseph Vento of a heroin conspiracy. The judge sentenced each of them to five years.

1951
The feds convicted Santoro of drug dealing. A judge sentenced him to two years.

June 4, 1958
Santoro and Ormento were fugitives from a drug indictment.

June 8, 1958
Santoro surrendered to US Attorney William D Walsh. He posted bail of $25,000 with Commissioner Earle W Bishop. Walsh told Bishop that "Santoro is a high overlord in the narcotics world, and his activities in narcotics can be traced back to 1942."

July 16, 1958
Federal Judge Edward J Dimock took Santoro's not guilty assertion and set bail at $25,000. He took the pleas of 18 other defendants.

October 3, 1958
Police arrested Santoro as a vagrant, but they were investigating the murder of Gambino Soldier John Robbilotto. The judge released Santoro for a later hearing.

January 5, 1959
The drug trial of Santoro, Vito Genovese et al began.

April 3, 1959
After a jury found Santoro and the other defendants guilty, Judge Dimock remanded Santora, Joseph DiPalermo, Charles Di Palermo, and Charles Barcellona into custody. He released Vito Genovese and some others on bail.

April 6, 1959
Judge Thomas F Murphy reduced John Ormento's bail from $150,000 to $100,000. He had avoided the original trial by going on the run.

April 17, 1959
Judge Dimock sentenced Santoro to twenty years, Joe DiPalermo to 20 years, and Charles DiPalermo to 12 years. He refused bail for Santoro and Joe DiPalermo due to their past drug convictions.

1960
The Second Circuit Court of Appeals affirmed Santoro's sentence.

May 1, 1961
The US District Court for the South District affirmed the convictions of Santoro et al.

October 16, 1964
The Second Circuit Court of Appeals rejected the appeals of Santoro, Genovese, and nine other defendants. They had claimed prosecution violated their rights by failing to provide the original notes of the feds interviews of turncoat Nelson Canteloupes.

March 1, 1965
The US Supreme Court rejected the appeals of Santoro, Genovese, and nine other defendants.

1978
BOP officials released Santoro. I cover Santoro's Mafia career after 1978 in Chapter Six, Anthony Corallo.

Note:
The feds convicted Santoro in the 1986 Commission case, and the judge hit him with a hundred-year sentence. He died behind bars on June 26, 2000.

Note:
The FBI listed Santoro as a Capo from 1960 to 1967, even though he was in prison.

CHAPTER EIGHTEEN

Capo James Plumeri

James "Jimmy Doyle" Plumeri

James "Jimmy Doyle" Plumeri was a long-time power in the Lucchese Family. He had come up from the rough streets of New York, making valuable connections along the way. In addition, the fact that his father was very successful in the construction business provided Plumeri with solid finances, especially when compared to most other hoods. His criminal record indicates that Plumeri was involved in lucrative union rackets centered on trucking in the garment center going back to the 1930s. Over the next three decades, he solidified and expanded those means of income, enriching his superiors along the way. The many federal and state investigations of organized crime in the 1950s and 60s made his name easily recognizable. Sadly for Plumeri, something went south in the early seventies, and he didn't die in bed.

DOB
April 14, 1903
Regalbuto, Italy

DOD
September 23, 1971
NYC

Description
5'7"
175 lbs
Brown eyes
Black/grey hair

The Daily News described Plumeri as short and chunky at the time of his death in 1971.

Wife
Mary Orapollo

Son
Thomas

Brothers
Vito, Joseph

Sisters
Four

Residences

169 Forsythe St, NYC
Circa 1923

187 Hester St, NYC
1943

46 Delancey St, NYC
Fall of 1943

Apartment 4C, 400 East 59th Street, NYC
Circa 1970

9224 Dickens Ave, Surfside, Florida
Winter months

Businesses

El Gee Carriers Corp

Dress Factory in Allentown, PA

Employment

MM Elish & Company
29 Beekman St, NYC
Chauffeur
Resigned 1929

Bike Repair Work
For three years

Livery Driver
In 1929s

President of the Five Borough Truckmen's Association
Resigned 1933.

Garment Center Truck Owners Association
Resigned 1935

Manager of Boxers
Thru 1937.

Richter Dress Company
218 W 35th St, NYC
1952

Bonnie Stewart Inc.
137 Broadway, NYC

Villa Mar Restaurant
74-05 37th Ave, Jackson Heights

Advance Junior Dress Corp.
501 7th Ave, NYC

Employed by his nephew Thomas Dioguardi in the following businesses.

Martin Pino Inc.
Sports Wear
35 Meadow St, Brooklyn.

New York Case Company
670 Broadway, NYC
Until 1943

Victory Dress Sports Shop
72 Spring St, Manhattan, NYC

VP of Read Shoulder Pad Co
Owned by John Dioguardi

December 22, 1913
Authorities charged Plumeri with delinquency but gave him a suspended sentence.

February 29, 1923
Plumeri filed a Declaration of Intention in the Supreme Court in New York City. This declaration was a step in the naturalization process.

March 12, 1923
Arrested for transporting liquor but was discharged.

April 26, 1923
Arrested for vagrancy but was discharged.

August 24, 1923
Fined $2 in traffic court.

October 4, 1923
Arrested for disorderly conduct but was discharged.

September 9, 1924
Fined $2 in traffic court for not having a functioning rear light.

September 30, 1924
Arrested for burglary but was discharged.

December 19, 1924
Arrested for receiving stolen goods.

June 17, 1925
Discharged from receiving stolen goods. (See December 19, 1924).

February 2, 1926
Plumeri filed some more forms for his naturalization in the Supreme Court in NYC.

February 19, 1926
Plumeri filed a petition for naturalization at the Supreme Court in NYC. He claimed he was a chauffeur.

July 29, 1926
Plumeri became naturalized on this date.

1932
Plumeri, John Dioguardi, and Domenic Didato forcibly took over the Five Boroughs Truckmen's Association. They immediately began forcing independent truckers to turn over their accounts or join the association.
The group extorted the Garment Center Truck Owners association by threatening violence. The principals at that group agreed to pay $500 a month to keep their association going. They would make checks to themselves then turn the cash over to Dioguardi.

May 11, 1933
Detectives arrested James Plumeri, Domenic Didato, and John Dioguardi, alleging that they were involved in extortion in the trucking industry.

June 2, 1933
Earlier, a grand jury indicted Plumeri, Didato, and Dioguardi for coercion, conspiracy, and assault in the trucking industry. Plumeri was the president of the Five Boroughs Truckmen's Association, while the other two were business agents. Assistant DA Morris H Panger announced the indictment at the arraignment for the three hoods.
A judge set bail at $75,000 for each man.

August 19, 1933
Someone shot Plumeri in his office at the Five Boroughs Truckmen's Association at 225 Lafayette Street. The shooters also wounded Dominick

Didato, who said it was bandits. Police took the two men to nearby St Vincent's Hospital in critical condition.

August 21, 1933
Dominick "Terry Burns" Didato died of his wounds. Plumeri, although seriously wounded, made a full recovery.

Note:
Vito Genovese had Didato hit because he was an obstacle to Genovese's desire to become the new Boss of the Genovese Family now that Luciano was in prison.

Note:
Old Mafioso Nicole Gentile wrote he helped set up Didato after Joe Biondo of the Gambino Family gave him a heads up on Genovese's intentions. In his account, the shooting took place outside a restaurant, and he held Didato's arm as the killer moved in. Gentile made no mention of Plumeri.

September 27, 1933
Officials dismissed homicide charges against Plumeri. Initially, they thought he and Didato fought a gun battle with each other.

March 19, 1937
Detectives arrested James Plumeri at his 65 Second Ave residence and John Dioguardi at 245 W 11th Street. A grand jury had indicted them for crimes in the trucking industry. Justice Ferdinand Pecora set bail at $50,000 for both men.

March 20, 1937
Judge Philip McCook took the not guilty pleas of James Plumeri and John Dioguardi in their trackmen's extortion case. He set bail at $50,000 for each man and sent them back to the Tombs (A jail).

June 2, 1937
The extortion trial of James Plumeri and John Dioguardi began in Judge Phillip J McCook's court. Murray I Gurfein handled the case for Special Prosecutor Thomas Dewey. The government alleged that the two hoods shook down 200 trucking firms, including 110 in the garment district.

Note:
The indictment also named Dominick "Terry Burns" Didato, but someone murdered him in 1933.

June 8, 1937
Benjamin Cohen, the Garment Center Truck Owners Association's former president, testified for the prosecution in the Plumeri/Dioguardi trial. He was a powerful witness detailing how Plumeri and Dioguardi forced his group to pay $500 a month to keep operating.

June 10, 1937
After seven days of prosecution testimony and 28 witnesses, Plumeri and Dioguardia pled guilty to a ten-count indictment. The counts included extortion, conspiracy, and assault. Justice Philip J McCook said they "Demoralized the great trucking industry by terror." The good guys alleged that the two hoods extorted $15,000 from the Garment Center Trucking Association.

June 28, 1937
Justice McCook sentenced Plumeri to five to ten years in Sing Sing. He gave Dioguardi three to five years. The judge said Plumeri was a "tough and a bully." Judge McCook described Dioguardi as possessing "a great vanity which was quite unjustified." Ouch!

July 29, 1937
Plumeri arrived at Sing Sing Prison.

December 30, 1937
Prison authorities transferred Plumeri to Clinton Prison.
Prison records show that Plumeri constantly wrote to his wife and other family members. Further information indicated that Ben Kessler took over Plumeri's stable of fighters while authorities had Plumeri locked up.

May 3, 1943
While in Clinton Prison, Plumeri arranged to register for the draft.

September 16, 1943
BOP officials released Plumeri from Clinton Prison.

February 12, 1947
Authorities served Plumeri with a grand jury subpoena at the Forrest Hotel at 224 W 49th Street in NYC.

February 13, 1947
Plumeri appeared before a grand jury investigating undercover boxing managers.

April 16, 1947
Plumeri was no longer on parole.

October 19, 1952
Plumeri was among the guests who attended the wedding of his nephew Thomas Dioguardi to Rosemary, daughter of hood Frank Livorsi. The nuptials took place at St Ignatius Church at Park Ave and 84th St.
An estimated 600 people went to the reception held at the Hotel Commodore.

May 4, 1954
The US government started denaturalization proceedings against Plumeri. The feds claimed he hid his criminal record before 1926.

January 2, 1956
Vanderbilt Hotel records indicate that Plumeri and John Dioguardi were registered there. An informer told the FBI that the two held a meeting with a Pennsylvania garment company owner. He added that Plumeri owned the Angelo Palanges Restaurant at 150 Sunny Isle Blvd. in Miami Beach.

December 29, 1956
Police charged Plumeri with disorderly conduct in Miami, but the court dropped the charges.

July 3, 1958
Before the McClellan Committee, Plumeri gave his marital status and address but took the 5th about 69 times.

December 19, 1958
Assistant US Attorney William Suglia informed the court that the feds had to drop their denaturalization case against Plumeri after failing to file the proper affidavit. However, he explained that the government might try again.

May 22, 1959
An informer told the FBI that Colombo Soldier John Franzese was behind the shady Retail Drug Employees Union. Franzese wanted Plumeri to help the Union gain recognition from Jimmy Hoffa and the Teamsters.

October 28, 1963
The feds arraigned Plumeri before Judge John FX McGohey on tax fraud. US Attorney Harold Baer explained that the government charged that Plumeri cheated on his 1960 and 1962 taxes. He asked for $10,000 bail, but the Judge settled on $5,000.

Russell Bufalino was the Boss of the Pittston, Pa Family. He had interests in the garment business in his home state and New York City. On many of his New York visits, he would meet up with Plumeri. Thanks to informer reports to the FBI, some of those events are listed below.

Unfortunately, we do not have any information about what would require the two hoods to meet so often. It would be reasonable to assume that the endless problems in the garment business would be a topic of discussion. The Commission's attempt to unseat Boss Joe Bonanno was another likely subject, along with the fed's long-standing attempt to deport Bufalino. Perhaps the two men liked each other's company.

April 16, 1964
Bufalino met with Plumeri.

April 21, 1964
Bufalino dined with Plumeri in the Villanova East Restaurant.

April 27, 1964
Bufalino met with Plumeri.

May 20, 1964
Bufalino met with Plumeri.

November 25, 1964
Bufalino met with Plumeri at the Brass Rail bar.

December 2, 1964
Bufalino met with Plumeri.

February 9, 1965
A jury convicted Plumeri of tax fraud. Judge Tyler released him on $30,000 bail.

March 12, 1965
Judge Harold Tyler listened as US Attorney Harold Baer outlined Plumeri's criminal career. Tyler then sentenced Plumeri to two and a half years in prison. There were two separate two-and-a-half-year sentences, but they were to run concurrently. The judge released Plumeri to appeal but raised his bail to $35,000. Before Plumeri left, Judge Tyler described him as a "lamprey-eel type of person." Unfortunately, it was not a compliment.

July 13, 1967
Boss Tommy Lucchese died of natural causes.

1967
Informers told the FBI about a series of meetings between Plumeri and other hoods while he was in Miami.

July 18, 1967
Plumeri met with John Dioguardi in a restaurant.

August 9, 1967
Plumeri told the informer that he had met with Jimmy Alo and Eddie Coco during the week of August 1. Therefore, it would be a reasonable guess that they discussed the recent death of Boss Lucchese.

November 6, 1967
Eddie Coco admitted to the FBI that he had met with Plumeri during the week of November 1, 1967. Coco was on lifetime parole.

July 18, 1968
The feds indicted Plumeri, John Dioguardi, and three others for conspiring to obtain a large loan from the Teamsters fraudulently. They hoped to get $1,350,000 to purchase a discount store chain, but the deal fell through. At the time, Plumeri was president of the Five Borough Truckmen's Association.

May 5, 1969
The judge granted Plumeri a severance in the Teamster fraud case. He would face trial on his own.

July 22, 1969
US Attorney Robert Morgenthau unsealed a massive indictment charging 13 men with conspiracy to defraud the Teamster's Central, Southwest, and Southeast Pension fund. He alleged that the conspirators conspired to pay an employee of the Pension Fund $5,000 to increase a loan already granted. Previously, the Mid-City Development Corporation of Detroit won a loan of $1,050,000, but the hoods wanted $1,250,000. Among those charged were Plumeri and the Mafia Boss of Pittsburgh, John La Rocca.

July 23, 1969
The FBI announced that it had arrested 9 of the 13 men named in the Teamster fraud indictment.

June 1971
Plumeri pled guilty to seven different indictments involving kickbacks and tax fraud. Judge Edward McLean sentenced him to two years and a fine of $1,500 on each count totaling 14 years and $10,500. However, after listening to a doctor say a prison term might shorten Plumeri's life, the judge suspended the sentence but kept the fines. Judge McLean said he made his decision, "With considerable reluctance, even though I believe he thoroughly deserves it." He put Plumeri on an installment plan for the fines and warned that a prison sentence would result if Plumeri did not pay.

Note:
The authorities had taken Plumeri to trial on these charges with a group of hoods, but he suffered a heart attack. Accordingly, the judge granted him severance. Plumeri then pled guilty.

September 16, 1971
Someone strangled Plumeri to death and left his body on Maspeth Street. At 7:30 AM the next day, an off-duty police officer discovered Plumeri's body lying face down on a grassy strip with his tie tight around his neck and a plastic bag over his head.

September 23, 1971
Monsignor Elwood Purick of St. Athanasius Church refused to hold a funeral mass for Plumeri since he was not a member of that church. So instead, the family had a service in Scarpaci's Funeral Home at 1401 86th Street in Bay Ridge, Brooklyn. Finally, they buried Plumeri in St John's Cemetery in Queens.

Comment:

There is no concrete evidence as to why someone killed Plumeri. However, it is reasonable to speculate that Boss Carmine Tramunti approved the hit for the Family took no revenge actions. Plumeri had always been a big money earner but slowed down with age and medical problems. Did the evidence in the kickback trials indicate to his Boss that Plumeri was making money but not sharing it? Perhaps. Did the Judge's decision to suspend Plumeri's 14 years sentence raise suspicions that he had made some secret deal? This possibility is my best GUESS as to the reason behind his murder.

Appendix A

The History of the Lucchese Family Administration

Lucchese Family
192? -1930

Boss
Gaetano "Tommy" Reina
192?-1930
Killed February 26, 1930

Underboss
Tommy Gagliano
192?-1930

Consigliere
Unknown

Lucchese Family
1930-1930

Boss
Joe Pinzolo
1930-1930
Killed September 5, 1930

Underboss
Unknown

Consigliere
Unknown

Lucchese Family
1930-1951

Boss
Tom Gagliano
1930-1951
Died February 16, 1951
Natural causes

Underboss
Tommy Lucchese
1930-1951

Consigliere
Steve Runnelli
1931-1953
Retired

Lucchese Family
1951-1967

Boss
Tommy Lucchese
1951-1967
Died July 13, 1967
Cancer

Acting Boss
Carmine Tramunti
1966-1967

Ettore Coco
1967
Resigned, legal problems

Underboss
Stephano LaSalle
1951-1967

Consigliere
Vince Rao
1951-1967
Prison in 1965

Acting Consigliere
Unknown
1965-1967

Lucchese Family
1967-1978

Boss
Carm Tramunti
1967-1978
Prison 1973
Died in jail October 15, 1978

Acting Boss
Anthony Corallo
1973-1978

Underboss
Stephano LaSalle
1967-1970
Retired

Paul Vario
1970-1978

Consigliere
Vince Rao
1967-1973
Prison in 1965-1970
Retired 1973

Acting Consigliere
Mariano Macaluso
1965-1970

Lucchese Family
1978-1986

Boss
Tony Corallo
1978-1986
Jailed for 100 yrs. January 13, 1987
Died in prison August 23, 2000

Underboss
Salvatore "Tom Mix" Santoro
1978-1986
Jailed for 100 yrs.

Acting Underboss
Mariano Macaluso
1986
Retired

Consigliere
Chris "Christy Trick" Furnari
1980-1986
Jailed for 100 yrs.

Lucchese Family
1986-20??

Boss
Vittorio "Vic" Amuso
1986-
Given life sentence June 15, 1992

Acting Boss
Al D'Arco
January 12, 1991-July 1991
Demoted
Rolled over September 1991

Committee
Frank Lastorino
Sal Avellino
Antonio Barratta
Danny Cutaia
Al D'Arco-informer 1991
July 91-December 1993

Acting Boss
Joe DeFede
1994-1998
Prison 1998-2002
Informer February 2002

Steve Crea
1998-September 2001
Parole violation November 4, 1999-March 2000
Arrested September 6, 2000
Convicted 2001, 5 years
Released August 24, 2006

Louis Daidone
2001-2003
Arrested March 2003
Life January 2004

<u>Committee</u>
Joe DiNapoli
Matthew Madonna
Neil Migliore
2003-2012

<u>Acting Boss</u>
Matthew Madonna
2012-2017
Stepped down
2020 life in prison

Michael DeSantis
2017-

<u>Underboss</u>
Mariano Macaluso
1986-1989
Retired

Tony "Gaspipe" Casso
1989-1994
Turned informer.
Life sentence July 1998

Steve Crea
1994-2017
Acting Boss 1998-2001
Prison November 4, 1999-March 2000
Arrested September 6, 2000
Prison 2001-2006
Released August 24, 2006
Stepped down 2017
Life 2020

Mikey DeSantis
2020-

Acting Underboss
Anthony Barratta
1992-1994

Eugene Castelle
1998-2001

Joe Caridi
2001-2002
Promoted to Consigliere

Patty Dellorusso
2017-

Consigliere
Frank Lastorino
1986-2002

Joe Caridi
2002-
Arrested November 15, 2002
Pleads March 19, 2003
Released November 27, 2009

Acting Consigliere
Louis Daidone
1993-2001
Promoted to Acting Boss

Joe DiNapoli
????-2019
Imprisoned

Andrew DeSimone
2019-2021

Patrick Delloruso
2021

Appendix B

Comedian Billy Crystal and Mafioso John Ormento

Billy Crystal Remembers Childhood in '700 Sundays'
By
ABC News
2 November 2005, 06:13
• 15 min read

Nov. 1, 2005 — -- *Comedian Billy Crystal's book "700 Sundays," based on his recent one-man play, is a tribute to his family -- especially his father, who died when Crystal was just 15. Crystal estimated that he shared only about 700 Sundays with his father, whom he deeply loves and admires.*

The book, which takes a nostalgic look at the Long Beach, Long Island of yesteryear, is available in stores now, from Warner Books.

Big John was scary, our Luca Brasi. While we were eating our egg rolls, and drinking our drinks with the little umbrellas in them, we had no idea that Big John Ormento was drunk driving his new car, a 1957, anti-Semitic Lincoln Continental. And he came roaring up Park Avenue, swerved and slammed into the back of the Belvedere, which then slammed into the back of the car in front of it, reducing our new car to a 1957 gray-on-gray Plymouth Belv! The crash was tremendous. We turned around so fast lo mein flew out of our mouths hitting and sticking to the window.

Big John staggered out of his car, surveyed the damage, shook his head a few times and started to laugh.

"Oh my God, it's Big John," Mom gasped.

"I'm going out there," said Dad as he started to push his way out of the black leather booth.

"Don't, Jack, what if he has a gun?" Dad ordered another gimlet.

Ormento ran to his car and took off.

Ten minutes later, Officer Miller was questioning my father.

"Did you see who did this, Mr. Crystal?"

Dad never hesitated.

"No, we heard the crash, and by the time we got out here, they were gone."

Mom looked at Dad, confused a bit, but knowing he probably did the right thing. Joel and Rip and I were dying to tell, but "dying" being the operative word here, we said nothing.

"Some people," the cop muttered. "Must have been some kid going too fast."

"Yeah," said Pop. "These kids today . . ."

It was a Sunday night, and Dad's service station, "Stan's," was closing early. Stan told Dad he didn't have any room for the car in the shop, but he would tow it to our house and pick it up in the morning.

The twisted piece of metal sat in front of our house, at 549 East Park in Long Beach, Long Island. A sleepy beach town of approximately ten thousand people, which nodded off in the winter and woke up in July to three times as many enjoying a beautiful summer at the sea, Long Beach was surrounded by water. The bay (Reynold's Channel) on one side of town, with its beautiful wetlands; and the Atlantic Ocean on the other, its thunderous waves hitting the shore of beautiful white sand beaches. The boardwalk stretched the length of the town and featured some amusement park rides. There were games of chance, and a batting cage, a soft ice cream shop, a knish place (Izzy's) and a large municipal swimming pool.

Modest homes, and the occasional thirties mansion, dotted the tree-lined streets. A few hotels near the boardwalk were once filled with people, making Long Beach at one time a sort of Atlantic City without the saltwater taffy and the diving horse. The abandoned submarine watch tower, left standing since World War II, was the place to take your girl for a kiss, or smoke a cigarette for the first time. At one time there was horseback riding on the beach, and supposedly George M. Cohan wrote "Only 45 Minutes from Broadway" about Long Beach.

It was known as America's healthiest city, which is why my sickly grandparents moved there from the Bronx and bought homes for my Uncle Danny and us, in 1951. It was a wonderful place to live. However, at nine o'clock that Monday morning, Long Beach didn't feel like the safest place to be. Stunned, the five of us sat in the living room bemoaning the loss of the Belvedere. The doorbell rang and I got it. I always got the door because I thought someday somebody's going to be there who would take me to Hollywood.

When I opened the door, there was an overcoat, a neck and an eyebrow. Big John Ormento was in the doorway. He looked down at me, which wasn't difficult. I was surprised to see his face. Usually gangsters like this are on television, sitting in silhouette confessing to their gruesome crimes, their voices electronically altered, sounding like Darth Vader on Quaaludes. Big John's voice was deep -- it actually seemed to echo -- and he had an accent as thick as his police file. "Can I see your father, please?"

My heart was beating so loud, I thought he could hear it. My throat was dry, making it a full octave higher than it already was.

"I will go and see if there is one here." And I ran into the living room, faster than a hyperactive midget wrestler.

"Dad, Big John Ormento's here. Big John Ormento's outside. He's going to kill us. He's going to kill all of us! We're doomed!"

"Billy, calm down. Calm down. He's not here to hurt us. He probably just wants to talk to me. Let him in."

"Me? I'm nine! I've got everything to live for!" (I became a better actor later.) "Please."

"Let him in."

I went back to the door to get Big John; he seemed even bigger, his head was so large it caused a total eclipse of the sun.

"Come on in."

He followed me into the living room. He stood there, looking menacing, and uncomfortable. He stared at my dad, took off his hat, and then he spoke.

"Hey, how fast do think your car was going when it backed into my car?"

We all froze. Big John broke out in a Pavarotti kind of laugh.

"I'm just kidding. How you doing? I'm John Ormento. Nice to meet you, Mr. Crystal, Mrs. Crystal, you boys here. Listen. I'm very sorry for what happened to your car last night. Very sorry. It was my fault, it was an accident, believe me, it was an accident. If it wasn't an accident, this would be a condolence call.

"I talked to my 'friends' and they told me you didn't tell the cops nothing. So I want to make it up to yous."

"Okay, Mr. Ormento. I have my insurance card. We'll just put it through the insurance company."

Big John interrupted Dad with an impatient laugh, the same way he probably interrupted somebody who wasn't beating up a guy properly.

"No, no, no, no. We're not going to do something stupid like put it through the insurance company, no. Cuz let's face it, we are the insurance company! "I want to do something special for yous."

Dad looked confused.

"What do you mean 'special'?" "I asked around about you, Mr. Crystal. People like you. They respect what you do, and they like your wife and your boys here. Don't you think you should be driving around in a car that more befits a man of your altitude?"

We all looked confused. "What are you trying to say, Mr. Ormento?"

"What I'm trying to say is this, Mr. Crystal. I want to buy you a new car, any car you want, the car of your choice."

Things were looking up! Any car we want? The car of our choice? Oh baby, I was overjoyed! All those great cars were now rolling around my brain, like a slot machine: the Impala, the Bel Air, the Thunderbird, the Corvette! Oh, a Corvette! Think with me, Pop, think with me, Corvette, Corvette, Corvette, I said to myself over and over, trying to send my message telepathically.

"Let's just get this car fixed," Dad said.

Shit! I said to myself.

Big John looked angry, and as he stepped forward, he got bigger.

"Let me ask you something, Mr. K . . ." I wanted to correct him, but I have this thing about dying.

"You are refusing my offer? Huh? That upsets me. You know, that really upsets me, and it confuses me. Why would you not want me to buy you a new car?"

Dad stood tall and simply said, "Because, Mr. Ormento, I bought this one."

There was silence as they stared at each other.

It got tense. Big John's shark eyes trying to intimidate, as they lasered into Dad's eyes, trying to push him to reconsider, and probably thinking, How can I get this guy's whole body into a can of tuna. Dad, only five foot nine and 160 pounds, just stared back at Big John, unafraid.

I looked at my mother. She looked at my father, and she smiled a smile of pride that I've never, ever forgotten. She took one step over next to him, put her arm around Pop, and together the two of them smiled at Big John Ormento.

Those were my parents.

Two weeks later, the car came back. Well, Big John knew a lot about bodywork because the car looked great, and after we opened the trunk to make sure there were no bodies in it, we took it out for a ride. And everything was great until

Dad tried to make a right turn. Almost impossible. The car barely reacted to Dad's turning of the steering wheel. It moaned and groaned; so did Dad. The car just couldn't make right turns very well. They couldn't fix that. You actually had to make three left turns in order to make one right turn. But it didn't matter; we had our new car.

Appendix C

The FBI's list of Lucchese Soldiers in 1963

NY 92-2300

LUCHESE "FAMILY"

Set forth below are individuals reported previously as being specifically named by sources as members of the THOMAS LUCHESE "family" or "borgata" within the framework of "Cosa Nostra":

Name	Alias	FBI Identification #
ARRA, FRANK		
BENDINELLI, JOSEPH	Joe Babes (Died 4/8/63)	296 870
BIANCO, DOMINICK	Danny Yankee (dead)	677 777
BONINA, NICHOLAS	The Baron	
BROCCHINI, JOSEPH	Joe Bikini	622 595 A
CALABRESE, JOSEPH		
CALLACE, FRANK	Chick 99 (dead)	
CAMPANELLO, FRANK	Frankie Bell	62 228
CANZONARI, (FNU)		
CARBO, PAUL JOHN	Frankie	187 972
CASTALDI, ANTHONY	Tony Higgins	546 748
CAVALIERI, SALVATORE	Big Sam	645 241
CICCONE, ANTHONY	Tony Moon	
CICCONE, SALVATORE		
CINTRANO, FRANK	Chick Wilson (dead)	

- 75 -

NY 92-2300

Name	Alias	FBI Identification #
COCO, ETTORE	Eddie	486 097
CORALLO, ANTONIO	Tony Ducks	269 969
CORREALE, PAUL	Paulie Ham (dead)	177 910
CURCIO, JOSEPH		2373 255
DE CARLO, JOHN		
DELGATO, LEO		
DEMPSEY (nickname)		
DE MARTINO, JOSEPH		
DE MINO, JIMMY		
DIOGUARDI, JOHN	Johnny Dio	665 273
DIOGUARDI, FRANK	Frank Dio	
DIOGUARDI, THOMAS	Tommy Dio	920 425
DI PALERMO, CHARLES	Charley Beck) (In Jail)	
DI PALERMO, JOSEPH	Joe Beck	1519 166
EMANUELE, JOSEPH	Joe Pelham Bay	
FOCERI, LOUIS	Louis Beans	
GAGLIANO, NUNZIE		
GAGLIANO, THOMAS		
GIANNONE, EUGENE	Little Gene	972 673 D
GORIO, CHARLES	Scupete	

- 76 -

NY 92-2300

Name	Alias	FBI Identification #
GUIGA, LOUIS		
LARATRO, JOSEPH	Joey Narrows	263 439 D
LA SALLA, STEPHANO	Steve	846 188 D
LA SALLA, VITO		
LASCALI, JOSEPH		
LAZZARO, CARMELLO		
LICATA, THOMAS	Tommy Bullets (dead)	
LOCASCIO, CARMINE	Willie Brown	246 742
LOIACANO, ANGELO	Puggy	4748 953
LO PINTO, ANTHONY	T. Balls	
LO PROTO, SALVATORE	Sally the Blond	921 798B
LUCHESE, JOSEPH	Joe Brown	
LUCHESE, THOMAS	Tommy Brown	168 275
MACALUSO, MARIANO		
MAGIARCINA, GASPAR		
MANERI, SALVATORE	Shears	
NESTE, ANGELO		

- 77 -

NY 92-2300

Name	Alias	FBI Identification #
NUNZIE (nickname)		
ORMENTO, JOHN	Big John	1321 383
PANICA, VIC	Little Victor (In Jail)	
PAPPADIO, ANDIMO	Tommy	1331 637
PETRELLI, DOMINICK	The Gap (dead)	
PLUMERI, JAMES	Jimmy Doyle	672 798
POTENZA, VINCENT	Jimmy Jones	
PRUNES, CHARLEY (nickname)		
RAO, CHARLES		
RAO, VINCENT JOHN		792 086 C
REINA, ANTHONY	Nino (dead)	
REINA, GIACOMO	Jack	
REINA, THOMAS	(dead)	
ROSATO, JOSEPH	Joe Palisades	416 5533
RUSSO, RALPH		
SANTORA, SALVATORE	Tom Mix (In Jail)	
SCOPERTO, CHARLES	Scoop	
SHILLITANI, SALVATORE	Sally Shields	

NY 92-2300

Name	Alias	FBI Identification #
SPECIALE, SALVATORE (dead)		
TOLENTINO, NICHOLAS	Big Nose Nick	
TRAMUNTI, CARMINE	Mr. Gribs	471 313
TUMINARO, ANGELO	Little Angie	270 010
VALENTE, SAM		
VALENTE, THOMAS (dead)		
VENTELARO, JAMES	Jimmy the Sniff	
VENTO, JOSEPH	Babo	143 2959
VIDALLA, ANTHONY	Grio	
BENENTI, DUTODO		

- 79 -

NY 92-2300

The following individuals were previously named as being in the THOMAS LUCHESE "family", and are now being deleted from this "family", since information has been received from a source, who is in a position to furnish reliable information, that they in fact are not members of the THOMAS LUCHESE "family". Their names are listed below with the source supplying the information, and the identity of the "family" to which the individuals actually belong:

Name	Source	"Family"
JOSEPH CARLINO aka Joe Woppi	NY T-14	JOSEPH BONANNO
VINCENT CORRAO aka Jimmy the Blond FBI #1378139	NY T-14	CARLO GAMBINO
NATALE EVOLA aka Joe Diamond FBI #449296	NY T-14	JOSEPH BONANNO
SALVATORE GRANELLO aka Sally Burns FBI #2120006	NY T-14	VITO GENOVESE
ANTHONY LISI aka Tony Lisi FBI #771146	NY T-14	JOSEPH BONANNO
JOSEPH SILESI aka Joe Rivers	NY T-14	CARLO GAMBINO
JOSEPH INDELICATO	NY T-1	CARLO GAMBINO

The following two individuals were previously named as being members of "Cosa Nostra", and in the THOMAS LUCHESE "family", and are now being deleted, since sources in a position to furnish reliable information have reported that although they are friendly with this group, they are not members of this "family":

Name	Source
JAMES LUCHESE	NY T-14 and NY T-1
JOSEPH MARINO	NY T-14 and NY T-1

- 80 -

Appendix D

The NYPD's List of the Lucchese Administration Circa 1988

LUCHESE
ORGANIZED CRIME NETWORK

APRIL, 1988

BOSS CORALLO, Antonio DOB 2/12/13 or
5 Grace Lane 2/13/13
Sough Oyster Bay Cove, NY SS# 78862

He was recently convicted and sentenced to 100 years in the "COMMISSION TRIAL," which was held in the SDNY. Although he is in Federal Prison, it is believed that he still continues to control this organized Crime Network.

UNDERBOSS SANTORA, Salvatore DOB 11/16/15
90 Irvy Island Avenue b# 210612
Bronx, NY

LEADERSHIP
OF
LUCHESE
ORGANIZED CRIME
NETWORK

He was recently convicted and sentenced to 100 years in the "COMMISSION TRIAL," which was held in the SDNY. Although he is in Federal Prison, it is believed that he still continues to control this network.

CONSIGLIERI FURNARI, Christopher DOB 4/20/24
66 Adams Court b# 213639
Staten Island, NY

He was recently convicted and sentenced to 100 years in the "COMMISSION TRIAL," which was held in the SDNY. Although he is in Federal Prison, it is believed that he still continues to control this network.

INTERIM AMUSO, Victor DOB 11,/4/34
BOSS 96-07 158th Avenue BS 322846
Howard Beach, NY NYSIIS D450383 L
FBI# 600774E

ACTING CASASSO, Antimo DOB 6/7/12
UNDERBOSS & 144-31 South Drive (10th Ave.)
CONSIGLIERI Whitestone, NY

Prepared by:

City of New York
Police Department
Intelligence Division

PAGE 01

LUCHESE
ORGANIZED CRIME NETWORK

APRIL, 1988

BOSS CORALLO, Antonio DOB 1/12/13 or 2/12/13
9 Grace Lane
South Oyster Bay Cove, NY B# 75882

He was recently convicted and sentenced to 100 years in the "COMMISSION TRIAL", which was held in the SDNY. Although he is in Federal Prison, it is believed that he still continues to control this Organized Crime Network.

UNDERBOSS SANTORA, Salvatore DOB 11/18/15
90 City Island Avenue B# 128622
Bronx, NY

He was recently convicted and sentenced to 100 years in the "COMMISSION TRIAL", which was held in the SDNY. Although he is in Federal Prison, it is believed that he still continues to control this network.

CONSIGLIERI FURNARI, Christopher DOB 4/30/24
66 Adams Court B# 213639
Staten Island, NY

He was recently convicted and sentenced to 100 years in the "COMMISSION TRIAL" which was held in the SDNY. Although he is in Federal Prison, it is believed that he still continues to control this network.

INTERIM BOSS AMUSO, Victor DOB 11/4/34
88-07 156th Avenue B# 322848
Howard Beach, NY NYSID# 0460283 L
 FBI# 698774B

ACTING UNDERBOSS & CONSIGLIERI MACALUSO, Mariano DOB 6/7/12
144-31 South Drive (10th Ave.)
Whitestone, NY

PAGE #1

941

LUCHESE
ORGANIZED CRIME NETWORK

APRIL, 1988

STREET BOSS	**CASSO, Anthony** 2148 East 72nd Street Brooklyn, NY	DOB 5/21/40 B# 509523 NYSID# 0900001 M
CAPOREGIMA	**ABATE, Joseph F.** 8905 Atlantic City Avenue Margate, NJ	DOB 7/8/02 FBI# 1-228-812
CAPOREGIMA	**ACCETURRO, Anthony** 5131 Jackson Street Hollywood, Fl. & PO Box 7089 Hollywood, Fl.	DOB 10/18/38 FBI# 938611C

He is currently on Federal trial in Newark, New Jersey.

CAPOREGIMA	**CASSO, Anthony** 2148 East 72nd Street Brooklyn, NY	DOB 5/21/40 B# 509523 NYSID# 0900001 M
CAPOREGIMA	**CASTALDI, Samuel** 335 Whipple Street Brentwood, NY	DOB 2/26/09 B# 254905 NYSID# 0257183 M FBI# 4981094
CAPOREGIMA	**CAVALIERI, Samuel** 149-45 Northern Blvd. Flushing, NY	DOB 4/11/11 B# 93580

He died of natural causes on November 4, 1987. It is not known who has replaced him at this time.

PAGE #2

LUCHESE
ORGANIZED CRIME NETWORK

APRIL, 1988

FORMER CAPOREGIMA   **CICCONE, Anthony** (Antonio)   DOB 7/18/18
67 Wyoming Drive   B# 172419
Huntington Station, NY

He is believed to have replaced **Anthony Luongo**, DOB 10/19/39, B# 393380, who has been missing since November 11, 1986, to date. He has not been officially reported missing. Anthony Ciccone died from natural causes in August of 1987. It is not known who has replaced him at this time.

CAPOREGIMA   **COCO, Ettore**   DOB 7/18/08
1261 Waring Avenue   B# 96208
Bronx, NY

It was believed that COCO was retired and living in Florida. Recent intelligence data indicates that he is back in New York. He has a current NY drivers license. From July to September of 1967, after the death of **Thomas LUCHESE**, he was the ACTING BOSS of this network.

CAPOREGIMA   **DeLUCA, Richard**   DOB 6/19/34
4 Horizon Road   B# 521879
Fort Lee, NJ   NYSID# 0943275 P
FBI# 486141C

CAPOREGIMA   **DiPALERMO, Joseph**   DOB 6/8/07
80 North Moore Street   B# 203135
New York, NY   NYSID# 0112283 M
FBI# 1519166

DiPalermo is a Federal Drug Enforcement fugitive since 7/3/86. It is believed that his brother **Peter DiPalermo**, B# 168069 is acting in his behalf.

DiPALERMO, Peter   DOB 10/18/14
801 Gramatan Avenue   B# 168069
Mount Vernon, NY   NYSID# 0032992 J
FBI# 518878

PAGE #3

943

LUCHESE
ORGANIZED CRIME NETWORK

APRIL, 1988

CAPOREGIMA **LARATRO, Joseph**   DOB 2/17/16
543 Palm Drive   NYSID# 1279607 Y
Hallandale, Fl.
&
12 Bouton Road
Lloyd Harbor, NY

      Intelligence data indicates that **Laratro**, is semi-retired and it is believed that **Aniello Migliore**, DOB 10/2/33, B# 522599 is acting in his behalf.

      MIGLIORE, Aniello (Neil) DOB 10/2/33
14 Grace Lane   B# 522599
South Oyster Bay Cove. NY
      NYSID# 0945003 J
      FBI# 284211E

CAPOREGIMA **SALERNO, Michael C.**   DOB 3/20/23
10 Dellwood Lane   B# 198299
Ardsley, NY

CAPOREGIMA **VARIO, Paul**   DOB 7/10/14
132 Island Parkway North   B# 98436
Island Park, NY   FBI# 516930

      Paul Vario was found guilty in the "AIRPORT TRIAL" which was held in the EDNY. On December 10, 1986, he was sentenced to serve 6 years consecutively in a Federal Prison. It is believed that his son, **Peter Vario**, B# 563733, is acting in his behalf.

      VARIO, Peter   DOB 6/26/36
968 Hemlock Street   B# 563733
Brooklyn, NY   NYSID# 0983580 M

PAGE #4

Appendix E

The FBI's List of Lucchese Soldiers Circa 1988

U. S. SENATE
PERMANENT SUBCOMMITTEE ON INVESTIGATIONS
FIVE NEW YORK LCN FAMILIES MEMBERSHIP

Name	Family	D.O.B.
VELLUCCI, ANTHONY J	GENOVESE	12/12/24
VERRA, JOHN	GENOVESE	01/27/22
VICARO, RALPH	GENOVESE	04/29/15
VIGORITO, FRED	GENOVESE	03/08/22
VISPISIANO, FRANK	GENOVESE	02/06/39
ZERBO, PAUL	GENOVESE	11/15/12
ABATE, JOSEPH	LUCHESE	07/08/02
ABINANTI, PETER	LUCHESE	06/12/12
ACCARDI, CARMINE N.	LUCHESE	12/18/39
ACCETTURO, ANTHONY	LUCHESE	10/18/38
AITA, VICTOR	LUCHESE	07/26/12
AMUSO, ROBERT	LUCHESE	/ / NYSIIS #0068875B
ARRA, NUNZIO F	LUCHESE	01/01/10
AVELLINO, SALVATORE	LUCHESE	11/19/35
BARATTA, ANTHONY	LUCHESE	07/08/38
BELLINO, FRANK	LUCHESE	09/26/16
BELMONT, VINCENT	LUCHESE	10/18/25
BONINA, NICHOLAS	LUCHESE	01/09/28
BORELLI, FRANK	LUCHESE	06/15/25
CAPRA, JOSEPH	LUCHESE	09/18/16
CAPUTO, JOHN	LUCHESE	08/31/11
CARLINO, CHARLES SALVATOR	LUCHESE	08/04/13
CASSO, ANTHONY	LUCHESE	05/21/40
CAVALIERI, SAMUEL JOSEPH	LUCHESE	08/14/11
CICCONE, SALVATORE	LUCHESE	07/28/16

Page No. 26
04/08/98

U. S. SENATE
PERMANENT SUBCOMMITTEE ON INVESTIGATIONS
FIVE NEW YORK LCN FAMILIES MEMBERSHIP

D.O.B.

CIRAULO, VINCENT	LUCHESE	09/18/19
COCO, ETTORE	LUCHESE	07/12/08
CONTI, JOHN JOSEPH	LUCHESE	07/28/35
CORALLO, ANTONIO	LUCHESE	01/12/13
CROCE, ANTHONY	LUCHESE	12/24/32
CURCIO, JOSEPH WILLIAM	LUCHESE	06/26/18
CUTAIA, DOMENICO	LUCHESE	11/22/36
DEBENEDICTUS, SAVINO	LUCHESE	04/27/22
DEFENDIS, ANGELO	LUCHESE	09/23/32
DELLACAGNA, MICHAEL	LUCHESE	12/12/18
DELLIPAOLI, ORLANDO	LUCHESE	10/09/12
DELUCA, RICHARD	LUCHESE	06/19/34
DESIMONE, ANDREW	LUCHESE	11/14/14
DICONSTANZA, NICHOLAS	LUCHESE	07/18/36
DIDONATO, THOMAS	LUCHESE	11/10/26
DIGUARDI, THOMAS T	LUCHESE	10/29/15
DILAPI, ANTHONY	LUCHESE	02/09/36
DIMEGLIO, ANTHONY J	LUCHESE	11/12/32
DIMEGLIO, ANTHONY JOSEPH	LUCHESE	11/12/32
DIPALERMO, CHARLES	LUCHESE	02/15/25
DIPALERMO, JOSEPH	LUCHESE	06/08/07
DIPALERMO, PETER	LUCHESE	10/18/14
DISIMONE, SALVATORE	LUCHESE	01/08/41
FACCIOLO, BRUNO	LUCHESE	12/30/36
FALCO, FELICE	LUCHESE	06/01/06

798

Page No. 27
04/08/88

U. S. SENATE
PERMANENT SUBCOMMITTEE ON INVESTIGATIONS
FIVE NEW YORK LCN FAMILIES MEMBERSHIP

D.O.B.

FALCO, JAMES MICHAEL	LUCHESE	03/19/12
FALCO, PHILIP	LUCHESE	07/01/08
FEDERICI, ANTHONY	LUCHESE	07/28/40
FOCERI, LOUIS N	LUCHESE	11/21/22
FRANGIAPANI, JOSEPH FRANK	LUCHESE	09/05/25
FURNARI, CHRISTOPHER	LUCHESE	04/30/24
GIAMPAOLA, CIRO CHARLES	LUCHESE	11/20/05
GIOIA, FRANK	LUCHESE	01/20/49
GRAFFAGNINO, SALVATORE	LUCHESE	12/20/12
IANNOTTA, MICHAEL	LUCHESE	12/08/16
LABARBARA, MICHAEL SR	LUCHESE	12/22/13
LAGANO, FRANK PETER	LUCHESE	11/24/39
LAIETTA, DONATO	LUCHESE	08/10/08
LAMELA, JOHN	LUCHESE	11/05/08
LARATRO, JOSEPH ALBER	LUCHESE	02/07/16
LAROSA, MICHAEL	LUCHESE	06/02/15
LASORSA, ANTHONY	LUCHESE	11/18/32
LASORSA, NICHOLAS	LUCHESE	/ / FBI #1577491
LATELLA, DANIEL JOSEPH	LUCHESE	10/12/40
LESSA, NICHOLAS	LUCHESE	02/19/21
LOCASCIO, PETER J	LUCHESE	06/10/16
LODUCA, PAUL	LUCHESE	04/10/40
LUCCHESE, JAMES J	LUCHESE	08/19/13
LUCCHESE, JOSEPH	LUCHESE	04/13/10
MACALUSO, MARIANO	LUCHESE	06/07/12

Page No.   28
04/08/88

U. S. SENATE
PERMANENT SUBCOMMITTEE ON INVESTIGATIONS
FIVE NEW YORK LCN FAMILIES MEMBERSHIP

D.O.B.

MAGISTRO, FRANK	LUCHESE	07/26/01
MANERI, SALVATORE	LUCHESE	08/15/11
MANGIAPANE, LEONARD P	LUCHESE	12/10/38
MANZO, FRANK	LUCHESE	02/02/25
MARONE, JOSEPH F	LUCHESE	02/11/04
MIGLIORE ANIELLO JOSEPH	LUCHESE	10/02/33
MOIA, FRANK	LUCHESE	07/05/34
NICCIO, VINCENT PETER	LUCHESE	03/05/12
NUCCIA, FRANK JOSEPH	LUCHESE	08/29/19
NUCCIO, SALVATORE JOHN	LUCHESE	07/20/16
ODDO, STEVEN V SR	LUCHESE	05/11/12
PANICA, VICTOR J	LUCHESE	04/17/24
PERNA, MICHAEL J	LUCHESE	04/28/42
PERRI, BRUNO	LUCHESE	06/06/24
PICCIOLI, CARLO ANTONIO	LUCHESE	02/24/30
PINTO, ANTONIO M	LUCHESE	10/27/26
PIZZOLATA, LEONARD	LUCHESE	06/01/05
PIZZOLATO, VITO	LUCHESE	08/01/09
PORCELLI, ANTHONY	LUCHESE	03/27/29
POTENZA, VINCENT	LUCHESE	08/25/26
RAO, VINCENT J	LUCHESE	04/27/07
REINA, GIACOMO	LUCHESE	09/21/08
RICCIARDI, THOMAS ANGELO	LUCHESE	03/25/52
RINALDI, ROSARIO	LUCHESE	03/07/17
RUSSO, ANTHONY PETER	LUCHESE	03/29/37

U. S. SENATE
PERMANENT SUBCOMMITTEE ON INVESTIGATIONS
FIVE NEW YORK LCN FAMILIES MEMBERSHIP

		D.O.B.
MAGISTRO, FRANK	LUCHESE	07/26/01
MANERI, SALVATORE	LUCHESE	08/15/11
MANGIAPANE, LEONARD P	LUCHESE	12/10/38
MANZO, FRANK	LUCHESE	02/02/25
MARONE, JOSEPH F	LUCHESE	02/11/04
MIGLIORE ANIELLO JOSEPH	LUCHESE	10/02/33
MOIA, FRANK	LUCHESE	07/05/34
NICCIO, VINCENT PETER	LUCHESE	03/05/12
NUCCIA, FRANK JOSEPH	LUCHESE	08/29/19
NUCCIO, SALVATORE JOHN	LUCHESE	07/20/16
ODDO, STEVEN V SR	LUCHESE	05/11/12
PANICA, VICTOR J	LUCHESE	04/17/24
PERNA, MICHAEL J	LUCHESE	04/28/42
PERRI, BRUNO	LUCHESE	06/06/24
PICCIOLI, CARLO ANTONIO	LUCHESE	02/24/30
PINTO, ANTONIO M	LUCHESE	10/27/26
PIZZOLATA, LEONARD	LUCHESE	06/01/05
PIZZOLATO, VITO	LUCHESE	08/01/09
PORCELLI, ANTHONY	LUCHESE	03/27/29
POTENZA, VINCENT	LUCHESE	08/25/26
RAO, VINCENT J	LUCHESE	04/27/07
REINA, GIACOMO	LUCHESE	09/21/08
RICCIARDI, THOMAS ANGELO	LUCHESE	03/25/52
RINALDI, ROSARIO	LUCHESE	03/07/17
RUSSO, ANTHONY PETER	LUCHESE	03/29/37

Page No.   29
04/08/88

U. S. SENATE
PERMANENT SUBCOMMITTEE ON INVESTIGATIONS
FIVE NEW YORK LCN FAMILIES MEMBERSHIP

D.O.B.

SALERNO, MICHAEL C	LUCHESE	03/20/23
SANTORA, SALVATORE	LUCHESE	11/18/15
SICA, JOSEPH	LUCHESE	08/20/11
SORRENTINO, JON	LUCHESE	06/04/49
TACCETTA, MARTIN RALPH	LUCHESE	05/02/51
TACCETTA, MICHAEL STANLEY	LUCHESE	09/16/47
TORTORELLO, ANTHONY	LUCHESE	10/06/36
TRUSCELLO, DOMINICK J	LUCHESE	04/29/34
TUMINARO, ANGELO	LUCHESE	02/22/09
TUSO, CHARLES	LUCHESE	01/14/12
TUTINO, RALPH JOSEPH	LUCHESE	05/12/28
URGITANO, ANGELO ANTHONY	LUCHESE	12/25/28
VARIO, PAUL	LUCHESE	07/10/14 may 3/88
VARIO, PAUL JR	LUCHESE	06/02/38
VARIO, PETER	LUCHESE	06/26/36
VARIO, THOMAS	LUCHESE	/ / B #158-208
VINTALORO, JAMES	LUCHESE	07/01/11
ZACCARO, PASQUALE	LUCHESE	03/16/12
ZITO, ANTHONY	LUCHESE	06/18/08

Appendix F

NJ Commission of Investigation 1989 Report

The Lucchese/Corallo/Amuso Family

La Cosa Nostra – State of New Jersey Commission of Investigation 1989 Report
The Lucchese/Corallo/Amuso Family

The Lucchese group is the smallest of the five New York LCN families, with 100 members and 200 associates. Its principal base of operation in New York City is the Bronx and Brooklyn but the family also has a strong faction in northern New Jersey.

Since its inception in the 1930's, the group has been primarily involved in the illegal distribution of narcotics. This activity has provided a lucra- tive income that has been invested in both legitimate and illegitimate enterprises over the years. Although involvement in narcotics continues today, the group's current emphasis is more on the financ- ing of major narcotics shipments rather than on distribution.

In addition to narcotics, the family's criminal activities include hijacking, gambling, loan-sharking, illegal landfills, pornography and other fraudulent activities in New York City, Northern New Jersey, Florida and California. The family has also been successful in infiltrating legitimate industries in the region, particularly the construction, solid waste, garment and trucking industries.

The family's current boss is Victor Amuso of the Howard Beach section of Queens. His underboss is Anthony Casso of Brooklyn. Amuso and Casso assumed leadership of the group as a result of the indictment and recent convictions of the entire former New York hierarchy of the family. Those affected included boss Anthony "Ducks" Corallo, underboss Salvatore "Sonny" Santoro, consigliere Christopher "Tick" Furnari and significant soldier Salvatore Avellino Jr. All were convicted on charges of violating federal antitrust laws involving the Long Island garbage carting industry. Corallo was also convicted, along with the bosses of the four other New York LCN families, for participation in mob operations and being a member of the LCN's ruling "Commission."

Amuso and Casso have legal problems of their own. Both were indicted in May, 1990, on federal charges including mail fraud and labor law violations.

The powerful northern New Jersey faction of the group, headed by Michael Taccetta of Florham Park, has also experienced its share of pressure from law enforcement. In addition, there has been dissension among the leadership. The faction had long been under the control of Anthony "Tumac" Accetturo of Newark and Taccetta had been his protege. However, Accetturo fled New Jersey for Florida in the early 1970's to avoid a subpoena to testify before the SCI. Taccetta took over for Accetturo but remained his subordinate until sometime in 1987. That year, a 21-month federal narcotics and racketeering trial began against Accetturo, Taccetta and 17 of their operatives. During the trial, Accetturo and Taccetta's once close relationship, which had cooled over the years, deteriorated into a power struggle that culminated in a murder contract being put on Accetturo's life. A major cause of that animosity was resentment over the emergence of Anthony Accetturo Jr. as a soldier and rising star in the family, along with his refusal to show the traditional deference and respect Taccetta felt was due him. Young Accetturo, who also lives in Florida, attended his father's trial and has been observed by law enforcement agencies at high level meetings of organized crime figures there and in New Jersey.

After the trial ended in acquittals for all the defendants, Accetturo returned to Florida and remained out of sight for months. Eventually, he was traced to North Carolina, where he was taken into custody in 1988 for his refusal to honor a New Jersey state grand jury subpoena to testify regarding labor racketeering and other state offenses. On September'19,1989, he was returned to New Jersey and was jailed for contempt of the state grand jury. However, because of the contract on his life, he was placed in protective custody. Accetturo has since pleaded guilty to income tax evasion in Florida but was acquitted of race-fixing charges there.

In October, 1989, young Accetturo and three other Florida residents were charged in Tampa by

Printed in Great Britain
by Amazon